❧ RESHAW ❧

<hr />

THE LIFE AND TIMES OF JOHN BAPTISTE RICHARD

<hr />

Extraordinary Entrepreneur and Scoundrel
of the Western Frontier

 RESHAW

THE LIFE AND TIMES OF JOHN BAPTISTE RICHARD

Extraordinary Entrepreneur  Scoundrel
of the Western Frontier

Jefferson Glass

HIGH PLAINS PRESS

FIRST PRINTING

10 9 8 7 6 5 4 3

Library of Congress Cataloging-in-Publication Data

Glass, Jefferson, 1955-
Reshaw : the life and times of John Baptiste Richard : extraordinary entrepreneur and scoundrel of the western frontier / Jefferson Glass.
     pages cm
Includes bibliographical references and index.
ISBN 978-1-937147-04-4 (trade paper : alk. paper)
1. Richard, John Baptiste, 1810-1875. 2. Pioneers--West (U.S.)--Biography.
3. Merchants--West (U.S.)--Biography. 4. Indian traders--West (U.S.)--
Biography. 5. Frontier and pioneer life--West (U.S.) 6. West (U.S.)--History--
To 1848. I. Title.
                    F593.R43G63 2013
                    978'.02092--dc23
                         [B]
                                    2013012416

HIGH PLAINS PRESS
403 CASSA ROAD
GLENDO, WYOMING 82213

CATALOG AVAILABLE
WWW.HIGHPLAINSPRESS.COM

It is with courage and devotion that we must approach our challenges if we expect to reach our goals.

Be well!

❧ CONTENTS ❧

❧ PREFACE ❧

 HISTORY may be right outside your back door.

For the past several years I have researched the life and adventures of John Baptiste Richard. Initially, I was curious about the history of Richard's Bridge—located only a few hundred yards from my home. For the first few years, I was more interested in the site than the man. Then I read a newspaper article about Susan Badger Doyle's discovery that Allen Hurlbut had, in fact, led a wagon train that departed from Richard's Bridge and traveled up what became the Bozeman Trail even before John Bozeman's 1864 expedition. The article reported that very little was known about Hurlbut or how he came to be in the vicinity at the time. The name sounded familiar to me, so I dug through my notes and discovered Allen Hulburt (a slightly different spelling) at Richard's Bridge at the right time. I could hardly contain my excitement at the likelihood that Hulburt and Hurlbut were indeed the same man. Through an associate, I obtained Doyle's phone number and called her.

After I revealed my discovery and we discussed our sources, she asked how I came to find this information. When I told her I was interested in the history of Richard's Bridge, she said she'd send me a little information she had on the bridge. A few days later I received in the mail a huge envelope containing dozens of documents about John Richard and Richard's Bridge. This packet of papers became the foundation of my research, and it gave me much insight into further sources. For this information, advice and encouragement, I owe a great deal of gratitude to Susan Badger Doyle, Ph.D. and renowned expert on the Bozeman Trail.

Not long after, I obtained a copy of John D. McDermott's *Frontier Crossroads*. I was intrigued by the frankness of the book, which in some instances totally discredited previously published folklore about the history of the region. I had my own theories as to what actually occurred and found McDermott's account in agreement with most of my own ideas. After my encouraging encounter with Susan Doyle, I felt somewhat confident in contacting John McDermott. I had never met him and was not sure what to expect. I was overwhelmed by his off-the-cuff knowledge of Wyoming history. I told him that I was primarily interested in Richard's Bridge and was beginning to toy with the idea of writing about it. He agreed that I should write the story of the bridge and said that knowledge is of little worth if not shared with others. When he asked what was stopping me, I answered that I did not yet know the whole story. He laughed and said that if I was waiting to know everything before I started writing, I would never begin to write. He went on to say that when I did start writing I would find out how little I really knew. His words still remain in the back of my mind and should be engraved on the walls of every history and journalism classroom. If I had nothing else to thank John D. McDermott for, this would be enough. There is, however, much more. His books and articles have provided mountains of information for this book. For his recording of western history, we should be forever grateful.

I was not yet ready to begin writing but started to compile a chronological outline of everything I knew about Richard's Bridge. As the outline grew, I realized that John Richard was far too intriguing a character for me to focus only on his bridge. The project that began as an article about the first successful bridge to span the North Platte River became a book about the man who built it. The more information I discovered, the less I seemed to know. John McDermott's words were haunting my research.

For two more years I studied, searched, and added to the chronology. I noticed immense gaps when Richard disappeared from my material. I began tracking his business associates and, through them, located Richard in different parts of the country, engaged in new ventures. I began writing, but something was still missing about this mysterious man, something that I could not put my finger on. After several months of writing, it struck me. Throughout his life, John Richard was closely tied to his family. His two brothers were involved in many of his business schemes. His father was his mentor in the fur industry; some of his Indian children were worthy subjects for books of their own. But were there any others?

Nearly halfway through the writing of the book, I began researching the genealogy of the family. I met Stewart Monroe of California. Stewart is a descendant of one of John Richard's sisters and had researched an entirely different aspect of the Richard family history. We compared notes and the result was astonishing. Some of Richard's business partners were in fact his brothers-in-law. Other of his employees were nephews. Many of the men he was associated with were in some way related to him. Together with Stewart Monroe, I have compiled a brief history of the descendants of John Richard's father. This is included as an appendix. Many of these names appear throughout this text. Their relationship to John Richard not only cements the identities of some of these associations, but helps to explain the reasons some of the partnerships existed. For this information, Stewart Monroe is primarily responsible. The pieces of this puzzle would never have fallen into place without his material.

In addition to these three primary contributors to this work, many others cannot be left unrecognized. Since my research, some have retired, moved on, or passed away; however, I'm nevertheless indebted to them. I owe a great deal of thanks to the Goodstein Library at Casper (Wyoming) College. The staff has been exceedingly helpful. I need to specially thank Kevin Anderson, former Western History Specialist, and Laurie Lye, then Interlibrary Loan Specialist. I must also thank the late Bill Gallucci, who was involved in his own research project and shared many sources of material. LaVaughn Bresnahan also deserves special thanks at the Wyoming State Archives in Cheyenne. She saved me numerous trips and much time by mailing copies and pulling material for my study. I must thank Annette Wheeler, who has located many maps, survey notes, and homestead records at the Bureau of Land Management Office in Cheyenne, Wyoming. The late Jean Cerquoz, Johnny Chasteen, and Charles Clough, all then members of CHUG, the Chugwater (Wyoming) Historical Unity Group, helped me in locating information about the Kelly family. I thank Mrs. Jim (Marcelyn) Brown, who owned the headquarters of the Hiram Kelly Ranch at Chugwater, and her daughter and son-in-law, Amy and Steve LeSatz, for allowing me to investigate the Kelly family cemetery. Bob and Matt Grant guided me to the site of John Richard's dugout cabin on Richeau Creek and gave me a copy of Duncan Paul Grant's memoirs that contains a rich history of the valley. They also introduced me to the West family, the present owners of the site, who welcomed my companions and me on that rainy day to explore there. My sincere thanks are extended to the Grant and West families.

Other libraries and institutions that provided source material were the Library of the State Historical Society of Wisconsin and the Beinecke Rare Book and Manuscript Library at Yale University, who also gave permission to publish J. Robert Brown's journal. Other contributors are the Missouri Historical Society, the Stake Library of the Church of Jesus Christ of Latter Day Saints, the Colorado Springs Pioneer Museum, the Nebraska State Historical Society, the Washington State Historical Society, the New York Public Library, Claremont College, and the Huntington Library. Also included are the University of New Mexico and the Oregon State Historical Society. Special thanks go to the American Heritage Center at the University of Wyoming, the Evansville (Wyoming) Historical Commission and the Town of Evansville, the Natrona County Historical Society, the Wyoming State Historical Society, the Wyoming Chapter of the Oregon-California Trails Association, and the National Historic Trails Center.

A few foresighted individuals, at the turn of the twentieth century, saw that the old west that they had known was rapidly disappearing. Some wrote down what they knew, and others sought to record the stories remembered by old-timers. Many of these notes are kept in the aforementioned archives. I offer to these men my very special thanks: C. G. Coutant, F. W. Cragin, and Judge Eli S. Ricker.

Many individuals offered a vast amount of encouragement and support. In addition to those previously mentioned, I also thank Todd Guenther, former Director of the Fremont County Pioneer Museum, Lander, Wyoming; Jim Lowe, Historian for TRC Mariah Associates Inc. and expert on Bridger Trail history; and Nancy Weidel, Historian and Outreach Coordinator for the Wyoming State Historic Preservation Office.

Most importantly, I thank my family and friends who put up with all of my eccentricities throughout the writing of this book. I especially thank my wife. There is more history out the back door than most people realize.

JEFFERSON GLASS

"The American trappers present a different phase of character. . . . They ride and walk like men whose breasts have so long been exposed to the bullet and the arrow, that fear finds within them no resting place."

Thomas J. Farnham in
Travels in the Great Western Prairies, 1843

I

⤳A LEGACY OF ADVENTURERS ⤳

J OHN BAPTISTE RICHARD was a mountain man, fur trader, entrepreneur, and perhaps the most notorious whiskey smuggler ever to venture to the West. His career spanned more than half the nineteenth century, ending just a few months before the Battle of Little Big Horn in 1876. Young Richard headed West from his home in Missouri before the evolution of six-shooters and repeating rifles. His numerous enterprises, occupations, and partnerships led to associations with some of the most famous explorers, traders, and pioneers of the developing western United States, yet his story is virtually untold. Barely able to read or write, John Richard's genius for commerce outweighed his lack of formal education. His uncanny instinct for business won him the utmost respect of his peers and the bitter enmity of his rivals.

John Richard, a wiry little man about five feet six or eight inches tall, commonly wore buckskins and moccasins adorned with beads and porcupine quills. His long black hair, parted in the middle, fell in curls below his shoulders. His naturally dark complexion, weathered by the outdoors, made him almost indistinguishable from the Natives with whom he traded. Francis Parkman described his strength and agility with admiration: "There was no superfluity, and indeed every limb was compact and hard; every sinew had its full tone and elasticity, and the whole man wore an air of mingled hardihood and buoyancy."[1]

Richard, considered a scoundrel by many, lived by his own code of ethics. When it came to bartering, few could match his skill or his ruthlessness. He showed no favoritism. Given the opportunity, he would trade white-man, Indian, friend, or foe out of everything he owned. Richard is reputed to have been the first trader to smuggle in contraband whiskey and trade it to the Indians of the northern plains. Although he gained much of his notoriety by his successful trade of controversial wares, most certainly he was not the first. However he bragged that he was "the best of the best" at what he did. In 1841, he boasted that there would never be an Indian Agent good enough to stop him. He lived to prove it.[2]

But Richard was full of contradictions. Away from the bargaining table, he could be both generous and compassionate. Many novices to western life and those down on their luck were spared hardship or even death when Richard shared his food, shelter, and savvy. Thus he earned his Sioux name, which translates roughly into English as "Always Has Plenty Meat."

John Baptiste Richard's contributions to western development are undeniable. He was the first to import food products to trade with the tribes of the northern plains. Richard was first to report the news of the gold strike on Cherry Creek that prompted the Colorado Gold Rush. He made hundreds of thousands of dollars from a variety of commercial speculations, yet he was no longer a wealthy man when he died.

⋖⋛⋗⋖⋚⋗

The wildness of the West was in Reshaw's blood and fiber. John Richard was born into a French family of several generations of early western adventurers. Many men who shared the name John Baptiste Richard traveled into what is now the United States early in the eighteenth century. Direct lineage is hard to establish, but that is not the point. They are most assuredly members of the same family, and these men were almost uniformly rugged adventurers, eager to explore remote locations. They learned from their fathers, uncles, grandfathers, and Indians how to survive in some of the wildest of times and places in history. Many of them held a portion of Native American blood from their mothers, grandmothers, or great-grandmothers.

No fabricated yarns. No dime novel heroes. The Richards were the adrenaline junkies of their era. Were they brave? Certainly. Were they bold? Absolutely. Were they fearless? Of course not, but they never allowed it to show. When a veteran soldier in a tight spot once was asked if he was scared he calmly replied, "No, I've been scared before. I'm just concerned." That's the kind of men the Richards were. They were hard, tough, wily, and confident men. Money was not the only force that drove them to the frontier. It was the wildness of it all. It was in their blood, literally. To survive was to succeed. To succeed was to prosper.

Several men named Jean Baptiste Richard ventured into and around the United States early in the eighteenth century, making the trail of the Richard men blurry and hard to follow.

The first Jean Baptiste Richard we find in the United States was born in Montreal in 1682, the son of a French soldier. By 1715 he was living in the Miami Indian village of Ouiatanon near present-day Lafayette, Indiana, where he was employed by the French military as an interpreter and blacksmith. He met Marie-Anne You, the daughter of Pierre You and a Miami Indian, Elizabeth. Before returning to Montreal where they were officially married in 1718, they had their first of three children. In 1722 after the birth of their third child, named Jean Baptiste Richard after his father, the family returned to Ouiatanon at the request of François-Marie Bissot, Sieur de Vincennes, the commander of the post. Their stay was less than three years. The elder Mr. Richard died in Montreal in 1725.

The second Jean Baptiste Richard of record, son of Jean and Marie-Anne, was also a frontiersman. Early in his career he was wounded and captured by a band of Sioux or Arikara Indians somewhere along the upper Missouri River. He reportedly was kept as a slave for four years. After his long captivity Jean Richard eventually escaped and headed east cross-country, finally reaching civilization in a settlement along the Mohawk River. From this point he returned to Montreal where he served ten years as a Loyalist officer in the French Army.[3]

By 1738 another member of the Richard family sharing the same name had settled in the upper Mississippi valley near Kaskaskia in present-day Illinois. A French merchant, this Jean Baptiste Richard—yes, perhaps our subject's great-grandfather—killed Henri Cotan in a drunken brawl there. He was acquitted of the murder charge on the grounds of self-defense. This event supplies early evidence that the men of the Richard family sometimes had a violent streak.[4]

A second Jean Baptiste Richard from the Kaskaskia area, presumably the son of the aforementioned, moved with his wife to New Madrid in what is now Missouri in 1791. This couple was likely the grandparents of the John Richard who is the subject of this book.[5]

Near the first of December 1795, world-famous frontier botanist Andre Michaux hired a man named Richard at Kaskaskia to transport him to Cumberland.[6] In 1800 another rugged Richard man, Stephen, was captured with Nolan's Army by the Spanish in Nacogdoches, now Texas, and sent to prison.[7] John Richard's father had been West many times by the 1830s. He is likely the Richard listed as commander of the upper Missouri operations of Cabanne and Company in 1819.[8]

Thomas Nuttall, another frontier biologist, met a Richard man in Arkansas with a load of furs that he had acquired from the Osage Indians. Oliver Rashaw [Richard] was employed on William Ashley & Company's 1827 expedition, and the American Fur Company employed Noel Richard at Fort Tecumseh in 1830.[9]

Richard men were routinely found on the dangerous edge of the American frontier, breaking trails and establishing inroads.

⋘⋙

Jean Francois Xavier Richard was a resident of St. Charles, Missouri, near St. Louis, at the beginning of the nineteenth century. There he met Rosalie Cote, the daughter of Alexis Cote and Elizabeth Dodier, also of French ancestry. Jean and Rosalie were married early in 1810, presumably in a civil service. Their eldest son was "our" Jean Baptiste Richard, later known as John, born December 14, 1810, in St. Charles, Missouri. When a parish priest, Marie Joseph Dunard, finally arrived at St. Charles, the Richards repeated their vows before him in a Catholic ceremony at the St. Charles Borromeo Church on January 7, 1812. The birth of two sisters followed, Leanore on September 22, 1812, and Rosalie on July 15, 1818. Then a brother, Pierre, was born October 4, 1820, followed by two more sisters—Agnes Julia in 1822 and Mary Elizabeth in 1823—and brother Joseph B. Richard in 1825. Three more sisters, Susanne, Louisa and Victorie, were born from 1829 to 1833. John's family members continued to play a role in his life long after he left Missouri.[10]

A Jean Richard was licensed as a trapper with the William Sublette Expedition in April 1832. Sublette ordered his partner William Ashley to pay Madam Richard in three months if Jean Richard kept up his end of the bargain. The title "Madam" implies she was the wife, rather than the mother of the wage earner. This suggests that this Jean Richard was not our subject, but rather his father.

Rosalie Cote Richard, John's mother, died shortly after the birth of Victorie in 1833. John then took on some of the responsibility of raising his two younger brothers, Pierre and Joseph. Perhaps this surrogate father relationship to his younger siblings may be partially responsible for the extremely close family bond that persisted throughout their lives.[11]

John Baptiste Richard is a difficult man to follow through history, partially because of the many spellings of his name. Jean became John or even sometimes Jonathan, as could easily be expected by simple Americanization of the French name. The French pronounce Baptiste with the "p" silent, making the pronunciation "Bah tees," consequently the common nickname "Bat." Richard, however, when spoken in French is pronounced "Ree-Shard," with the uvular "ard" often mistaken for "aw."

We don't know how John himself pronounced his name. His heavy French accent had always made him difficult for English speakers to understand, and as he lived among various tribes, he probably picked up their accents and pronunciations. He likely became even more difficult to understand.[12]

To complicate things further, few Westerners of the nineteenth century were literate by current standards. Those who were able to read and write often spelled phonetically, resulting in dozens of different spellings of surnames. Richard adopted the first name of John, but through all the variations, he, himself, kept the original spelling of Richard. For the purpose of clarity and consistency, "John Baptiste Richard" will be used throughout this book.

Some of the most common variations of John Richard's name found in documents and placenames are:

Jean	Richard	Richarde	Risham	Rishaw
John	Richards	Richaud	Renshaw	Richieu
Jon	Reshaw	Richeau	Rashaw	Reishaw
Jonathan	Rieshaw	Reeshaw	Reshar	Reichard
	Reshau	Regshaw	Reshan	Rosseaux

With all these variations of his name available, it is ironic that some of those closest to him, the Sioux, called the generous John Richard by yet another name which translated to "Always Has Plenty Meat."

Notes to Chapter One:

1. Francis Parkman, *The Oregon Trail* (New York: Books), 76-77.

2. George E. Hyde, *Spotted Tail's Folk: A History of the Brule Sioux* (Norman: University of Oklahoma Press, 1974), 89-90.

3. Jean Baptiste Richard was born in Montreal in 1682, christened March 19, 1682. He married Marie Anne You on August 15, 1718, in Montreal and their daughter Suzanne was christened the same day. Their second child, Agnes, was born May 7, 1719, in Montreal. Jean Baptiste Richard, their third child, was born November 20, 1721, in Montreal. This second Jean Baptiste Richard died in Bay of Quinte in 1807 at the age of 85. James L. Richards and Warren K. Gordon, Correspondence with Jefferson Glass, 1999.

4. John D. McDermott, "John Baptiste Richard" in *Mountain Men and the Fur Trade of the Far West*, ed. LeRoy Hafen (Glendale, Calif: Arthur H. Clark, 1965-1972), 2:289-290. It has been reported that this Jean Richard was our subject's grandfather, but it seems far more likely that he was his great grandfather. Hila Gilbert, George Harris and Bernice Pourier Harris, *Big Bat Pourier Guide & Interpreter, Fort Laramie 1870-1880* (Sheridan, Wyo: Mills,1968), 4.

5. John D. McDermott, "John Baptiste Richard," in *Mountain Men* 2:289.

6. On December 2 and 3, 1795, Andre Michaux made arrangements with Richard to go by water to Cumberland from Kaskaskia. This is believed to be the Pierre Richard listed as a head of family in the 1783 and 1790 census, most likely an uncle or great-uncle of our subject. Reuben Gold Thwaites, "Andre Micheaux's Travels" in *Early Western Travels, 1748-1846: A Series of Annotated Reprints of Some of the Best and Rarest...* (Glendale, Calif: Arthur H. Clark,1904), 3:78.

7. Stephen Reshar [Richard], an Anglo-American, was captured with Nolan by the Spaniards at Nacogdoches on March 21, 1800. It is not known if he was one of the eight survivors of the imprisonment that followed who were released five years later. Noel M. Loomis, Abraham Phineas Nasatir and Pedro Vial, *Pedro Vial and the Roads to Santa Fe* (Norman: University of Oklahoma Press, 1967), 225-226. Phillip Nolan was a horse trader and freebooter from Natchez, MS, operating primarily in what is now Texas from 1790-1800. Time-Life Books and David Nevin, *The Texans* (New York: Time-Life Books, 1975), 16.

8. Dale Lowell Morgan and William Henry Ashley, *The West of William H. Ashley* (Denver: Old West, 1964), 172.

9. Thomas Nuttall and Reuben Gold Thwaites, *Journal of Travels into the Arkansas Territory : During the Year 1919* (Cleveland, Ohio: A.H. Clark, 1966), 13:138. According to family genealogists, Oliver and Noel Richard were John Richard's uncles.

10. The author has contacted several genealogists who have done extensive research on the Richard family in America including Stewart Monroe of California. Monroe is a descendant of John Baptiste Richard's sister Mary Elizabeth Richard and has undoubtedly done more research on the immediate family from St. Charles than any other. Confirming both the birth of John Richard

and that his parents were married prior to his birth is the following note from the records of the St. Charles Borromeo Church, transcribed by Stewart Monroe: "The third of January, 1811, I baptized Jean, born the 14th of last December of the legal marriage of Jean Francois Xavier Richard and Rosalie Cote...." (Signed by Brother Urbain, Religious Trappist). McDermott, "Jean Baptiste Richard," in *Mountain Men*, 2: 289; Brian Jones, *Those Wild Reshaw Boys* (from *Sidelights of the Sioux Wars;* London: English Westerners Society, 1967), 40. Rosalie Cote was born in 1790 in St. Charles, Missouri. St. Charles Borromeo Church, St. Charles, Missouri, Records, 1792-1846. Joan Leaneagh, Correspondence with Jefferson Glass, 1999. Emily Levine stated in an editorial note that John Richard was born April 5, 1823. The source of this date is unknown. The date in question has been cited by other historians as the date of birth of John Richard's wife, Mary Gardiner. Susan Bordeaux Bettelyoun, Josephine Waggoner, and Emily Levine, *With My Own Eyes,* (Lincoln: University of Nebraska Press, 1998), 145.

11. Stewart Monroe, Correspondence with Jefferson Glass, 1999; Janet Lecompte, "Archibald Charles Metcalf," in *Mountain Men and the Fur Trade of the Far West,* ed. LeRoy Hafen (Glendale, Calif.: Arthur H. Clark, 1965-1972), 4: 217.

12. McDermott, "John Baptiste Richard" in *Mountain Men*, 2:289.

This photograph disputedly shows John Baptiste Richard, standing on left. The identifications of the photographs taken by Alexander Gardner at the Treaty of 1868 in Fort Laramie vary from museum to museum and publication to publication, partly because prints were identified by different people, sometimes years after they were taken. Some publications and libraries identify the man standing at the left as John Richard with his wife Mary Gardiner Richard on his left and his grandson Alfred in front of Mary. Other sources, including the Smithsonian Institution, identify the man as George Colhobo (Colhoff). Colhoff worked at the fort, first as a hospital steward and later in the sutler's store. (*Minnesota Historical Society*)

2

⊰ GONE WEST ⊱

B Y 1834 William Sublette and Robert Campbell had established the company of Sublette & Campbell. In June they constructed Fort William, the first trading post on the North Platte River route in what is now Wyoming, near the confluence of the Laramie and North Platte Rivers. The following year they sold the log wood post to Sublette's brother Milton, Tom Fitzpatrick, and Jim Bridger of the American Fur Company. They renamed the post Fort John in honor of John Berald Sarpy. In 1841 it was moved to a new adobe stockade up the Laramie River. The post, already nicknamed Fort Laramie due to its location, was not officially named Fort Laramie until it was sold to the United States Army in 1849.[1]

In 1837 Peter L. Sarpy erected Fort Sarpy about eight miles below Fort John to rival the American Fur Company's operation, but abandoned it unfinished in 1838. By then John Richard had come west with his father, an independent trader who did not work under contract with the larger fur companies.

Trade in buffalo robes was rapidly replacing the demand for beaver pelts. Buffalo robes were considerably less valuable than furs, and the increased bulk of a season's inventory required a different mode of transportation. A pack train could easily handle the season's load of trade goods from St. Louis, but was incapable of hauling huge packs of buffalo robes to eastern markets. The change in commodities increased the use of wagons and Mackinaws, flat-bottomed boats built on site to carry cargo downriver during high water. A large Mackinaw boat could carry up to three hundred packs of ten buffalo robes. If the spring thaw was late and the rivers remained unnavigable, the traders resorted to overland travel by wagon. The only feasible wagon route followed the Platte River and later became known as the Oregon Trail or Platte River Road. Caching the buffalo robes near both land and water routes allowed the traders to make several trips into the hunting grounds with pack trains to haul the robes out. Preference for river travel now became a necessity.[2]

About 1836 the Richards established a base of operation known as Reshaw's Fort on the south side of the North Platte River between the present towns of Lisco and Broadwater, Nebraska.[3] When John Richard received his own license to trade with the Sioux in 1838, he established a sub-post, later known as Reshaw's Houses, located on the Cheyenne River about three miles from the Old Woman Fork. From that location Richard established trade with the Brule Sioux who wintered near Bear Butte. In January 1839, Richard took thirty gallons of contraband whiskey to trade with the Brule, thus beginning his long and notorious career as a whiskey trader and a life-long friendship with the tribe.[4]

By the summer of 1840 John Richard had formed a business partnership with Archibald Metcalf, an eastern gentleman about five years Richard's junior. What Metcalf brought to this venture is uncertain, but since Richard had the experience and finesse to trade with the Sioux (not to mention the license) Metcalf probably contributed the finances. The fur and robe trade was a cutthroat business so we can assume John Richard must have had a tough go of it with the competition of big companies like American Fur.

Archibald Charles Metcalf was said to be a fine looking man about six feet tall and weighing about 225 pounds. He was strongly built and very active. The reasons why Metcalf came west from his New York home are as mysterious as his later disappearance from the western scene. Perhaps he was infatuated with the romance of the frontier or fascinated by the tales of young John Richard, who had recently returned from a season of trading. Metcalf was twenty-five years old when he met Richard in St. Louis. Nothing is known of the first meeting of Metcalf and Richard. They could have met in one of the wild, raucous waterfront saloons or in the lobby of one of St. Louis's finest luxury hotels. A partnership was formed, and on July 9, 1840, the *St. Louis Daily Argus* reported, "The company of Metcalf & Richard will depart for the Rocky Mountains in 10 or 15 days."[5]

Metcalf apparently had great difficulty dealing with the Sioux and was content to mind the post while Richard made trading expeditions to the Indian camps. More accustomed to the company and culture of a larger city like St. Louis than to months of wintry isolation at Reshaw's Houses on the Cheyenne River, Metcalf must have suffered a most severe case of "cabin fever." Richard's occasional visits, when he stopped by to cache his robes and pick up additional trade goods, were not enough companionship for the eastern gentleman.

The following spring Metcalf dissolved their brief partnership, headed south, and settled on the Greenhorn just south of the Arkansas River near present-day Pueblo, Colorado, along with three ex-trappers, John Brown, William New, and Marcelino Baca. Metcalf was far from the northern plains, but his association with John Richard had just begun. Metcalf soon made connections in Taos to supply him with plenty of liquor or "Taos Lightning" to sell to northern traders in years to come.[6]

In June 1834 Congress had passed the Indian Intercourse Act which governed the relations between the Americans and surrounding Indian tribes for many years. The sale of liquor to Indians was strictly forbidden. In 1841 the Attorney of the United States authorized payment to informants of illegal activities in the trade of "Spirituous Liquors." A month later, a circular was published detailing the particulars of the Act of 1834 and the payments to informants.[7]

Metcalf's associates in Taos are unknown, but distilling "Taos Lightning" was well established as early as 1825. The distilleries were of little interest to the authorities, but bootlegging of alcohol into the United States or the northern frontier was an entirely different story. In 1826 William Workman and two partners built the first American-made distillery in Taos. They had the components built in St. Louis on the sly, and family members smuggled the parts on a westbound Santa Fe freight wagon. Workman was loosely associated with Sylvestre Pratte, the son of St. Louis fur magnate Bernard Pratte. John Richard and Archibald or A.C. Metcalf probably dealt with Bernard Pratte, but a connection to Workman is uncertain. In 1841 Workman and one of his partners, suspected of conspiring with the Texan-Santa Fe expedition, fled to California.[8]

Not long after Metcalf arrived on the Greenhorn, John Richard was leading pack trains of alcohol over the mountain trails to the North Platte from the Mexican settlements. An agent for the American Fur

Company knew what Richard was up to, but the slippery frontiersman eluded him continually. John Richard had the advantage. He knew all the trails and had a network of Indian informants to apprise him of the agent's activities. If the agent staked out one trail in anticipation of ambushing Richard's pack trains, Richard simply took another. By the time the agent realized he had missed him, Richard had already cached or dispersed his goods.[9]

John Richard was not well liked by the American Fur Company. Ironically he later become associated with some of its partners. By the fall of 1841 John Richard was a partner with John Sibille and David Adams, founders of the company of Sibille & Adams, one of American Fur's new rivals. Sibille & Adams established Fort Adams, a trading post two miles up the Laramie River from the North Platte.

To further erode the American Fur Company's stronghold, another trading post opened nearby that season. Lancaster P. Lupton, an established trader on the South Platte and Arkansas rivers, built Fort Platte near the confluence of the North Platte and Laramie rivers, only two miles from Fort John. A man named Lock built another trading post two miles above Fort Adams on the Laramie River later that fall. Thus, three new trading posts were operating within a three-mile radius of the American Fur Company's Fort John. Competition was fierce.[10]

⋐⋑∘⋐⋑

John Richard's life is fairly well documented over the next few years. David Adams evidently liked Richard. Perhaps he even admired him and his daring escapades. David Adams's journals and letters shed much light on the life of John Richard during his thirties. Richard's two younger brothers, Pierre and Joseph, were also in the employ of Sibille and Adams. Pierre, who had by then assumed the name of Peter, was twenty-one. Joseph, the youngest, was seventeen years old.

On November 13, 1841, Mr. Adams wrote that John Richard left Fort Adams for the Cheyenne River with four carts pulled by unbroken horses and oxen. John Sibille accompanied Richard as far as Fort Platte. An Indian accosted them, and Sibille bargained for their passage by offering five pints of whiskey. By the Adams account, they bought the whiskey from Mr. Lupton's post to bribe the Indian, although it seems likely that a notorious whiskey trader such as Richard would not be without his most precious ware on a trading expedition. If Adams's account is true, Richard must have cached his main liquor supply at his father's nearby camp away from the eyes of the Indian Agents and retrieved it as he needed it.

Richard had trouble with the half-wild oxen. Later he sent word by his father for Sibille and Adams to send packsaddles, and he would send back the oxcart. Richard's father was still an independent trader at that time.

The next day Richard's father arrived at the camp with the packsaddles, only to find that his son's four best horses had been stolen the night before. Not disheartened by his misfortunes, Richard loaded his goods on three horse carts and seven packhorses and sent the oxcart back to Fort Adams with his father. Richard was on his way again by mid-day. Only a mile from camp the overloaded horse carts bogged down. John sent his brother Joseph after the oxcart again, but Joseph was unable to catch his father before he reached Fort Adams.

Finally underway again on November 15, Richard soon found the Indian camp he was looking for. When he started the barter, Richard discovered the Indians had more robes than expected. He sent an Indian messenger to Fort Adams with a letter requesting two more men, packhorses, and more trade goods. Adams dispatched Iott and Dubray with the horses and goods. Meanwhile John's brother Peter arrived at Fort Adams from the LeBorne Sioux village on the Chug.[11] Peter and Sibille packed up their own merchandise and headed back to their camp on Chugwater Creek.

About that same time Richard's old partner Archibald Metcalf camped near Lock's Fort and soon moved in at Fort Platte. The purpose of his return to the North Platte is uncertain, but he may have brought a shipment of Taos Lightning north. The chroniclers of the time may have excluded this information to keep from implicating themselves. On November 20 John Richard's father, whom Adams called "Old Man Reshaw," wandered into Fort Adams in a blizzard with an employee of Sibille & Adams named Sigler. By Adams's description, the two were nearly frozen to death. They told Adams that Indians had accosted three of Hubert Papin's buffalo hunters from the American Fur Company. Many Indians were quite hostile toward the white traders, especially if they believed the traders were hunting buffalo. Although they seemed unconcerned about other wild game, the Indians believed the buffalo belonged only to them, and the whites had no right to them even for food.

The Indians were going to kill the buffalo hunters, but chief Man Afraid of his Horses intervened. Instead, they killed the hunters' horses and sent them on their way, warning them not to hunt buffalo again. Later Old Man Richard and Sigler discovered the trio afoot. Richard loaned them a mule and bade them good luck. The next day one of the three arrived at Fort Adams to return the borrowed mule. David Adams thought it peculiar that he never offered a single word of thanks.

A few days later Old Man Richard left to trade with the Brule Sioux who were camped down the Platte near Horse Creek. Sibille returned from the Oglala village on Chugwater Creek, bringing twenty-eight robes, one horse, one white bear skin, and a large quantity of meat.

Sibille thought that while he was gone from Chugwater Creek, Joseph Bissonette from the American Fur Company had tried to have their kegs of whiskey destroyed. American Fur hired a group of Indians to help keep the peace among the Indians. These men were known as "soldiers," but had the reputation of being enforcers and thugs. One of Bissonette's soldiers named Left Hand had tried to break the kegs, but Smoke, an Oglala from a nearby village, stopped him. Sibille thought Bissonette was behind it.[12]

Meanwhile, Iott and Dubray, the two traders whom David Adams had sent to meet John Richard two weeks earlier, had still not returned to Fort Adams. Adams was deeply concerned for their safety. At ten o'clock on December 1, 1841, Adams and Sigler left to find the missing traders. After a grueling trip through a blizzard, they finally found Iott, Dubray, John Richard, and the others snowed in at Reshaw's Houses on the Cheyenne River. When the storm broke, Richard convinced Adams to establish a sub-post at that location while he prepared to go on to Bear Butte to trade.[13]

The next day, a party of young Sioux warriors, who were camped on nearby Hat Creek, came to Reshaw's Houses on their way to fight the Snake tribe (Shoshone). John Richard was their friend, and they wanted to give Richard a dance before they left because it might be the last time they would see him. The fact that the warriors wanted to perform this ceremony for Richard before their possible deaths confirms the strength of the bond between Richard and this tribe.

Trade was disrupted between the Sibille & Adams traders and the two Oglala villages on the Cheyenne River for several days when traders from the American Fur Company arrived at the villages. David Adams dispatched a messenger to Fort Adams requesting that more trade goods be sent to the post on the Cheyenne River. Adams, hoping to agitate the American Fur Company further, sent Sigler to the Oglala camp with five gallons of watered down whiskey. Trade did not improve.

The following day John Richard and his men left for Bear Butte in the Black Hills. After a slow day of travel through deep snow, Richard was forced to send two men back to the post with the horse carts. He had to rely on his pack train to carry his goods to the butte.

John Richard and his youngest brother, Joseph, spent the rest of the season trading with the Brule Sioux. Since Joseph Richard was never listed as a trader for Sibille & Adams, he probably worked directly for his brother. David Adams remained at the post on the Cheyenne River, trading with the nearby villages throughout the winter. In March 1842 Adams returned to the North Platte. John Sibille had stayed the winter at Fort Adams. When the Adams party arrived at the fort, they began building two Mackinaws to transport their merchandise to St. Louis.

On March 20 about the time that Lancaster Lupton declared bankruptcy and sold his trading posts, David Adams, John Sibille, and Sigler visited Lupton at Fort Platte. The details of Lupton's transactions are vague. Fort Platte was sold either to Sibille & Adams, the most likely buyer, or to Pratte, Cabanne, & Company. Pratte and Cabanne later became partners of Sibille & Adams and eventually bought them out. On March 23 Hubert Papin, Joseph Bissonette, and Charles Lajeunesse of the American Fur Company visited Fort Adams with news that they were leaving for St. Louis in a few days. On March 26 David Adams left Fort Adams with Daniel Simons for St. Louis. Hubert Papin and his group had left Fort John earlier the same day, but Adams and Simons soon caught up to them at "Sarpy's old fort." Adams's meeting with Lupton was probably to discuss the purchase of Fort Platte. If so, then David Adams's sudden trip to St. Louis may have been to secure the finances necessary to close the deal. Otherwise Adams would not likely have chosen his rivals as traveling companions for the long journey east. In St. Louis Adams negotiated the financing for the purchase of Fort Platte with Bernard Pratte. Later entries in the Adams journal suggest a substantial indebtedness to Pratte, a burden which eventually led to the demise of the Sibille & Adams Company.

⊰≯⋅⊰≱⋅

John Richard returned to Fort Adams from Bear Butte sometime in April. By the end of that month, he and Sibille were operating from Fort Platte. In a letter to David Adams dated April 25, Richard stated his disgust with Sibille and wrote that he only stayed at the post for Adams's benefit. The next day Richard wrote to Adams that he had sent word to the South Platte to send some Spaniards to help build boats, but they had not yet arrived.[14]

After many delays the boats were finally completed. On May 7 Richard and Sibille left Fort Platte with two boats heavily loaded with robes and furs, but their troubles were not over. The high springtime waters had ebbed. The waters were no longer navigable 200 miles downriver. Richard returned to Fort Platte and sent wagons. Sibille and his men eventually got to St. Louis with their load. John Richard stayed at Fort Platte through the summer.

James Bordeaux, a long time employee of the American Fur Company, was operating Fort John in Hubert Papin's absence and was trying to prove himself against Richard.[15] In mid-June animosities between the Sibille & Adams traders and James Bordeaux erupted into violence at Fort Platte. Bordeaux was in a complete rage over the competition by the men from Fort Platte. John Richard had four men with him to carry on trade through the summer, make repairs, complete new construction, collect hay, and all the other necessities of preparing for next winter's trade. With a liberal supply of whiskey, Bordeaux convinced half a dozen Brule Sioux that Richard, as well as Sibille & Adams, had been cheating them. It was not unusual for James Bordeaux to visit Fort Platte, so Richard was not alarmed when Bordeaux showed up at the post. He continued his work inside the post while carrying on a casual conversation with his back to Bordeaux. When Richard bent over, Bordeaux cocked his gun, stepped up behind him, and hollered to his accomplices that now was "a good time to kill these Damned dogs."

John Richard was quite alone in the room with Bordeaux and his friends. With a cool head, he managed to face Bordeaux with the latter's pistol still held at his chest. While pretending to back away from Bordeaux, he worked his way toward his own pistol and rifle. He told Bordeaux that if he had any grievances he should present them like a gentleman, but if he had come only to commit murder then to get on with it. Bordeaux seemed not to notice Richard's change in position. While Bordeaux continued his cursing rage, he followed Richard across the room. John Richard sprang for his rifle and was about to shoot when Kellogg, the clerk from Fort John, with two or three Indians clinched with him. A frantic scuffle followed. Hearing the commotion, LeClair, one of Richard's men, burst into the room. One of Bordeaux's friends shot LeClair down as he came through the door.[16] Bordeaux and his group then broke and ran. Richard chased them out of the fort firing several ineffective shots in their direction.

The story of the melee quickly spread through the Indian camps. In Bordeaux's attempt to turn the Indians against the Sibille & Adams traders, he had turned them against himself and the American Fur Company. Several of Richard's Indian friends threatened to retaliate against Fort John and would have done so had Richard and his companions not convinced them that they would take care of the problem themselves.[17]

In July Richard was in charge when John C. Frémont's 1842 expedition arrived at Fort Platte. Joseph Bissonette, who had worked for the American Fur Company for some time, evidently disagreeing with Bordeaux's actions, had mutinied. In a letter to David Adams on Independence Day, Richard informed him that he had taken Bissonette into the firm according to Adams's wishes. Frémont enlisted Bissonette as scout and interpreter for his expedition until they arrived at Red Buttes, some 130 miles up the Platte. About the time they reached Red Buttes, Bissonette was summoned to a parlay with a band of Indians. The Indians told Bissonette that certain doom awaited the expedition if they did not turn back. When he translated this message to Frémont, the surveyor scoffed. Since he had fulfilled his obligation, Bissonette returned to Fort Platte. Frémont continued on unmolested. The incident unfortunately bolstered Frémont's low opinion of Bissonette's character and abilities, and undoubtedly affected future opportunities for Bissonette with government sponsored expeditions.[18]

In the Fourth of July letter to Adams, John Richard also commented on the progress of the new construction at Fort Platte. He expressed the necessity for Adams to acquire a good blacksmith and a gunsmith. Richard then added his own shopping list: "two to three thousand pounds of tobacco, as much ammunition as you can get, plenty of trade goods, and as much liquor as last year." This would seem to be a whopping order when you consider the transportation of the era. However, William Sublette considered it a "small outfit" in a letter to his partners when the entourage departed St. Louis in September. Sublette's letter confirms John Richard's partnership with Sibille and Adams. He referred to the company as Adams, Sibille, and Richard. Sublette also hinted their affiliation with Bernard Pratte.[19]

John Sibille evidently left St. Louis on the return trip to Fort Platte prior to David Adams's departure. Shortly after Adams left Westport, Missouri, Alexander Barclay overtook him. Barclay was embarking on his first season as an independent trader with a hired man and a three-horse wagon. He had operated Bent's Fort just off the Santa Fe Trail on the Arkansas River before undertaking this venture. From Fort Platte, Sibille wrote to Adams that the fort was finished. When Adams arrived two weeks later, he complimented Richard's accomplishments over the summer. Trade through the summer was normally slow, but in his partners' absence Richard had managed a fair amount of trade as well as the construction work on Fort Platte. Perhaps his most important contribution to Fort Platte that summer was swaying the savvy young trader Joseph Bissonette from the American Fur Company into Sibille and Adams's camp.

While Sibille and Adams were preparing for expeditions into the wintering grounds of the various villages, a shipment of corn, flour, and peas arrived from the south. John Richard's former partner A. C. Metcalf had made another trip up the Old Trapper's Trail. This is the first known record of an expedition for the primary purpose of trading food from the south with the Northern Plains tribes. Sibille and Adams traded a wagon and six packs of robes for Metcalf's food staples on the agreement that he would abstain from trading with the Sioux.

Fort Platte was bustling with no less than sixty men on November 1, 1842. Joseph Bissonette's trading party departed for his post on Horse Creek on November 7. The following day John Richard's party left for Bear Butte. A.C. Metcalf, Alexander Barclay, Abel Baker, and a man named Patterson left for the Spanish settlements in the South. Alexis Godey with his Indian wife had made the trip north with Metcalf, but he stayed to work with Sibille and Adams on the North Platte. [20]

Little is known of John Richard's trading expedition to Bear Butte that season, but a man David Adams called "Buscay" deserted Richard's party and was seen at Fort John two days after the expedition had left

Fort Platte. Given Richard and Metcalf's history of smuggling, Buscay may have been a spy for the American Fur Company or for Deputy Indian Agent James V. Hamilton. If so, John Richard had eluded his pursuers once again. The simultaneous departure of Richard to Bear Butte and Metcalf's return south suggests they had rendezvoused to transfer liquor. The infiltrator Buscay had no chance to catch Richard with the goods because the meeting never took place. Richard had apparently arranged for Metcalf to haul whiskey from the "Spanish Settlements" and hide it away near Reshaw's Houses. Buscay either deserted Richard's party as soon as he realized the plan had not worked, or Richard discovered his plot shortly after departing Fort Platte and sent him packing.[21]

Major Andrew Drips was appointed as the United States Indian Agent for the Upper Missouri Country in 1842 and made Fort Pierre on the Missouri River his base of operations. With his deputy at Fort John, Drips was able to keep a fairly close eye on the operations of John Sibille, trading from Reshaw's Houses on the Cheyenne River, and John Richard, trading at Bear Butte. In April 1843 Sibille evidently left the houses on Cheyenne River with the season's robes, while Richard stayed until the other traders had left for the season.

According to Andrew Drips, John Richard truly began his trading season after the others had left the Cheyenne River, and the Indian Agents had lessened their vigilance. Then he brought out his cached liquor and traded it for some 500 buffalo robes. He promised the Indians that he would have all the liquor they wanted by the next fall. If he was unable to bring whiskey from St. Louis, he would order it again from Metcalf.[22]

The death of an Indian reportedly resulted from a quarrel during the spree following Richard's "big trade," but he had already left the area. By May 7, 1843, John Richard loaded half a dozen wagons with buffalo robes and left Fort Platte for St. Louis. A few days later Major Andrew Drips vented his frustration by authorizing his deputy at Fort John, James Hamilton, to destroy any "Spirituous Liquor you can lay your hands on" whether carried by Indians or whites. He also empowered Hamilton to confiscate the trade goods, wagons, and livestock of any trader who possessed liquor, and to call on any respectable Indians or any "American Traders" (employees of the American Fur Company) for assistance, if necessary, in carrying out the orders.[23]

Competitors had certainly noticed the "one eye closed" politics of Major Andrew Drips, but now the former employee of the American Fur Company had put his prejudices in writing. With such biased support from the Indian Agents towards the American Fur Company, the independents and smaller companies had more difficulty competing for a share of the available buffalo robes than ever before. John Richard and his associates were willing to challenge this liability.

The American Fur Company had operated its own still at Fort Union for the purpose of distilling corn whiskey to trade to the Indians for several years. Major Drips was undoubtedly aware of the operation, but had continually ignored it. The distillery remained in operation until 1850 when the United States government sent more than fifty special detectives to locate and destroy it. The successful expedition employed scouts and interpreters from the Arikara, Gros Ventre, Mandan, Crow, and Assiniboin tribes. Honore Picotte, in charge of trading operations for the American Fur Company, managed to bribe enough of the agents that the owners and operators of the still were never disclosed.[24]

Notes to Chapter Two:

1. B. Jones, *Those* , 40; John D. McDermott "James Bordeaux" in *Mountain Men and the Fur Trade of the Far West*, ed. LeRoy Reuben Hafen (Glendale, Calif: Arthur H. Clark Co., 1965-72), 5:71.

2. Dale Lowell Morgan, *Overland in 1846: Diaries and Letters of the California-Oregon Trail* (Georgetown, Calif: Talisman Press, 1963), 2:53. Changes in the fur trade are described in detail in LeRoy Reuben Hafen, "Decline of the fur trade," in *Mountain Men and the Fur Trade of the Far West*, LeRoy Hafen (Glendale, Calif: Arthur H. Clark, 1965-72), 1-169. Transportation changes, the uses of trading posts, and descriptions and construction methods of both Mackinaw and bull boats, were described by Magloire Mosseau. Eli S. Ricker, "Interview of Magloire Alexis Mosseau, Buzzard Basin, Pine Ridge Reservation, South Dakota, on October 30, 1906," Nebraska State Historical Society Library, Lincoln, Nebraska, tablet 28, 6-8.

3. The name and location of the remains of "Reshaw's Fort" were described by David Adams in his journal entry for April 1, 1841. Later, Adams refers to a wildfire in the same vicinity. Reshaw's Fort may have been destroyed in this or a similar wildfire about the same time, since later diarists fail to mention the fort. David Adams and Charles E. Hanson, *The David Adams Journals*, (Chadron, NE: Museum of the Fur Trade, 1994), 34.

4. Reference to John Richard obtaining his trading license is found in Lecompte, "Archibald Charles Metcalf," in *Mountain Men*, 4:217. David Adams described the post vividly in his journals after his arrival on December 7, 1841. Adams, *Journals*, 24-25. The confluence of the Old Woman Fork with the South Fork of the Cheyenne River is about ninety miles due north of Fort Laramie. The tributary, now known as Old Woman Creek, is a few miles due north of present-day Lusk, Wyoming. On the 1869 Wyoming Territorial Map it was still shown as Old Woman Fork. Bear Butte was about ninety miles northeast of Reshaw's Houses beyond the Black Hills near present-day Sturgis, South Dakota. John Richard may have used what fifty years later became the Cheyenne /Deadwood route to reach this destination.

5. According to the Family Search International Genealogical Index v.5.0 at Familysearch.org, Archibald Charles Metcalf was born in New York State about 1815, the son of Thomas and Mary Metcalf; McDermott, "John Baptiste Richard" in *Mountain Men*, 2:290; Lecompte, "Archibald Charles Metcalf" in *Mountain Men*, 4:217; F. W. Cragin, "Interview of Josiah F. Smith on July 18, 1903," in F. W. Cragin Papers, Colorado Springs, CO: Colorado Springs Pioneers Museum, Notebook XVII, 6; Louise Barry, *The Beginning of the West* (Topeka, KS: Kansas State Historical Society, 1972), 415.

6. Lecompte, "Archibald Charles Metcalf" in *Mountain Men*, 4: 217-219. After Texas won independence from Mexico in 1836, the area between the Arkansas and Rio Grande Rivers west of the one-hundredth meridian was part of the Republic of Texas. Both Taos and Santa Fe were within Texas boundaries, but because of the distance from Austin, law enforcement by the Texas Rangers was minimal. Nevin, *Texans*, 16, 155-156.

7. J. Loughborough to Maj. Andrew Drips, May 10, 1843, in Andrew Drips Papers, Missouri Historical Society, St. Louis, Missouri.

8. William Workman, "A Letter from Taos, 1826," *New Mexico Historical Review* 41 (1966): 155-164.

9. B. Jones, *Those Wild Reshaw Boys*, 5.

10. John Sibille is often written John Sybille and several other spelling variations. The spelling used here is how John Sibille signed company documents for Sibille & Adams. Adams, Journals, 16-17; B. Jones, *Those Wild Reshaw Boys*, 5.

11. Chugwater Creek was originally called "The Chug." The tributary of the Laramie River was named for its source—Chug Springs—where legend has it Indians stampeded buffalo over the chalk cliffs to their deaths. The Indians called the spring "Water at the place where the buffalo chug." Mae Urbanek, *Wyoming Place Names* (Boulder: Johnson, 1967), 44-45.

12. Adams, *Journals*, 6-21. Joseph Bissonette (1818-1894) was the son of Louis Bissonette (1774-1836). He should not be confused with his uncle Joseph Bissonette who became known as José Bissonette after obtaining Mexican

citizenship in the early 1800s in Taos. McDermott, "Joseph Bissonette" in *Mountain Men*, 4: 49-60. Joseph Bissonette was also the nephew of Paul Primeau who was appointed the administrator of Bissonette's father's estate on January 2, 1837. His uncle, Joseph "Jose" Bissonette, was still living in Taos at that time. John C. Luttig and Stella Madeleine Drumm, *Journal of a Fur Trading Expedition on the Upper Missouri 1812-1813* (New York: Argosy-Antiquarian Ltd., 1964), 148-149.

13. Iott is presumably Sefroy Iott, considered "another old timer" at Fort Laramie when Susan Bordeaux Bettelyoun was a young girl twenty years later. Dubray is either Michael Dubray who died a few years later or Antoine Dubray who remained in the Fort Laramie area for many years. Adams, *Journals*, 61; Bettelyoun, Waggoner and Levine, *With My Own Eyes*, 41, 73, 157.

14. Adams, *Journals*, 21-34.

15. McDermott, "John Baptiste Richard" in *Mountain Men*, 2:291; McDermott, "Joseph Bissonette" in *Mountain Men*, 4:50; James Bordeaux was second-in-command of Fort John. If Papin was away from the fort, Bordeaux was usually left in charge. McDermott, "James Bordeaux" in *Mountain Men*, 5:65-80.

16. Very little is known about LeClair. According to Stewart Monroe, he had an Indian wife and with her had a daughter, Susan, who was born about the time her father was killed. Susan LeClair later married Eli Plant.

17. On June 21, 1842, James Bordeaux wrote a letter of apology to Richard, following this incident. Adams, *Journals*, 43-44. James Bordeaux's extreme dislike for John Richard often comes to the surface in other episodes as well. Many years later he still referred to him by the derogatory Sioux name of Owasakala, meaning cheap or easily bought. Bettelyoun, Waggoner, and Levine, *With My Own Eyes*, 145.

18. McDermott, "Joseph Bissonette" in *Mountain Men*, 4:50.

19. B. Jones, *Those Wild Reshaw Boys*, 6; Adams, *Journals*, 48.

20. George P. Hammond and Alexander Barclay, *The Adventures of Alexander Barclay, Mountain Man* (Denver: Old West Pub. Co., 1976), 224.

21. Adams, *Journals*, 39-48.

22. Maj. Andrew Drips to Maj. D.D. Mitchell, May 10, 1843, Drips Papers; Lecompte, "Archibald Charles Metcalf" in *Mountain Men*, 4: 217-219.

23. Maj. Andrew Drips to Maj. D. D. Mitchell, May 10, 1843, Drips Papers; McDermott, "John Baptiste Richard" in *Mountain Men*, 2:291; Maj. Andrew Drips to Maj. James V. Hamilton, May 12, 1843, Drips Papers.

24. Ricker, "Interview of Magloire Mosseau," tablet 28, 1-5.

3

❧ EXPANDING VIRTUES ❧

JOHN RICHARD WAS NOT a man to keep all of his eggs in one basket. He was both imaginative and aggressive in his exploits in a time when few of his counterparts were willing to gamble on uncertain ventures. Perhaps his most important virtue was his ability to put his ideas into action. Many of his adventures put him at both personal and financial risk, but his uncanny ability to successfully carry out the most extreme tasks created admiration among his associates and hatred from his competitors.

The next two years put all of Richard's abilities to the test. Relying on his trading experience, he diversified his business. Through his daring exploits as a whiskey smuggler, he overcame his greatest challenge to date. The consequence, however, was the end of a longtime partnership and the creation of new enmities not soon to be forgotten.

In 1833 Sir William Drummond Stewart began amassing a vast collection of wildlife specimens from America to take home to Scotland. Solomon and William Sublette were responsible for arranging many of Stewart's expeditions into the American West, and they assisted him in contracting "hunters" to capture many specimens for his collection. Over the next ten years, Stewart had many successful expeditions along the Platte and Arkansas Rivers. Collecting the fauna from the region was not unique to Sir William Stewart. Many eastern Americans, as well as Europeans, were greatly intrigued by the new and strange species in the West. Collecting specimens for public zoos and private collections was often a profitable enterprise.[1]

While the Sublettes were guiding Sir William on his 1843 expedition, they met John Richard with his wagons loaded with robes. What makes this meeting interesting is that Richard's entourage included specimens for another collector. On June 6 William Sublette recorded in his diary: "Met John Risham [Richard] this evening . . . He had some cows & 6 buffalo calves & one young elk ...."[2] John Richard was the epitome of frontier entrepreneurs. He had learned early that diversifying into the buffalo robe market increased his profits. Now he had expanded his interests into yet another realm.

Another member of the 1843 Stewart expedition was Joseph Pourier, an old timer on the frontier who had enlisted with the "one hundred men, to ascend the Missouri to the Rocky Mountains" on the famous 1823 Ashley and Henry expedition. The meeting between Richard and Pourier was probably not their first; their families had resided in close proximity in St. Charles, Missouri, for many years. Little did they suspect, however, that Pourier's two-year-old son, Baptiste, would one day become John Richard's son-in-law. This would also be their last meeting. Joseph Pourier became ill on the trip and died shortly after his return to St. Charles that autumn.[3]

John Richard's stay in St. Louis during the summer of 1843 was short. He quickly disposed of his robes, wagons, and wildlife and purchased three hundred gallons of whiskey for the return trip. His actions did not go unnoticed by the American Fur Company. On July 27, 1843, John Berald Sarpy wrote from St. Louis to Major Andrew Drips in Westport (near Kansas City) about rumors that Richard planned to transport a large supply of whiskey on mules to the Indian Country.[4]

Major Drips's response to this letter opens the door for more speculation. He told Sarpy that nothing was known of the movements or intentions of "certain persons" and that he was inclined to believe that such (whiskey smuggling) was not their intention.[5] That was an unusual response since Drips himself had written to his superior the previous spring expressing his own suspicions about Richard's whiskey purchases.[6] Why did Major Drips change his opinion of Richard and partners Sibille and Adams? By the time John Richard arrived back at Fort Platte from St. Louis on August 16, Sibille & Adams was under the control of Pratte, Cabanne & Company,[7] the St. Louis merchants who had substantially financed Sibille and Adams in the past. In a letter to his wife on August 4, David Adams hinted that he and his partners had become a subsidiary of the St. Louis company.[8] It is possible that Major Drips was more trustful of the new management than he had been of Sibille & Adams.

Regardless of the circumstances affecting Drips's change of heart, J. B. Sarpy was outraged. In his fury, he all but accused Drips of corruption. Drips had returned to Fort Pierre by the time Sarpy fired a heated

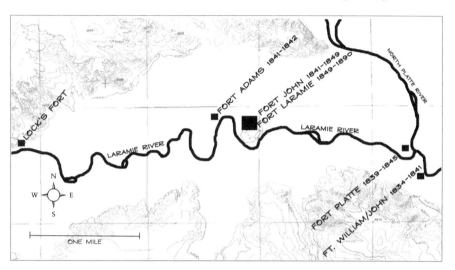

The confluence of the North Platte and the Laramie Rivers was the site of a progression of both privately-owned and military forts, often referred to as Fort Laramie even when they were officially named something else. Finally in 1849, the military established a fort officially named Fort Laramie. (*Based on USGS map*)

response regarding Drips's disinterest in Richard's illegal wares. "Now it seems to me somewhat strange that there people can so easily elude your vigilance—It is matter next to certainty that they dispatched 10 horses loaded with liquor ... that the operation was conducted at night—in traveling they avoided all roads & pathes—the party was conducted by Richard—that they crossed the Kanzas at the old agencies.... This transaction occurred before the time of your packing up [to leave Westport] and it therefore seems strange that you did not get any clue to it at all ... this I fear has resulted from the want of a proper vigilance...."[9]

Joseph Bissonette, who had been left in charge of Fort Platte, wrote to Sibille and Adams in St. Louis with the news that at the end of June Alexander Montgomery and Jose Portelance had arrived at Fort Platte from Taos with a large supply of flour and abalone shells. The goods were put into inventory at the post and Bissonette reported making "...considerable sales of it and animals to Captain Stewart's party.... We are putting up the Barn & Office and shall have plenty of Hay for the Winter."[10]

Although the American Fur Company always proclaimed innocence when it came to trading liquor with the Indians, Archibald

Joseph Bissonette was a fur trader and interpreter who explored the Rocky Mountains with John C. Frémont and was a friend and sometimes partner of John Richard. (*Nebraska State Historical Society, [Digital ID, RG2411-0459]*)

Metcalf carried a load of Taos Lightning to Fort John that summer. On July 5 James Bordeaux, who was once more in charge of Fort John, threw a drunken Crow Indian from the wall of the fort resulting in the Indian's death, thus acquiring the Sioux name Mato (Bear). Richard was already aware of Bordeaux's presumptuous attitude toward fellow members of the human race. Bordeaux, it could be argued, was probably not the source of the Indian's intoxicating liquor except that Metcalf had received the suspiciously large sum of $415 from James Bordeaux at that very time.[11]

The exact dates of John Richard's departure from St. Louis or Westport are unknown. Sarpy wrote that his pack train traveled strictly by night and far from the normal trails along the Platte. They hid during the day with watchful guards posted to alert the sleeping company of any movement that might require a hasty departure. With the stealth and speed of veterans, Richard and his companions arrived near Fort Platte on the night of August 16, 1843. Early the next morning, Richard made a personal reconnaissance and entered the fort. Finding no government agent, he dispatched a messenger back to where the pack train was camped. Fifteen pack animals loaded with kegs were slipped into the fort. The gates were closed and locked. The men then unloaded the kegs, containing some three hundred gallons of whiskey, and buried them inside a storeroom at Fort Platte.[12]

John Richard succeeded in smuggling the whiskey to Fort Platte, but was not in the clear yet. Several officers of Captain Stewart's Company arrived at Fort John shortly after the first of September. Richard, fearing discovery of his illegal merchandise, dug up his cache and reburied it away from the post. Furthermore, two spies from Fort John, Oscar Sarpy and J. Loughborough, had infiltrated Fort Platte. Loughborough wrote to Andrew Drips, enclosing a lengthy sworn statement from Oscar Sarpy with explicit details about Richard's pack train arrival and the caching of the whiskey at Fort Platte. He also added instructions that the Attorney of the United States should issue the "tinder" for this information to him as informant.[13]

Major Drips immediately sent Major James V. Hamilton to Fort Platte to confiscate the contraband. He followed up with a letter to his supervisor D. D. Mitchell boasting about how quickly he had responded to Loughborough's letter. Drips failed to mention that John B. Sarpy had warned him of John Richard's expedition before he or Richard had ever left Westport.[14]

Major Hamilton began his search of Fort Platte on the morning of September 16, 1843. When he could find no whiskey, he gave up looking. The traders taunted Hamilton, telling him that they had moved the whiskey and defying him to find it. Post clerk W. D. Hodgekiss, who was in charge of bookkeeping, told Hamilton not to expect any cooperation from the traders, but that soon Mr. Cabanne, one of the new owners of the fort, would arrive and perhaps attitudes would improve then. Hodgekiss told Hamilton that he knew where the kegs were hidden and, if it came to it, he personally would tell Hamilton where the kegs were cached on the condition that Hamilton provide him with a safe refuge for the winter plus funds to return to Cincinnati in the spring. If Hodgekiss had indeed revealed the location of the whiskey, the traders probably would have seen to it that he did not survive until spring, even holed up in the protection of Fort John.[15]

It is worth noting that John Richard had left Westport about August 1 with his heavily loaded mule train. Two weeks later he arrived at Fort Platte about seven hundred miles away, so he had covered between thirty-five and fifty miles each day, an astonishing feat even if he had traveled the regular road in the daylight. He, however, traveled only at night avoiding all known trails. On the other hand Major Hamilton left Fort Pierre with Drips's interpreter on September 7 and arrived at Fort John on September 15. Traveling lightly equipped on a well-used trail for long days and into the nights, they covered about three hundred miles averaging only thirty-eight miles per day. Apparently John Richard had also set up relay points where he obtained fresh mules, since he left Westport with ten mules and arrived at Fort Platte with fifteen.

The absence of evidence at Fort Platte did not deter Major Hamilton. At Fort John he became acquainted with John Hill, a respectable gentleman from Washington, D.C. who had accompanied Captain Stewart on his specimen collecting expedition. Prior to Hamilton's arrival, Hill had purchased eighty dollars worth of whiskey from John Richard at Fort Platte while Joseph Bissonette was in charge of the post. At Hamilton's request, Hill submitted a sworn statement to Major Drips substantiating the whiskey purchase, adding that he would stay the winter at Fort John and would accompany Major Hamilton to St. Louis in the spring where he would turn over his evidence. Although any hint of liquor trade had ceased upon Hamilton's arrival, he was still suspicious of John Richard. A village of Brule Sioux camped near Fort Platte even tried to trade their most valuable possession, horses, for Richard's whiskey, perhaps at Hamilton's instigation. Richard flatly refused. Hamilton warned Major Drips that he thought Richard would try to take the whiskey to the Cheyenne River for the season's trade.[16]

Jean Pierre Cabanne arrived at Fort Platte the first part of October. The particulars of his agreement with Hamilton are vague. Richard was reportedly discharged from the company and departed for Taos shortly after Cabanne's arrival. If Cabanne had authority to discharge John Richard, then certainly Pratte, Cabanne & Company now had complete control of Sibille & Adams. Richard was a partner prior to Cabanne's arrival, trading under the license of Sibille & Adams, and was not employed by Pratte, Cabanne & Company unless P.C.&Co. had absorbed Sibille & Adams. Cabanne possibly expelled him from the fort as a ruse to get Hamilton off the track, but Richard's later animosity toward Cabanne suggests the dismissal was genuine. By the time David Adams and Cabanne's son, Julius, arrived at the fort a few days later, John Richard was gone. Adams remained at Fort Platte to prepare for the season's trade while John Sibille took a keelboat up the Missouri River to establish a post near the mouth of the Cheyenne River.[17]

Major Drips planned to leave Fort Pierre for the Platte River around the first of November, but after hearing that Hamilton had things under control there, he changed his mind. He wrote Hamilton commending him on his success in stopping the liquor traffic in the area. Drips wrote that a company of dragoons were being stationed at Bent's Fort on the Arkansas River to curtail the "Whiskey Peddlers" coming up from the Spanish settlements. He also told Hamilton there would be a "tightening of the cinches" on the traders. They would no longer be allowed to go to Indian lodges or villages to trade. Instead they would be required to operate strictly from the points or posts designated on their licenses.[18]

John Richard did not go to Taos as some believed. Instead he smuggled his whiskey to the vicinity of his old post on the Cheyenne River as Hamilton suspected he might. Getting booted out of Fort Platte by Cabanne did not sit lightly with Richard. He had been trading without a license for nearly a month when he got word of Drips's new trade restrictions. Richard seemed to fear the possibility of getting caught trading without a license more than he had ever feared apprehension for dealing in whiskey. He swallowed his pride and asked Walter Riddick of Pratte & Cabanne to help. Riddick, trading from "Abbot's Wintering Ground," sent a messenger to Drips requesting that John and Peter Richard and four other traders be included on Pratte & Cabanne's license. Adding yet another twist to his questionable integrity, Andrew Drips approved the request without question.[19]

About this time John Richard married Mary Gardiner. Some scholars have suggested that his marriage might have been a ploy to give Richard access to the Indian villages, a hopeful loophole in Drips's new trading regulation. This theory holds little merit since the love John had for Mary was shown on many occasions in years to come. Unlike many mountain traders who took a different Indian wife each trade season, John was devoted to Mary, and their marriage has been reported by descendants to be one of the true romances of the frontier. John and Mary Richard remained together for the rest of their lives.

Mary Gardiner was the daughter of William Gardiner, a white trader, and White Thunder Woman of the Northern Oglala Sioux. After her marriage to Gardiner, the tribe disowned White Thunder Woman who died when Mary was just an infant. At the request of her Sioux relatives, Mary was raised with her two half-brothers, Rocky Bear and Black Tiger, in the same village as her cousin Red Cloud. Descendants say that William Gardiner took Mary away to Rulo, Nebraska, as a young girl. Her Sioux relatives kidnapped her, but Gardiner managed to get her back and took her to St. Charles, Missouri, where she stayed with members of the Pourier family and attended school. When her father returned to the Indian country to trade in 1841, he took Mary with him.[20]

⟨⟩ ⟨⟩

The traders of Pratte, Cabanne & Company were well set up at their various stations for the season of 1843. John Sibille was at his new post on the Missouri River. Joseph Bissonette had set up operations on Horse Creek near the North Platte River, and David Adams was on the Cache la Poudre. Peter Richard was at Reshaw's Houses on the Cheyenne River. John Richard was at Bear Butte. Jean Pierre Cabanne was running Fort Platte with clerk W. D. Hodgekiss.[21]

In November A. C. Metcalf arrived at Fort John with a load of trade goods and liquor from Taos. He asked Major Hamilton for a license to trade with the Sioux. When Hamilton examined his inventory, he gave Metcalf his walking papers. Metcalf returned to Fort Lancaster on the South Platte River and sold his inventory to Lancaster Lupton, who was running his old post for Wilson & Rich. He then contracted to trade the whiskey for Wilson & Rich with the Cheyenne villages in the vicinity. Although Hamilton did not confiscate Metcalf's liquor or his trade goods, he vowed to Major Drips that he would do just that if any other peddlers from the Spanish country should arrive in the area.[22]

Major Andrew Drips was pleased with Hamilton's actions thus far and agreed with his future enforcement plans. He traveled up the Cheyenne River in the fall of 1843 to observe the traders. Although he had yet to uncover any illegal activity, he planned to return to the area "for the purpose of watching the whiskey merchant" who was building at the forks of the river. Drips may have been referring to John Richard, but more likely John Sibille was the "whiskey merchant" concerned. Sibille had started constructing a new post just below the mouth of the Cheyenne on the Missouri River.[23]

By late January 1844 the company had sent Richard to help David Adams build boats to float robes down the South Platte River. In February they had already assembled nearly six hundred packs of buffalo robes at Fort Platte to float down the North Platte River. High spring waters on both forks of the Platte River aided the traders in transporting their goods to market. The arrival of Pratte, Cabanne & Company's Fort Platte flotilla in St. Louis was announced in the *St. Louis Reveille* on June 22, 1844: "Six Mackinaw boats arrived yesterday from the North Fork of the Platte River with valuable freights of peltries. A party of Pawnee Indians attacked them on the way down, but they were repulsed without loss of life." Cabanne reported that trading had been very successful that year on the North Platte.[24]

In St. Louis the company sold their buffalo robes and paid their men. Joseph Bissonette purchased supplies and immediately began assembling a pack train to return to Fort Platte. John Richard severed his ties with his partners and equipped himself for his return west. Richard's solo movements become more difficult to follow over the next several months.[25]

Major D. D. Mitchell, Superintendent of Indian Affairs, had forecast that the trading of "Spirituous Liquor" would be stopped that year. The illegal trade was greatly curtailed thanks primarily to the vigilance of Deputy Indian Agent Major James V. Hamilton. Most of the seven hundred lodges of Sioux Indians who encamped on the North Platte River spent the winter hunting instead of drinking. Consequently they produced twelve hundred packs of buffalo robes compared to the usual eight hundred packs.[26]

Mary Richard traveled to St. Charles with her husband. When John returned to the North Platte, he left Mary behind. She was to rejoin him after giving birth to their first child. John's return to the Platte, however, was delayed. Now that he was a free trader, Richard evidently could not afford to buy his trading liquor at Westport prices, so he chose the more circuitous route back to the North Platte, going via Taos or Pueblo where he could restock his liquor supply.[27]

On September 3, 1844, David Adams left the Westport area on his return to Fort Platte. He and his companions, including Lancaster Lupton, had a difficult trip west. Adams was nearly broke before he departed St. Louis. His heavy debt to Pratte and Cabanne must have consumed most of his gains from the previous season. Adams complained that the road was in terrible condition due to heavy emigrant traffic that year. They had no trouble with Indians other than delays from several lost horses. On September 17, one of the group, Michael Dubray, died from "the nurvus fever." He had been ill for several days and "we hadnt now way of helping him." Lupton and several others were also ill.[28]

On October 9 the Adams party spotted a group of men with horses traveling on the north side of the Platte River. Assuming they might be hostile Indians, the traders prepared to defend themselves and their livestock from possible attack. A Frenchman was sent across the river to check out the strangers. Their caution, although wise, was unnecessary. The party across the river was Major Hamilton's group also headed for the mouth of the Laramie River to observe the trade season. Hamilton and his men joined Adams's party for the next four days until Hamilton became irritated with a fellow in Adams's company and separated from the group.[29]

Lupton and his men also left the Adams party and continued up the South Platte River to Fort Lancaster. Lupton had been operating the fort for Wilson & Rich since he had sold it to them in 1842. Later in December 1844 Lupton abandoned the post all together and moved south to the Arkansas River. However, the routine of the early season's trading commenced with John Sibille working with the Sioux from a post established on Horse Creek. Joseph Bissonette, David Adams, and others were occupying the Horse Creek post from time to time, though Adams stayed primarily at Fort Platte.[30]

When Mary Richard returned to the vicinity of Fort Platte from St. Charles with her infant son, John Baptiste Richard Jr., her husband was nowhere to be found. No one had seen or heard from John Richard since he had departed Westport. Upon hearing that he had arranged to meet his beloved wife at Fort Platte, everyone assumed Richard was dead. Mary was persuaded to return with her son to her Sioux family. The tribal elders arranged for the young widow to marry Black Moon, an eligible warrior. Soon Mary was again with child.[31]

On December 10, 1844, David Adams recorded in his journal: "mr tucker arived with a letr from hors crek a stating that the tous pedlors had arived thair with corn and flour and licker . . . mr sebel wishes us to send mr drips the agnt . . . we mad our report to him and he started this morning."[32] Adams did not name the Taos Peddlers who were at Horse Creek. Sibille might not have recognized them, although John Richard was in the area and might have been in the group.

Meanwhile John Richard was alive and well and had acquired a new partner named Matterson. The two eluded agent Drips's raid on Horse Creek and spent the next few months trading on Chugwater Creek. They were having a poor season when they visited Fort Platte in February. The Sioux were building a medicine lodge on the Laramie River and preparing to go to war with the Crows. Man Afraid of His Horses was wounded, and Iron Frenchman was killed in a skirmish. The war party disbanded and fifty lodges of Sioux moved back to the Sandhills.

A party of Sioux and Cheyenne attacked a village of Ute and Shoshone Indians on the Sweetwater River and stole a large number of horses. The Utes and Shoshones prevailed in the fight that followed. Only one Sioux survived. The fighting among the Indian tribes left little time for hunting. "The Richard Brothers, Lieutenant Lupton, and the Company [American Fur] had the Sioux drunk, vomiting, and murdering one another and all comers whenever they had robes to sell. All earlier debaucheries seem sweet by comparison."[33] The result was devastating to the small independents like Richard and Matterson.

During that chaotic time among the tribes and his visit to Fort Platte, John Richard must have discovered that he was "dead." By tribal custom his wife had married the Sioux warrior Black Moon and was now carrying

Black Moon's child. Richard did not blame Mary or his many friends along the Platte for this incredible predicament. Instead, with extraordinary devotion and respect for the tribal law, he consulted with the tribal elders for a resolution. They proposed that Richard should bring gifts to Black Moon and offer to buy Mary back. Richard's offer so enraged Black Moon that he threatened to kill Richard. Before his threats could be carried out, Black Moon left with a war party to lay siege on a neighboring tribe, and he was killed in the skirmish.

The death of Black Moon did not yet free Mary to return to John Richard. By tribal custom, she was still property of Black Moon's family. Realizing how badly Richard wanted her back, they did not let her go without substantial compensation.[34] John Richard paid Black Moon's family a large percentage of his own and his partner's goods for the return of his cherished wife. Thus, by mid-February Richard and Matterson had run out of food and were unable to trade for meat let alone robes. In desperation they sent a messenger to David Adams to beg for food, but Adams was suffering himself. Adams told the messenger that he would oblige the request with pleasure if he had any goods to spare.[35]

Three days later Major Hamilton, under the direction of Major Drips, came to Fort Platte seeking help with confiscating Richard's robes at his Chugwater Creek camp. Hamilton said it was on behalf of the government, but Adams was enraged. Though dead set against it, he gave permission for any of his men to join Hamilton's crusade if they desired. Only Beauvais left with Hamilton. When Hamilton returned to Fort John with only one man, Drips cancelled the mission, and Beauvais returned to Fort Platte. Adams never forgave Beauvais for volunteering to perform such a dastardly deed: "I know that if it was me I wold dy befor I wold be robed of evry thing that I posesed …."[36]

A few days later, John Richard's brother Joseph arrived at Fort Platte with Matterson's son. They tried to sell Adams ten gallons of whiskey, two mules, and two *fanegas*[37] of corn and were undoubtedly told how close they had come to a run-in with Hamilton. The fact that Richard still had corn to trade indicates that perhaps they were not as "starving" as previously suggested. Unable to agree with Adams on a price, the two went on to Fort John to attempt a sale. There they found Major Drips. They discreetly offered the mules and corn for sale, but the presence of Drips put such a scare into them that they failed to make a deal there

Maria de la Luz Trujillo was born in 1830 and married trader Archibald Charles Metcalf in 1845. (*Ceferino Ahuero-Baca collection*)

also. They returned to Chugwater Creek spending the night at Fort Platte on the way. In fact, there is no record that Joseph Richard and young Matterson ever made the sale to any of the traders in the area.[38]

On the last day of February, Peter Richard arrived at Fort Platte. He told Adams he had been trading at a village below Smith Fork about 130 miles downriver from Fort Platte. Peter said that he had passed the trader Sigler about sixty miles from the fort with a cart heavily loaded with robes. The next day when an overnight snowstorm let up, Peter Richard left for his brother's camp on Chugwater Creek. A few days later Matterson with his son and a young black man who belonged to Matterson came to Fort Platte with whiskey and were finally able to sell it to Adams.[39] Adams does not report on Peter's trading success on Chugwater Creek, but records other traders' failure to locate the village.

David Adams was severely in debt to Pratte & Cabanne. Sibille & Adams still officially owned Fort Platte and had agreed to give it to Pratte & Cabanne along with most of their merchandise in order to satisfy some or all of the debt. To have something to show for his labors, David Adams set out in mid-March on a trapping expedition on tributaries of the Laramie River. The Adams party ate lunch with Richard and Matterson on March 13, 1845, at their camp on Chugwater Creek.[40]

On April 7, Pierre Chouteau Jr. & Co. paid Pratte & Cabanne $10,036.36 for Fort Platte and selected portions of the inventory. On April 18, Chouteau paid $379.75, the balance of wages owed to Joseph Bissonette and $176.37 to John Sibille. The merchandise was removed, and Fort Platte was abandoned. John and Peter Richard with Joseph Bissonette packed up the remaining inventory and moved into the long-vacant Sarpy's Fort and re-established it as Fort Bernard (named in honor of Bernard Pratte). The post was located on the south side of the North Platte River about eight miles downriver from Fort John near the present town of Lingle, Wyoming.[41]

In June 1845 Colonel Stephen Watts Kearny addressed the Sioux at Fort John warning the Indians against drinking alcohol. Joseph Bissonette interpreted Kearny's address. Alexander Culbertson, a partner of the American Fur Company, visited Fort John and was not at all impressed with James Bordeaux. He left him "temporarily" in charge of the post. Bordeaux managed to redeem himself with the company by trading for one hundred packs of robes over the next two months. Why Culbertson was so displeased with Bordeaux is uncertain, although Bordeaux's purchase of several hundred dollars worth of whiskey from Archibald Metcalf might be suspected. That purchase probably contributed to Bordeaux's unusually high trade that summer and got him back on the good side of the company.[42]

Meanwhile in Taos, Archibald Metcalf married Maria de la Luz Trujillo, known as Luz, the fifteen-year-old daughter of Don Jose Francisco Trujillo. The couple moved to Pueblo. Thanks to Alexander Barclay, Pueblo was rapidly becoming a successful farming and trading community. Metcalf was primarily involved in trading whiskey and coffee for furs and robes with the Cheyenne and Arapaho in the area of Manitou Springs where the soda in the spring's water was sufficient leavening for Luz's bread.[43]

A man named John Wells murdered his estranged wife Candelaria and her lover LeFontaine near Pueblo about this time. Wells was banished from the Arkansas River valley for his crime. Although the punishment might seem a mere scolding by today's standards, Wells's chances of survival were narrow for a man alone in the wilderness. Metcalf, Barclay, and other friends of Wells spent the next several weeks helping to move Wells's grain, livestock, and other belongings out of the valley.[44]

Notes to Chapter Three:

1. Janet Lecompte, *Pueblo-Hardscrabble-Greenhorn: the Upper Arkansas, 1832-1856* (Norman: University of Oklahoma Press, 1978), 128.

2. Barry, *Beginning of the West,* 486; B. Jones, *Those Wild Reshaw Boys*, 6.

3. Gilbert, *Big Bat Pourier*, 2. The legendary one hundred men included a multitude of characters of campfire lore: a very young Jim Bridger, John Fitzpatrick, and Hugh Glass, to name only three of those whose names were connected to that famous trek. John Myers Myers, *The Saga of Hugh Glass: Pirate, Pawnee, and Mountain Man*, (Lincoln: University of Nebraska Press, 1963, reprinted by Bison Books, 1976), 68.

4. Barry, *Beginning of the West*, 486; John B. Sarpy to Maj. Andrew Drips, July 27, 1843, Drips Papers.

5. John B. Sarpy to Maj. Andrew Drips, August 29, 1843, Drips Papers.

6. Drips to D.D. Mitchell, May 10, 1843, Drips Papers.

7. J. Loughborough to Maj. Andrew Drips, September 7, 1843, Drips Papers.

8. David Adams to his wife, August 4, 1843, cited in Adams, *Journals*, 49.

9. Sarpy to Drips, August 29, 1843, Drips Papers.

10. Joseph Bissonette to Sibille & Adams, July 25, 1843, cited in Adams, *Journals*, 47-48. The abalone shells made the trip to the plains all the way from the Pacific coast in California. They were a highly praised commodity among the Plains Tribes.

11. Lecompte, "Archibald Charles Metcalf" in *Mountain Men*, 4:218-219; McDermott, "James Bordeaux" in *Mountain Men*, 5:69.

12. Loughborough to Drips, September 7, 1843, Drips Papers.

13. Maj. James V. Hamilton to Maj. Andrew Drips, September 17, 1843, Drips Papers; Loughborough to Drips, September 7, 1843, Drips Papers.

14. Maj. Andrew Drips to Maj. D. D. Mitchell, September 7, 1843, Drips Papers.

15. Hamilton to Drips, September 17, 1843, Drips Papers.

16. John Hill to Maj. Andrew Drips, September 17, 1843, Drips Papers; Hamilton to Drips, September 17, 1843, Drips Papers.

17. Adams, *Journals*, 50; McDermott, "John Baptiste Richard" in *Mountain Men*, 2:292; Drips to Hamilton, November 4, 1843, Drips Papers.

18. Maj. Andrew Drips to William Laidlou, November 1, 1843, Drips Papers; Drips to Hamilton, November 4, 1843, Drips Papers.

19. Walter J. Riddick to Maj. Andrew Drips, November 5, 1843, Drips Papers. Drips to Riddick, November 5, 1843, Drips Papers.

20. White Thunder Woman was a sister of Red Cloud's mother. She was first married to a Sioux warrior who was reportedly killed in battle against the Pawnees. Mary Gardiner was born somewhere along the Yellowstone River in what is now Montana on April 5, 1823. Some sources cite Rosebud, daughter of Conquering Bear, as Mary Gardiner's mother. If so, this Conquering Bear was not likely to have been the same Conquering Bear who was killed as a result of the Grattan Massacre. William Gardiner is believed to have died around 1845. B. Jones, *Those Wild Reshaw Boys*, 6, 41; McDermott, "John Baptiste Richard" in *Mountain Men*, 2:293; Gilbert, *Big Bat Pourier*, 11, 33-34.

21. Drips to Hamilton, November 4, 1843, Drips Papers; Riddick to Drips, November 5, 1843, Drips Papers; Adams, *Journals*, 50, 54-55.

22. Wilson & Rich had purchased Fort Lancaster, now known as Fort Lupton, from Lancaster P. Lupton about the same time that Sibille & Adams purchased Fort Platte. Hamilton to Drips, December 4, 1843, Drips Papers.

23. Drips to Hamilton, December 21, 1843, Drips Papers.

24. Adams, *Journals*, 50; McDermott, "John Baptiste Richard" in *Mountain Men*, 2:294.

25. Adams, *Journals*, 50; McDermott, "Joseph Bissonette" in *Mountain Men*, 4:50.

26 Lecompte, *Pueblo-Hardscrabble-Greenhorn*, 93-94.

27 Gilbert, *Big Bat Pourier*, 4, 8.

28 Adams, *Journals*, 50-63, 96; Michael Dubray had been an employee of Sibille & Adams since as early as 1841. Adams, Journals, 25; He was "a person acting as Steward of said Company [Pratte, Cabanne, & Co.]" in 1843. Loughborough to Drips, September 7, 1843, Drips Papers.

29. Adams, *Journals*, 66-67.

30. Although Adams does not mention Lupton's departure from the group, neither does he mention his presence on this journey after crossing the South Platte River. Adams, *Journals*, 70-74; Lecompte, *Pueblo-Hardscrabble-Greenhorn*, 133.

31. Gilbert, *Big Bat Pourier*, 7-8.

32. If David Adams had known that his old partner John Richard was among the traders from Taos at Horse Creek, he probably would have never sent Drips after them. Adams, *Journals*, 74.

33. Bernard Augustine DeVoto and Alfred Jacob Miller, *Across the Wide Missouri* (Boston: Houghton Mifflin Company, 1947), 374.

34. Gilbert, *Big Bat Pourier*, 8.

35. Adams, *Journals*, 74, 86-87, 90.

36. David Adams's anger with Hamilton and Beauvais further exemplifies the compassion he had for his old friend, John Richard. Adams, *Journals*, 90-91.

37. In Mexico a *fanega* is approximately equivalent to 90 liters or 2.5 bushels.

38. Adams, *Journals*, 92-93.

39. Adams, *Journals*, 94-95. This is the first known instance of black slaves being used in this part of the country, although there are occasional references to Indians enslaving captives from other tribes prior to this (and even whites, although rarely).

40. David Adams, Letter to Mrs. Adams, March 9, 1845. Adams, *Journals*, 96-97.

41. Pierre Chouteau Jr., Chouteau Papers, Missouri Historical Society, St. Louis, Missouri; Adams, *Journals*, 103; McDermott, "John Baptiste Richard" in *Mountain Men*, 2:294; B. Jones, *Those Wild Reshaw Boys*, 6-7.

42. McDermott, "Joseph Bissonette" in *Mountain Men*, 4:51; McDermott, "James Bordeaux" in *Mountain Men*, 5:69; Lecompte, "Archibald Charles Metcalf" in *Mountain Men*, 4:219.

43. Lecompte, *Pueblo-Hardscrabble-Greenhorn*, 135, 169-170. The Trujillo family was well established in Taos. In 1828 Vincente Trujillo was the *alcalde* there. Workman, "Letter from Taos," 163; F. W. Cragin, "Interview of Luz Trujillo Metcalf Ledoux on February 13, 1908," Cragin Papers, Notebook VII; Lecompte, "Archibald Charles Metcalf" in *Mountain Men*, 4: 218-220.

44. Hammond, *Alexander Barclay*, 135-136, 186.

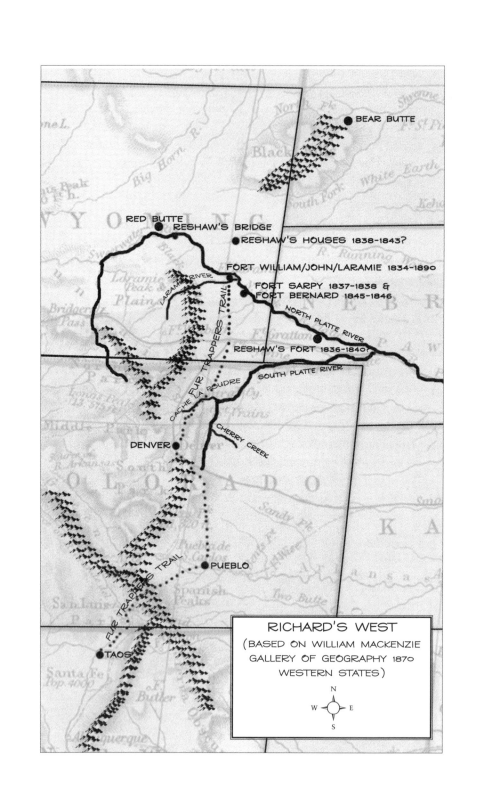

BEAR BUTTE

RED BUTTE
RESHAW'S BRIDGE
RESHAW'S HOUSES 1838-1843?
FORT WILLIAM/JOHN/LARAMIE 1834-1890
FORT SARPY 1837-1838 &
FORT BERNARD 1845-1846
NORTH PLATTE RIVER
RESHAW'S FORT 1836-1840?
SOUTH PLATTE RIVER
CACHE LA POUDRE
CHERRY CREEK
DENVER
FUR TRAPPERS TRAIL
PUEBLO
FUR TRAPPERS TRAIL
TAOS

RICHARD'S WEST
(BASED ON WILLIAM MACKENZIE
GALLERY OF GEOGRAPHY 1870
WESTERN STATES)

N
W E
S

4
❧ YEAR OF DECISION ❧

A UTHOR BERNARD DeVoto, in the title of his seminal book, referred
to the year 1846 as *The Year of Decision*. There is no question that
this was a critical year in the shaping of western history. The entire area
west of the Mississippi River was beginning to show signs of growth.
During this year the United States truly adopted the policy of "Manifest
Destiny," the idea that expansion across the continent by U.S. citizens
was destined. Many believed the spreading expansion was what God
intended. The phrase, coined by a newspaper in 1845, became a concept
of American thinking that would remain well into the next century.

The year 1846 surely was a year of decision for John Richard, and a
year that influenced events for the remainder of his life. He regained
prominence as a trader on the North Platte River and began a relationship with followers of the Mormon Church that would both help and
hinder him over the next two decades.[1]

The activities of John Richard that year were documented in an
unusually detailed manner, considering he lived and worked in an iso-
lated and obscure part of the frontier. In spite of Richard's remote location, author Francis Parkman and diarists Edwin Bryant and John Brown
each encountered Richard and recorded details of his life.

❧ ❧

John Richard rang in the New Year with his brother Peter, Joseph Bissonette, and his brothers-in-law Charles B. Branham and Charles Bordeaux. They were residing at the half-finished trading post they called
Fort Bernard and spent the winter there trading corn from Pueblo to
the Indians for buffalo robes. These five men had formed a partnership
called Richard & Company. Levin "Mitch" Mitchell had delivered a
shipment of corn from Alexander Barclay in early December, and trade
was good. Richard's brother Joseph was running a store in *Fuerte el
Pueblo*. He may have been working for Archibald Metcalf or Alexander

55

Barclay, or perhaps this was yet another enterprise of John Richard's. The fact that he conducted other business with Metcalf may make that the most likely.[2]

Alexander Barclay made the next trip from Pueblo to Fort Bernard himself. He was accompanied by a hired man and John Wells, and they carried a considerable load of corn and whiskey on three droves of mules. The three men arrived on the Spring Branch of Horse Creek on February 1, but they were delayed there by a succession of storms which kept them holed up until the end of the month.

The reason Barclay made the trip himself was partially of a personal nature. He needed to ask a favor of Richard that he would not have been comfortable asking by messenger. When Barclay's group finally arrived at Fort Bernard on February 25, he asked John Richard if Wells could stay there until a suitable opportunity arrived for him to ride west with other travelers. Richard agreed, and Barclay left with his man, Benito, and one pack mule on March 2 to return to Pueblo.[3]

Within a few days, on March 8, 1846, President Polk ordered General Zachary Taylor and his troops into the disputed territory between the Nueces and Rio Grande Rivers. That action would later result in the Mexican War. The United States had annexed the Republic of Texas the previous year and admitted Texas to the union as the twenty-ninth state. With this, the U.S. inherited a dispute with Mexico's President Jose Joaquin de Herrera over the border between Texas and Mexico. Mexico considered the annexation of *Tejas* an act of aggression by the United States. A short time later, General Mariano Paredes overthrew Herrera, and Mexico began mobilizing troops near the Rio Grande.[4]

Before Barclay could complete his trip back to Pueblo, Honore Picotte wrote to his employer, Pierre Chouteau, that the "Taos Peddlers" were a great annoyance. They were trading corn from Kansas (actually from Pueblo) and were controlling the trade. He suggested that Chouteau import four to five hundred bushels of corn as quickly as possible. Chouteau immediately sent the corn. It arrived too late to do Picotte any good with his trading with Indians, but he hoped to make up for his winter losses by selling the corn to emigrants along the trails at inflated prices. Before Picotte's corn had arrived, however, Richard had already received another large train loaded with corn from Pueblo plus pigs, cats, and whiskey from Taos. Richard and his partners further aggravated the competition by cutting their prices to emigrants by up to forty percent.[5]

Early in May, Peter Richard, Charles Bordeaux, Charles Branham, and several others shoved off in their Mackinaws from Fort Bernard with a large shipment of buffalo robes headed for St. Louis.

Joseph Bissonette built a cabin on Bitter Cottonwood Creek, a few miles above Fort Laramie, and began a farming operation to supplement supplies for Fort Bernard. John Richard and a few others stayed behind to mind business at the post.[6]

On June 1, Richard and a "Negro" left Fort Bernard to trade with the Indians on Horse Creek. A few days later Richard's companion, astride one of their mules, got lost while hunting for some oxen that had strayed from camp; he never returned. After searching for both the man and the oxen to no avail, Richard returned to Fort Bernard.

Meanwhile, the United States troops stationed along the Rio Grande had engaged in their first skirmish with Mexican troops from across the river. On May 8, 1846, President Polk signed a Declaration of War with Mexico.[7]

⋘≫ ⋘≫

On June 11, diarist Edwin Bryant was a considerable distance in front of his westward bound wagon train near Willow Island when he noticed a man ahead, standing in the trail, and leaning against his rifle. He wore the dress of the mountains: buckskin shirt and pants and moccasins. The man informed Bryant that his name was Bordeaux and that he originally hailed from St. Charles, Missouri. Bordeaux went on to tell Bryant that he was one of several men in a party that had been on the river for nearly six weeks. They were navigating two boats loaded with buffalo robes to the Missouri, but had continually run aground due to low water in the Platte. They had been forced to land their craft and were searching for arrangements to continue their journey overland.

Bryant and his wagon train proceeded with Bordeaux to the spot where the rest of Bordeaux's party was camped, and there took their noon rest. The meeting of this group of English-speaking men in such a remote area was to Bryant's party a pleasant surprise. They traded news and enjoyed a somewhat festive gathering that certainly broke the monotony of travel on the trail. Many members of the train took the opportunity to send letters back to the States with the mountaineers while others traded flour, sugar, bacon, and coffee for buffalo robes. The leaders of the *voyageurs* were identified as Bordeaux, Richard, and Branham (of Scott County, Kentucky), indeed the same men who had left Fort Bernard on May 1. The party included a Mexican, an Indian, and several Creole Frenchmen from Missouri.[8]

Bryant wrote in his journal that the whole party presented a half-civilized, half-savage appearance in both dress and manners. He added that, "The Americans were all well-formed, athletic, and hardy young men, with that daring resolute, and intelligent expression of countenance which generally characterizes the trappers, hunters, and traders of the mountains. Their avocation, position, and connections forces them to be ever watchful and ever ready to meet danger in its most threatening forms." Bryant was appalled by the lack of cleanliness of the Mexican and Indian's cooking arrangement, but chose to ignore it after sampling the bread they fried in buffalo tallow. He said, "…but the result of their culinary operations were such as to excite the appetite of the epicure of the mountains."

Bordeaux, Richard, and Branham accompanied Bryant's wagon train to their afternoon camp, and stayed the night with them. That evening they procured a horse and other supplies they needed to continue their journey to the settlements. The next morning Peter Richard presented Bryant with a letter of introduction to his brother John Richard at Fort Bernard, which also detailed the *voyageurs'* journey thus far.[9]

⟨⟩ ⟨⟩

Historian and author Francis Parkman spent the summer of 1846 naively hoping to witness a battle between two warring tribes of Indians. Travelling ahead of Edwin Bryant by a few days, he arrived at Fort Bernard with Henry Chatillon, his guide, on June 15. He was seemingly astonished by the crudeness of the unfinished fort, but remarked that countless battles had been won by settlers against insurmountable numbers of Indians in structures less suitable than the one he now observed. Only two sides of the stockade had been completed with log and adobe buildings, providing rooms for storage and lodging opening into the center of the stockade. Two Indian lodges occupied the sun-baked yard in front of the fort and the only sign of human life was a squaw who peered out from the nearest lodge as they approached.

In a moment a door opened and John Richard, the *bourgeois*, came out to meet them. Richard beckoned a Navajo to take charge of their horses and, after politely relieving them of their rifles, led them inside the principal room of the establishment. Parkman was impressed with Richard's appearance. Dressed in elaborately decorated buckskin clothing and moccasins, he moved easily with a high degree of athletic agility and vigor; he looked every bit the mountain man that he was. The small room contained a huge fireplace built from four massive rocks and was decorated with the highest degree of Rocky Mountain finery; an Indian bow with otter-skin quiver, a medicine bag, and a pipe with tobacco pouch adorned the walls and a brace of rifles rested in the corner.[10]

Parkman and his guide took rest there and enjoyed the passing of the pipe (Indian style) that Reynal had prepared, but declined Richard's offer to stay. Instead Parkman purchased a pair of "radiant" moccasins from Mary Richard and invited the Richards to join his party for coffee at the nearby Platte River. Parkman then proceeded to bathe and shave at the river, donned his new moccasins and prepared biscuits and coffee for his guests, who soon arrived. After entertaining Richard, Parkman bid them adieu and continued on to Fort Laramie (Fort John).[11]

⊰⊱ ⊰⊱

Eight days later Edwin Bryant's wagon train arrived at Fort Bernard. Approaching the fort, he noticed a large herd of mules grazing on the prairie. Bryant and his associates much desired these animals, but they learned they belonged to traders recently arrived from Pueblo and Taos. Bryant presented John Richard with the letter of introduction that Peter Richard had prepared. Richard received Bryant and his party with "mountain cordiality" and invited them to remain overnight. Bryant also declined Richard's offer, but admitted that "An inhabited house, although of the rudest construction and with accommodations far inferior to an ordinary stable, was nevertheless a cheering sight." Bryant learned that the traders from Taos had packed several hundred pounds of flour from Pueblo for the purpose of trading with the Indians and emigrants along the Platte.

The following afternoon Bryant and some of his companions returned to Fort Bernard in hope of procuring some of the Taos traders' mules. They arranged to trade their oxen and wagons for mules. Bryant and his group were in a hurry to reach California and had become quite disgusted with the slow pace of their oxen. He was elated with the prospect of acquiring mules to continue the journey. The inconvenience of reducing his cargo to what could be loaded on pack mules was of small consequence to him. Bryant sent for the wagons that had been left at Fort John and set up camp near Fort Bernard. Soon Bryant and his party entertained all the trappers and traders from Fort Bernard at their camp. "The mountaineer who has subsisted for months on nothing but fresh meat, would proclaim bread, sugar, and coffee to be high orders of luxury," he wrote.

The following morning Edwin Bryant concluded his barter for mules with Mr. New, a trader from Pueblo. Bryant and his companion, Mr. Jacobs, received seven mules with packsaddles and trappings in exchange for their wagon and three yoke of oxen. Bryant and Jacobs then sorted through their cargo to decide what had to be discarded or sold before continuing their journey.[12]

That same day Francis Parkman rode into Fort Bernard with Paul Dorion. Dorion wanted to trade a horse with one of the men from Taos. When they arrived there they found some of Bryant's company, "engaged in drinking and refitting, and a host of Canadians besides. Russell, drunk as a pigeon.... A motley crew appeared in Richard's rooms; squaws, children, Spaniards, French, and emigrants." Parkman mentions a number of emigrants and mountain men at the post, Russell and Jacobs, both of Bryant's party, included. Some fine-looking Kentucky men, Daniel Boone's grandsons, were among them. "The Boones had clearly inherited the adventurous character of that prince of pioneers [their grandfather] but saw no signs of the quiet and tranquil spirit that so remarkably distinguished him," although they did seem more educated than any others he had met in the West, Parkman said.[13]

Parkman's greatest concern was that some of Bryant's party intended to sell their whiskey to the Indians, since they were obligated to dispose of it before resuming their journey. He was not concerned about the Indians' welfare, but rather was afraid that they might lose interest in the battle with the Crows he was so eager to witness. Filled with disappointment and disgust, he beckoned Dorion to return to Fort Laramie with him.[14]

Artist Alfred Jacob Miller visited the fort in 1837 and left the only known illustrations of Fort William. (*Courtesy, Everett D. Graff Collection, American Heritage Center, University of Wyoming*)

Bryant meanwhile spent most of the day arranging his packs and preparing to get back on the trail west. Just before sunset he took a break to watch an impromptu shooting match. He was amazed with the accuracy, force, and distance the Sioux could attain with a bow and arrow and the skill some showed with a rifle. He was amused by the Indians' astonishment at Colt's five-shot revolving pistol. They regarded this firearm with such awe that they would not even touch it. When the demonstration ended, Bryant returned to his labors, then retired.[15]

George L. Curry was another member of Edwin Bryant's wagon train. He had evidently contracted with the *St. Louis Reveille* to report the news of his adventure to California. Curry was among the party that wished to continue the journey via pack train. On June 25, he sent a lengthy letter from Fort Bernard to the newspaper to report their progress. He described the fort in the following manner: "I returned to Fort Bernard yesterday, and have received much attention from the gentlemen of the establishment. This post was almost reconstructed last year by J.F.X. Richard and brothers, of St. Charles, Missouri, is yet in an unfinished state, but when completed it will be an admirable place for the transaction of mountain commerce. Already it has become, though situated so near its more powerful rival, a position of no small importance. Its proprietors and inmates are agreeable and courteous in the extreme, and among them a stranger feels himself at home." Once again John Richard's hospitality had won himself a friend and this time some free advertisement for Fort Bernard in the *St. Louis Reveille*.[16]

Parkman concluded from his visits to Fort Bernard that, "Gifts pass here as freely as the winds. Visit a Trader, and his last cup of coffee and sugar, his last pound of flour are brought out for your entertainment, and if you admire something he has, he gives it to you. Little thanks expected or given on either side." Bryant was in agreement when he said, "The mountain Traders and Trappers are not rich in luxuries; but whatever they possess they are ever ready to divide with their guests." He added that, "In a trade, however, they are as keen as the shrewdest Yankee that ever peddled clocks or wooden nutmegs."[17]

Edwin Bryant, with the help of some of the Taos traders, learned the basics of packing a mule for the trail. On June 28, 1846, he and his party left Fort Bernard for the last time and resumed their journey to California. He recounted with humor, his own ignorance in traveling by pack train. "The mules, stupid as we regarded them, knew more about this business than we did; and several times I thought I could detect them in giving a wise wink and sly leer, as much as to say, that we were perfect novices, and if they could speak, they would give us the benefit of their advice and instruction. A Mexican pack-mule is one of the most sagacious and intelligent quadrupeds that I have ever met with." A few days after their departure from Fort Bernard they were joined by John Wells, who then accompanied them on to California.[18]

Francis Parkman was spending Independence Day camped on Chugwater Creek, when three Indians brought into camp a "wretchedly emaciated *Negro*." This was the same man who had camped with Richard over a month before and had become lost while looking for their oxen. How he had survived without a gun, knife, or moccasins may never be known. All who saw him, too starved and weak to even speak, considered it nothing short of a miracle that he was alive. Parkman left Chugwater Creek and rode to Bitter Cottonwood Creek to meet Joseph Bissonette to travel with him to La Bonte Creek. Bissonette was not there and after waiting a day Parkman continued on for La Bonte Creek without him, still hoping to witness the battle between the Sioux and Crow.[19]

⋙⋘

In late June, John Brown was in a company of Mormons traveling the emigrant trail in search of "Zion." Brown picked up a Spaniard who he called Hosea [José] along the trail. This Spaniard had started down the river with a party of traders transporting their robes by boat to St. Louis. Due to low water these traders were forced to land their craft and search for means to continue their journey overland. Fearing attack by Pawnee Indians, Hosea hit the trail back for the mountains on foot, until Brown picked him up. The circumstances and timing of these events suggest that he most likely was a member of the party from Fort Bernard. John Brown was immensely thankful for his frontier experience. "He was of great service to me in camp life and helping care for the animals; also taught us how to approach buffalo." At Ash Hollow, a rattlesnake bit "the Spaniard." Though not fatal, it laid him up for a week or more.

This company of Mormons became known as the "Mississippi Saints." Up to this point they thought that Brigham Young and his "Pioneer Battalion" were ahead of them on the trail. Early in July they met John Richard, who was trading for buffalo robes in Goshen's Hole. When they asked Richard about another company of Mormons, he told them that they were the first he had seen, but that he had heard that the Mormons were going up the South Platte River. These Mississippi Saints held a council and concluded to go no farther west, but to find a place to stay the winter east of the Rocky Mountains.[20]

Richard suggested that they go to the upper Arkansas River, where there was corn growing and they would be close enough to Taos to get supplies. After some discussion John Richard agreed to guide them to Pueblo, since he had planned to go that direction on his way to Taos soon anyway. Richard returned to Fort Bernard and prepared to take two wagons with oxen to Taos. On July 10, 1846, he departed Goshen's Hole leading nineteen wagons of Saints to Pueblo. In his autobiography Brown wrote, "Mr. Reshaw proved faithful to us and rendered all the assistance he could on the plains and among the Indians."[21]

Two weeks into the journey, one of the Mormons spotted what he thought was a herd of buffalo in the distance just before nightfall. Early the next morning Richard led a group of Saints on a buffalo hunt near Crow Creek. The herd of buffalo turned out to be a herd of wild horses. The Mormons spread out in an attempt to capture some of the mustangs, but soon were discovered by a large party of Indians who were attempting a capture of their own. The Indians turned and immediately rushed the white men. "Mr. Reshaw was with us and I watched him all the time to see if he was alarmed, but he betrayed no fear." The Indians were a band of Arapaho led by Slim Face, an acquaintance of Richard's. Recognizing Richard, Slim Face dismounted and began a parlay. Soon a campfire was made, and the groups gathered round for a smoke from the chief's pipe. The Arapaho then accompanied the Mormons back to their camp. The next day at Cache la Poudre, they were joined by hundreds more Indians with their lodges. They traveled with the Mormons until they reached the South Platte River.[22]

The Mississippi Saints searched in vain for signs of the Pioneer Battalion at the South Platte River. Unable to find any indication of them, they crossed the South Platte River on July 27 and continued on to Pueblo. John Richard arrived at "the Pueblo" on August 7, 1846, with sixteen families and several single men of the Mississippi Saints. Here they found, "several mountaineers living with their Spanish and Indian wives."[23]

Upon arriving at Pueblo the Mormons received the first news of the whereabouts of Brigham Young. The Saints from Nauvoo, Illinois, had stopped after crossing the Missouri River and established Winter Quarters near the present-day city of Omaha, Nebraska. With the war with Mexico escalating, some five hundred Mormon Volunteers had been enlisted to aid the United States in the conflict. The soldiers, the only religious-based military unit in the history of the U.S., marched from Iowa to the southwest and eventually to San Diego. News of the Mormon Brigade's approach on the Santa Fe Trail had reached Pueblo.[24]

What had been good news to the Mormons turned out to be bad news for John Richard. He was halted at Pueblo and ordered not to proceed to Taos, due to the conflict. His old friend, A. C. Metcalf, whom Richard probably expected to find at Pueblo, was gone, purchasing mules for the United States Army. He had been in Pueblo to buy mules from Alexander Barclay a few days earlier, but was now thought to be back at Bent's Fort. To Richard's undoubted surprise Metcalf was now Lt. Charles Metcalf, second in command of Capt. Ceran St. Vrain's company of New Mexico mounted volunteers with Col. Sterling Price. John Richard could do nothing but wait for the conquest to subside. [25]

Pueblo was full of surprises. A few days after their arrival, who should come riding through the gate? None other than Francis Parkman. Neither Richard or Parkman was expecting to see the other anywhere near Pueblo. Richard was strolling near the gate when Parkman rode in, and it seemed to Parkman that Richard greeted him as though he was expecting him. Typical of John Richard, he made Parkman most welcome in his temporary home. "Richard entertained us hospitably in the little mud room, the best in the Fort." After feeding the party a hearty dinner, Richard sent corn and vegetables to Parkman's camp and sent a Mexican to supply them with a generous supply of firewood. [26]

Parkman noted the beautiful valley surrounding Pueblo and thought that it should sustain more than the few men and Spanish women who lived there. He found the pueblo itself to be built like a rude adobe trading fort and noted Richard's large Santa Fe wagons standing together idly in the compound. When he crossed the valley to observe the Mormons erecting cabins for their winter stay, he saw the abundant cornfields surrounding the fort. In all he found the place to be a very hospitable environment. He expressed his prejudices in his writings when it came to the residents. "The human race in this part of the world," he said, "is divided into three divisions, arranged in order of their merits; white men, Indians and Mexicans." [27]

The Mormons at Pueblo had both good times and bad. Upon their arrival two of the men wounded a deer while hunting. When they went into the brush after the animal, one of the men was attacked by a grizzly bear and badly mauled. He survived the attack, but suffered from the consequences. On September 1, after assisting in the erecting of the cabins, William Crosby, John Brown, and a few others left Pueblo to return to Mississippi for their families. On their return east, they met the Mormon Military Brigade and had an opportunity to exchange pleasantries with them, some of whom they knew. Meanwhile back at Pueblo on September 13, the Saints held a *fandango* at Mormontown, as their little settlement nearby was known. Barclay, Metcalf, and Richard were all in attendance and Metcalf was "the soul of fun." [28]

After the *fandango*, Richard finally managed to make his way to Taos to purchase his whiskey. The war with Mexico was far from over, but enough of a reprieve existed momentarily to allow some civilian travel on the road to Taos. On November 6, 1846, he left Pueblo on his return trip to the North Platte River. What had started out to be a five- or six-week journey, had turned into a five- or six-month trip. He left Pueblo and started up the *Font qui Bouille* with his two Santa Fe wagons heavily loaded with whiskey and corn.

He arrived back at Fort Bernard to find it had been burned to the ground while he was away. The partners suspected the American Fur Company was responsible, but with the Indian Agents backing the opposition and no other law enforcement in the area, the partners could do little to recoup their losses.[29]

John Richard had developed into a man of such diverse character and personality that it is difficult to shoehorn him into a categorical description that does not contradict itself. On one hand he was a shrewd and ruthless trader and a smuggler; on another, he was a kind and hospitable westerner who would share his last scrap of food with a stranger. His 1846 trip to Pueblo was a signature of this conundrum of human nature. He did not hesitate to reschedule his plans to go to Taos on an illegal mission to smuggle whiskey, in order to assist a group of devoutly religious Latter Day Saints in search of a place to call home for the winter. Perhaps it can be summed up in this way, where one might see a scalawag another sees a "good ol' boy."

Of all the events that took place in 1846, one happened in this "year of decision" that would affect John Richard the most, and he was not even aware of it. A young man named Moses Milner proved himself as an Army Scout in the Mexican War. The expansion of his dubious career over the next several years would eventually land him at Fort Laramie and a fateful meeting with John Richard. Bernard DeVoto, when discussing the roles of the variety of characters involved with the events of the year, summed it all up by saying: "…though it is about a good many things, one theme that recurs is the basic courage and honor in the face of adversity which we call gallantry. It is always good to remember human gallantry…."[30]

Notes to Chapter Four:

1. DeVoto, Bernard, *The Year of Decision, 1846, (Little, Brown and Company,* Boston, 1943), p. ix–xii, 3, 8–10.

2. Charles B. Branham married Mary Elizabeth Richard (his second wife) August 2, 1843, in St. Charles, Missouri. He was born in Kentucky in 1811 and remarried twice more in later years. He died and was buried in Boone County, Missouri, in 1893. Charles Bordeaux married Rosalie Richard in St. Charles, Missouri, February 11, 1839. Monroe; Many references to the Bordeaux of the Richard & Company partnership state that this was James Bordeaux of the American Fur Company. This has always seemed unlikely due to the long enmity between James Bordeaux and John Richard. A few years ago this author proved that James Bordeaux was not the Bordeaux in this partnership, but the puzzle of which Bordeaux was Richard's partner at Fort Bernard has yet to be solved. Recent studies are yet to be proven but strongly suggest John Richard's brother-in-law Charles Bordeaux. Levin (pronounced "Leveen") Mitchell was known to most of his friends as Mitch. He arrived back at Pueblo on December 30, 1845, after his trip to the North Platte River. Hammond, p. 136 and 186; McDermott, "John Baptiste Richard" in *Mountain Men*, 2:294; Vincente Trujillo traveled from Taos to Pueblo with Metcalf in 1846. He listed "Jo Rashaw" among the residents and stated that he was involved in the trading and trapping industry there. Cragin, F. W., "Interview of Vincente Trujillo on November 9, 1907, at Avondale, Colorado," (Unpublished Notebooks, Cragin Papers, Colorado Springs Pioneers Museum, Colorado Springs, Colorado) Notebook X, p. 6/29–6/30; Tom Autobees stated that Joe Richard had a store at Pueblo and although John and Peter visited there, Joe was the only one of the brothers who actually resided there. Cragin, F. W., "Interview of Tom Autobees on July 28, 1908, at Avondale, Colorado," (Unpublished Notebooks, Cragin Papers, Colorado Springs Pioneer Museum, Colorado Springs, Colorado) Notebook I, p. 2/9–2/10.

3. Hammond, p. 136.

4. Raat, William Dirk, "The Mexican War," *Encarta 98 Encyclopedia*, (Microsoft, 1993–1997).

5. Jones, p. 7; Cats were a valuable commodity in the west. Without them there was no hope of keeping rodents out of stored food and grain. Hammond, p. 136–139; McDermott, "Joseph Bissonette" in *Mountain Men*, 4:52.

6. The Richard stated to be on this expedition to St. Louis is often mistaken for John. This is another case of mistaken identity. Peter Richard is believed to be the one to participate in this journey as his younger brother Joseph was living in Pueblo, and John definitely stayed at Fort Bernard. Bryant, Edwin, *What I Saw in California: Being the Journal of a Tour*, (Ross & Haynes, Inc. Minneapolis, 1967), p. 82–84

7. Francis Parkman visited Bissonette's farm on Bitter Cottonwood Creek. This creek enters the North Platte River from the south side between the Laramie River and Horseshoe Creek and is now known as Cottonwood Creek. The black man survived a lengthy ordeal in the wilderness before being discovered by Indians and taken to Francis Parkman's camp. Further description follows later in this chapter. Wade, Mason, *Francis Parkman: Heroic Historian*, (Viking Press, New York, 1942), p. 265–267; Raat.

8. Bryant, p. 82–84; The Mexican that Bryant mentions is likely the same man that John Brown called "The Spaniard, Hosea [Jose]" who accompanied him to Pueblo a short time later. Brown, John: Brown, John Zimmerman, editor, *The Autobiography of Pioneer John Brown*, (Stevens & Wallace, Inc., Publishers, Salt Lake City, Utah, 1941), p. 67.

9. Bryant, p. 82–84.

10. Parkman, p. 76–77.

11. Reynal was presumably Antoine Reynal, born in 1809 in Missouri. He was the father of Louisa and Jane "Jennie" Reynal. Jane, born in 1850, later married John Richard's son Louis, born in 1847. *Ibid.* p. 77–78; Wade, p. 258–259; Census of Fort Laramie, Laramie County, Wyoming Territory, 1860, 1870.

12. Bryant, p. 106–107, 112–114.

13. DeVoto, *The Year of Decision, 1846*, p. 174.

14. Wade, p. 263–264; DeVoto, *The Year of Decision, 1846*, p. 175.

15. Bryant, p. 113–114.

16. Morgan, *Overland in 1846*, vol. II, p. 574–575.

17. Wade, p. 262; Bryant, p. 112–113.

18. Bryant, p. 114–115.

19. Wade, p. 265–267.

20. Brown, p. 67–68.

21. Jones, p. 8; Barry, p. 486; Brown, p. 68.

22. Brown, p. 69–70; Slim Face and Left Hand were with Black Kettle at the Sand Creek Massacre. Cragin, F. W., (Unpublished Notebooks, Cragin Papers, Colorado Springs Pioneer Museum, Colorado Springs, Colorado).

23. Brown, p. 69–70; Charles Kelly, editor, *Journals of John D. Lee*, (Western Printing Company, Salt Lake City, Utah, 1938), p. 31–32.

24. Brown, p. 70.

25. McDermott, "John Baptiste Richard" in *Mountain Men*, 2:296; On August 4, 1846, Archibald Metcalf found Alexander Barclay hunting on Shepherd's Fork, where he and Beckworth purchased several mules from him. On August

25, Briggs paid Barclay for the mules Metcalf had received on August 4. Hammond, p. 141–142; In August Luz Metcalf was one of the ladies who entertained Kearny at Bent's Fort. Lecompte, "Archibald Charles Metcalf," in *Mountain Men*, 4:220.

26. Wade, p. 278; Parkman, p. 239–242.

27. Wade, p. 278–279; Parkman, p. 239–242.

28. Parkman, p. 239–242; Kelly, p. 32; Brown, p. 70; Hammond, p. 142.

29. Hammond, p. 144; McDermott, "John Baptiste Richard" in *Mountain Men*, 2:296; Gilbert, p. 7.

30. Milner, Joe E., and Forrest, Earle R., *California Joe; Noted Scout and Indian Fighter*, (The Caxton Printers, Ltd., Caldwell, Idaho 1935); DeVoto, *The Year of Decision*, 1846, p. i.

This photograph, taken at Fort Laramie by Alexander Gardner in 1868, shows Indians crossing the North Platte River in a boat. This seems to show a small craft specifically for transporting people. Larger vessels were used for ferrying animals and wagons. Note the rigging which allowed the current of the river to propel the craft across the river. *(Minnesota Historical Society)*

5
⋙ IF AT FIRST... ⋘

ONE OF THE MOST prominent features of John Richard's complex personality was his amazing resiliency. With all manner of elasticity, he continued to rebound from numerous failures. This singular characteristic separated him from many of his counterparts and provided him with the opportunity to succeed. With each new venture he added to the experiences of his past of both success and failure, yet shortfalls never seemed to lessen his enthusiasm or vigor when embarking on a new endeavor.

John Richard started the year of 1847 with nothing to lose. With Fort Bernard burned, he had started a new trading post somewhere in the Fort Laramie area, probably near the site of the Upper Platte Agency. He may have merely been trading from an Indian lodge and a Santa Fe wagon, with his pregnant wife, three-year-old son, John Jr., and stepdaughter, Mary, close at hand. He received a shipment of corn from Alexander Barclay in Pueblo around the middle of February and about that time he and Mary's second son, Louis, was born.[1]

John Richard was planning an early departure from the area in the hope of arriving in St. Louis ahead of the competition which would result in his buffalo robes bringing top prices. With the spring thaw still months away, river transportation was out of the question. But he was caught without sufficient draft animals on hand to haul his season's yield overland, so he needed to acquire additional workhorses and mules before he could start. Before Barclay's freight wagons left Fort Laramie on his return to Pueblo, Richard ordered mules and horses from him. They were delivered a few weeks later.[2]

Richard left Fort Laramie on March 26, 1847, with two traders and more than thirty packs of buffalo robes. While crossing Kansas in May, they met some four hundred Delaware and Shawnee Indians at Elm Grove. These Indians were on their way to do battle with the Pawnees.

The traders took the Oregon Trail route and met a party of emigrants just outside of St. Joseph, Missouri. Their eastward journey came to an end when they arrived in St. Louis on June 11.[3]

⌘ ⌘

In April 1847 Brigham Young departed with his first Pioneer Company from Winter Quarters to Zion with approximately 147 emigrants and 72 wagons. Zion would turn out to be the valley of the Great Salt Lake, but when they left the Missouri River they only knew Zion was westward. The Mississippi Saints who had traveled to Pueblo the previous year had also started back up the Old Trappers' Trail to the North Platte River. William Empey, who was with Brigham Young recorded in his diary on June 1, 1847: " …came to fort-larramie and camped for the night in peace and found some of our Brethren from the missippie 3 famleys 9 men 5 women and 3 children wich came out in the year 1836 [1846] they went to fort perbolo and came to meet the rest of the saints in the spring…."

When leaving Fort Laramie, Brigham Young split the company into two segments. The first, smaller group traveled ahead to establish a crossing of the North Platte with their leather boat, the *Revenue Cutter*. Young and the majority of the Saints followed behind. The night that John Richard arrived in St. Louis, the second group of Brigham Young's Saints camped at the mouth of Dry Muddy Creek, near the present Natrona/Converse county line of Wyoming. William Empey recalled, "…camped a Long side of the platt in a butifull valley we rested in peace for the night."[4]

The following day the second group arrived at the crossing point on the North Platte River and found the advance group ferrying a party of non-Mormon emigrants across the river with the *Revenue Cutter*. Here the Mormons were exercising their ingenuity in supplementing the church coffers while waiting for the remainder of their own company to arrive. The ferry site they had chosen was directly across the river from the mouth of Cannon Creek. Cannon Creek is now called Casper Creek, and this location is about one mile downstream from the later location of Guinard's Bridge and Fort Casper in present-day Casper, Wyoming.[5]

Brigham Young, seeing both the potential income for his church and the convenience of the ferry for future emigration of his own flock, concluded to establish a genuine ferry at this location. He ordered that two ferry boats, or rafts, be constructed of timber from the "Black Hills" to the south (now known as Casper Mountain). These rafts were built by first constructing several dugout canoes then lashing them together with timbers to form something like a deck. Tom Empey, a longtime contemporary resident of Casper and the great-grandson of William Empey, constructed a similar ferry, built to specifications, that is on display at Fort Caspar Museum. Pioneers used this method to construct many ferries to cross rivers in the West.[6]

William Empey was among the men Brigham Young appointed to operate the ferry in 1847. Shortly after this appointment, Empey and another man were sent back to Deer Creek, near present-day Glenrock, Wyoming, to dig coal from a bank that had been noted a few days earlier. This coal was used to fire the forge at a temporary blacksmith's shop operated in conjunction with the ferry. While at Deer Creek, Empey and his partner erected a sign along the trail announcing their ferry ahead. This sign is reported to have been the first commercial advertisement displayed in what is now Wyoming.[7]

Shortly after the Mormon ferry began operation, the Hill Ferry, a private company, began operation downstream from them. After suffering a loss of business, the Mormons approached Hill and asked if he was interested in a partnership. Hill flatly refused. Not wishing to lose any more business, the Mormons packed up their equipment and floated downriver to a new location below Mr. Hill's operation. This new location would be seen first by arriving emigrants. A few days later the Mormons witnessed the remains of Hill's ferry floating down the river. He had given up the contest, but destroyed his ferry to keep anyone else from profiting from his labors. After several weeks the waters of the Platte subsided, and business slowed drastically as the river became fordable by wagon. The Mormon men then moved back to their first location and, aside from occasional blacksmith's work, the camp became mournfully lonely as they waited for the last Mormon wagon train scheduled for the season. They planned to accompany that train to its final destination.[8]

After a season of hard work, the ferrymen finally had time to reflect on their labors as they winterized the location. They beached their crafts and prepared them for storage until the following spring.

A close call with a grizzly bear by one of the men while hunting game reminded them all that danger was never far away. Wesley Dustin, who was just a young boy, had drowned earlier that summer in the raging Platte, and they also feared being taken by surprise and killed in a brush with Indians. Yes, life here was very different than it had been back home.[9]

⊲⊱·⊰⊳

In the fall of 1847, Alexander Barclay moved his base of operations from Pueblo south to the Santa Fe Trail. He sold his store there to A.C. Metcalf, who had recently been the sheriff of Taos but had since resumed his career as a trader. Traders Ward and Guerrier left Pueblo on an expedition to the North Platte in November, followed by Metcalf a few weeks later.

⊲⊱·⊰⊳

The following summer of 1848, John Richard brought a shipment of corn up the trail from Pueblo and was trading in partnership with F. Robidoux below Fort John. It appears that this new partnership also included Joseph Bissonette and Charles Bordeaux from the earlier Fort Bernard team.

Two hundred Apaches at Manco de Burro Pass, in the Raton Mountains, attacked the wagon train of Maxwell and Quinn from Taos. A short time later Metcalf moved his wife from Pueblo to Santa Fe.[10]

⊲⊱·⊰⊳

By early 1849, A.C. Metcalf was apparently becoming somewhat distanced from his young wife Luz. He spent the winter trading with the Kiowas near present-day Dodge City, Kansas, and returned to Barclay's Fort often, but only occasionally made the trip to Santa Fe. Spring waters were high on the North Platte that year so John Richard and his partners, F. Robidoux, Joseph Bissonette, Charles Bordeaux, and McLean, carried their robes downriver in Mackinaws. They left their post near Fort John at the end of March and stopped to pick up mail at the new military post of Fort Kearny (Nebraska) in the middle of April. By the end of the month, they arrived at St. Joseph then continued on to St. Louis with their cargo. The season's trade must have been outstanding that year. In May, Ward and Guerrier's eastbound wagon train was carrying six thousand robes over the Santa Fe Trail.[11]

On June 26, 1849, the American Fur Company sold Fort John to the United States Army. The Army then officially renamed the location

Fort Laramie, though it had been referred to by that name for many years. The Richard partners now expanded their livestock business to supply beef (often trail-weary oxen), horses, and mules to the United States Army. They also added Charles Primeau, a cousin of Bissonette's, into the partnership.

⪦⪧

Later that summer, Richard had left the trading post near Fort Laramie to visit St. Louis when he met Lt. J. W. Gunnison, second in command of a U.S. Corps of Engineers topographical expedition (Stansbury's Utah Expedition), at Joseph Robidoux's trading post near present-day Scottsbuff, Nebraska. Richard recommended that Gunnison take the route through Mitchell Pass, stating that it was "not much of a trail" but that he had used it the previous winter. The selling point was that it was at least eight miles shorter.[12]

An epidemic of cholera took its toll among the tribes along the Platte that summer. In early July, the rest of Captain Stansbury's topographical party arrived on the North Platte. Near Ash Hollow they happened upon five lodges filled with Sioux, all dead from cholera. Further along they met James Bordeaux who had been trading with ten lodges of Brules. This band was now recovering from the mysterious illness and, after suffering tremendous losses, was in great fear of the disease returning. Joseph Bissonette was trading a short distance west of Bordeaux with thirty lodges of Brules who were in the height of the sickness. After losing faith in their Medicine Man they pitifully begged for medicine to fight their dilemma. Captain Stansbury sent his doctor among them, and they anxiously swallowed the medication offered them.[13]

⪦⪧

That same summer A. C. Metcalf returned to the North Platte River with Kit Carson and Calvin Jones. They went to the mouth of Deer Creek, and there erected the first bridge ever to span the North Platte River. This bridge, which is sometimes referred to as the "Trapper's Bridge," was poorly constructed and failed miserably in the high waters of the following spring. Carson and Jones returned to Taos while Metcalf vanished seemingly into thin air. The accounts of Metcalf's death are so varied (and some so far fetched) that none can be believed. He may have died or simply left the country to escape his many creditors. Luz Metcalf remarried and stated in an interview many years later that her husband had died in a cholera epidemic at Fort Laramie in 1848. This is possible since an epidemic existed there at the time, except that he was reportedly still alive and well and in the vicinity when the Trapper's Bridge washed out in 1849. Another report states that he was killed at Pawnee or Walnut Fork on the Santa Fe Trail. We may never know the details of his leaving, but Archibald Charles Metcalf departed from the West as mysteriously as he had appeared there some ten years earlier.[14]

On John Richard's return from St. Louis, he and one of his brothers boarded a steamboat headed west only to find that also aboard were Alexander Barclay and the Indian Agents Majors Drips and Thomas Fitzpatrick: "…Majors Fitzpatrick, Dripps and Isaac Adamson came up on same boat with Richard (John & brother) and some of the old fur trade remnants. Arrived at Kansas in due course.…" Barclay wrote in his diary, September 1, 1849.

This trip up the Missouri River must have been amusing, to say the least. It would have been entertaining to be the proverbial fly on the wall and listen to the conversations of the two Indian Agents on one side of the boat and the trappers and notorious whiskey traders, such as Richard, on the other.[15]

❖ ❖

In the summer of 1850, the old Fort Bernard partnership was dissolved. Joseph Bissonette opened a trading post near the trail at his farm on Bitter Cottonwood Creek. John Richard was still a partner in the farm there, but otherwise appears not to have been involved. John and Peter Richard were running a trading post at Ash Point, some twenty miles downriver from Fort Laramie. They apparently were supplying emigrant traffic with goods purchased from their old rival the American Fur Company. It was about this time that John's third son, Peter S., was born into the growing Richard family. Joseph Richard had acquired the old Barclay/Metcalf store at Pueblo and, though there is little documentation about the family during this period, the Richards seemed to be prospering.[16]

During the "low water season" in the fall of 1850 John Richard, hoping to have learned from Metcalf's mistakes, began construction of a second bridge across the North Platte River. He chose a site a few miles west of the former Trapper's Bridge at a place near Muddy Creek that would later be known as Parkerton. Richard risked everything he owned on the emigrant trade of the year to come. It was a gamble he could not resist. Very much aware of the dangers involved in crossing the Platte at high water, he was positive that Metcalf's idea would pay off. He was convinced that a toll bridge across the Platte was the answer. He felt most assuredly that the emigrants would pay nearly any price to cross the river quickly and safely.[17]

John Richard was so enthusiastic about the plan that he managed to convince Miller, Langdon, Steele, and Randall to invest in the scheme. His new partners thought that if one bridge was a good idea, two would be even better. They obtained permission from the United States Army to also construct a bridge across the Laramie River, within the domain of Fort Laramie. Due to the proximity, the military would regulate the amount that could be charged for tolls, but it would still be a lucrative venture. To ensure that potential customers would know of the bridge's existence before attempting to ford the river at some downstream crossing, Richard placed an advertisement in the *St. Joseph Gazette* on February 26, 1851. The advertisement stated that he would have 150 to 200 ponies for sale at Ash Point. It continued that he had "very nearly completed a bridge across the North Platte."[18]

A short time later the *Missouri Republican* reported that John Richard had completed his project: "…a fine and substantial bridge has been built over the Platte 100 miles above [Fort] Laramie." The *Frontier Guardian* in Kanesville, Iowa, reported on May 16, 1851: "William and T. Randell (en route to [Richard's] new North Platte River bridge) with groceries and provisions for emigrants; J. B. Nichols (for Fort Laramie); "Richard's & Co." (trader John Richard's outfit) with Provisions, &c." In May John Richard was so optimistic about the coming success of the bridge that he moved his brother Peter, who had been running the post at Ash Point, to the bridge at Parkerton and sold the Ash Point Trading Post to Ward and Guerrier from Pueblo.[19]

John Richard's optimism for the success of the bridge was unwarranted. Traffic on the Oregon Trail in 1851 was unusually slow that year, and the waters of the North Platte River remained low. The emigrant trains passed by Richard's Bridge, with few even noting its existence in their diaries. They forded the river at any of the many convenient locations along the route.

You would think that the financial failure of this first year of operation for the new bridge might have defeated John Richard. Instead he

simply packed up and in August moved to the farm on Bitter Cottonwood Creek with Bissonette. Richard and Bissonette worked in the
corn and vegetable fields and the apple and plum orchard. Other than
filing a claim against the Army at Fort Laramie for $560 worth of dam-
age done to the farm by the Army's livestock, their late summer and fall
was uneventful while they waited for the next year's migration.[20]

⟨⟩⟨⟩

John Richard was still at the farm on Bitter Cottonwood Creek when
William T. Eubank, an early freighter on both the Oregon and Santa Fe
Trails, first met him that spring in 1852. Early on, the high spring
waters were rising in the Platte, and John Richard hoped for a profitable season at the bridge. He relocated to the bridge to solicit the
business of the first emigrant trains. All his hopes were soon floating
down the Platte. The high waters he had wished for all winter took the
bridge away with them on July 16. The Fort Laramie bridge, which
Richard had little involvement with, had been somewhat successful
these two years. John Richard relinquished his share of that bridge to
the other partners in trade for his freedom from the debt incurred by
the loss of the bridge at Parkerton.[21]

⟨⟩⟨⟩

That spring (1852) Magloire Mosseau had gone to work as a clerk at
the Devil's Gate Trading Post. This trading post had been erected by
the partnership of Charles Lajeunesse, Hubert Papin, and Moses and
Charley Perat. All of these men had earlier been either partners or
employees of the American Fur Company. At some later point, Louis
Guinard joined the partnership. The partners erected a toll bridge
spanning the Sweetwater River seven miles below the trading post, just
downstream from Independence Rock.[22]

⟨⟩⟨⟩

John Richard returned to the farm on Bitter Cottonwood Creek where
he and Joseph Bissonette sold and traded fruit and vegetables with the
pioneers along the trail. Together they headed for St. Louis in late
summer. By early September, they were already returning westbound
on the trail.

On September 12, 1852, Major Winslow F. Sanderson, with two
companies of mounted riflemen met Joseph Bissonette's wagon train,
loaded with goods, at Cottonwood Point. At the junction of the road to

Independence and St. Joseph, he then met John Richard. Richard was herding a flock of three thousand sheep to the Mormon settlements in Utah. The potential profitability of this excursion is obvious. Richard knew and understood the value of livestock west of the Mississippi.[23]

This late season departure on such a venture may have left some people questioning his sanity. When considering the possible consequences, it must be reasoned that few men could have succeeded in arriving in Utah with a band of healthy sheep. On the other hand, John Richard had an uncanny ability to successfully complete what seem to be impossible missions. He'd previously transported contraband whiskey over great distances with amazing speed all the while eluding authorities. His daring whiskey run in 1843 demonstrated that he had the skills and provided him with experience. While John was en route with the sheep, his wife Mary gave birth to twins, Charles and Josephine, on November 9, 1852. The Richard family was growing, but no more rapidly than was common for any other American family in that era.[24]

John Richard must have succeeded on his mission with the huge flock of sheep for that same winter, he erected yet another bridge across the North Platte River. This time Richard joined with his former partners Joseph Bissonette and Charles Bordeaux plus a group of five new partners. He chose a new site some twenty miles above the Parkerton Bridge. The new bridge was constructed only two hundred feet upstream from the second location of the 1847 Mormon Ferry; this was a quarter-mile above a popular ford that in 1849 had become known as the California Crossing. Prior to the California Gold Rush, this crossing was called the Old Indian Ford and had been used by many western travelers including John C. Frémont. This new bridge was simply known as "the bridge" or Platte Bridge until 1860, when Louis Guinard built another bridge a few miles upstream. The earlier bridge then became known as Reshaw's (Richard's) Bridge or Lower Platte Bridge. The other was called Guinard's Bridge or Upper Platte Bridge.[25]

It seems obvious that Joseph Bissonette was heavily involved in the partnership of Richard's Bridge from its onset. The wagon train he led west ahead of Richard and his sheep in the fall of 1852 had been carrying tools, hardware, and other materials for the bridge's construction. In January 1853, he wrote to Thomas Pim in St. Louis. The nature of this

Lt. John C. Frémont visited Fort Laramie on his first exploring trip to the Rocky Mountains. He recommended the establishment of a military post at the site. (*Wyoming State Archives, Department of State Parks and Cultural Resources*)

correspondence was a request for his services. Bissonette asked Pim to come to the North Platte to keep books for their company that was building a new bridge across the river.[26]

In a "Notice to Californians," Bissonette, Kenceleur & Co. stated in the *St. Joseph Gazette* on February 23, 1853, that a "substantial" bridge across the North Platte River would be finished "in time for the earliest trains." The advertisement continued: "There will be at the Bridge two Blacksmith and Wagon maker's shops, for the accommodation of emigrants. The company will have a good Grocery Store and eating house, and all kinds of Indian handled peltries, also oxen, cows, horses, and mules at low prices…. Bissonette, Kenceleur, & Co.'s. St. Joseph agent, R. L. McGhee." At the bridge Richard constructed a log cabin, blacksmith shop, and other buildings on the south side of the river, awaiting the first wagon train's arrival. Perhaps good fortune was finally smiling on John Richard as the Fort Laramie Bridge washed out that spring. He had liquidated that previous partnership before further losses had occurred.[27]

❖⊱⊰❖

John Richard had learned his lessons in bridge building well. Richard employed Joseph McKnight at the bridge for several years. McKnight described the bridge as follows: the new bridge was built on several wooden piers, made of heavy timbers in a diamond shape to divert the water around them; they were then filled with rock for stability. The north abutment was a sandstone cliff that rose several feet above the high water line. The south end of the bridge was slightly lower as it extended some distance to meet the sloping prairie. To further strengthen the piers they were cross-timbered internally before the rock was added. These piers were thirty to forty feet apart and spanned by logs hauled from the mountain, seven miles to the south. After all had been braced, stayed, and fastened together with iron bolts, the deck was laid. Made from four-inch thick hand-sawn planks, each was hand fit tightly together and spiked to the span logs. Afterward a heavy railing was installed to prevent livestock from drifting over the side. This railing carried extra bracing at each of the piers to further strengthen the structure. The completed bridge overall was about one thousand feet long and fifteen or eighteen feet wide. McKnight also reported that the bridge cost some forty thousand dollars to build. It is likely that this hefty sum was an exaggeration, as Richard quoted to others considerably lower figures.[28]

Traveler John Murray reported a very similar description of the bridge in his journal, when he saw it in 1853: "…The bridge is a substantial structure— It has 8 wood framed piers filled & sunk with rock & the reaches are supported by heavy braces—The sides are railed up & bottom planked &c…. Some of the timbers look to be sawed perhaps by hand—Where they got the timber I cant see….". Murray's wagon train was traveling the north side of the river, or Child's Route. The nearest native timber was located on what is now called Casper Mountain, a distance of several miles, and was perhaps not visible on the cloudy day he reported in his journal.[29]

Ward & Guerrier also constructed a trading post and ferry nine miles upstream from Fort Laramie. When the bridge at the fort washed out, the Army realized the important service it had provided for the fort. They consequently contracted Seth Ward and a man named Major or Majors to reconstruct it. This made the Laramie River Bridge property of the United States military and ended the tolls at that crossing.

In May 1853, Ward & Guerrier presented to Richard and Bordeaux a promissory note for a one-year supply of trade goods. What was given in return may never be known, but this note certainly indicates a substantial debt was incurred.[30]

On June 11, 1853, a wagon train carrying diarist Sarah Sutton crossed Richard's Bridge. Her opinion of Richard's toll was not very amiable. She felt the five hundred dollars that Richard charged for the crossing of their train was little short of highway robbery. Nathaniel Myer, who dealt with Richard that same day from another train, was forced to sell him one of his oxen. "…Campment all around us. Passed two trading places… Sold one of our oxen at $18; he got lame." The animal must have been in considerably better condition than Myer thought for Richard to pay eighteen dollars for him. He was known to pay much less.

The migration season of 1853 was enormous. When Myer stated, "campment all around us," he did not exaggerate. Literally thousands of settlers crossed the trail that year. These two wagon trains both had diarists that coincidentally mentioned John Richard on the same day. There are undoubtedly hundreds of other diary entries that are yet to be found. Richard's ill-fated luck of the past few years was soon to change if the first season for the new bridge continued as it started.[31]

⟨≋⟩ ⟨≋⟩

Richard evidently used the expense of the bridge to explain his high toll to his potential customers. It is obvious when studying these diary accounts that Richard claimed varying costs of construction and charged varying toll rates, depending on the conditions of the river or the customer. When J. R. Bradway crossed the bridge at the end of June, Richard charged eight dollars per wagon. He also told Bradway that the bridge cost fifteen thousand dollars to build, his way of rationalizing the higher toll. As the water in the North Platte River rose, so did the toll and so did Richard's reported financial investment in the bridge.[32]

Richard performed another valuable service for his customers at the bridge. Bradway left a letter and a portion of his journal with Richard to be sent back home via the first eastbound traveler who happened by. He also reported a coal mine in the north bank of the river that Richard used to fuel the fires in his blacksmith shops as well as to heat his home and his other business enterprises at the bridge.

When John Murray arrived at the bridge a few days later, he utilized Richard's blacksmith's shop and trading posts. He reported trading posts on both sides of the river to take advantage of all possible customers. William Brown substantiated this fact by stating, "…passed a fine bridge made of pine…last crossing place on Platte River. At the bridge there was 2 trading posts, blacksmith shop & several Indian Wigwams." At the trading post Murray purchased flour at ten dollars per hundredweight. After having his team shod, he bought extra shoes at a dollar per pair and nails at seventy-five cents per dozen. The water was beginning to recede, lowering the toll rate that day to six dollars per wagon.[33]

On July 1, 1853, Dr. John Smith arrived at the bridge and his wagon train camped there that night. He was told that the bridge cost sixteen thousand dollars to build, and Richard charged the train the six-dollars-per-wagon rate. John Richard also told Dr. Smith that so far that year three thousand wagons had crossed the bridge. The following day in his diary Smith noted passing the old site of the Mormon Ferry, writing that it was abandoned due to the competition from the new bridge. At the old ferry site he states that the road forked: the fork to the right was the old road which took a route over the hills away from the river, while the new fork, to the left, followed the river for another nine miles to rejoin the old road at Red Buttes, where Smith's party camped the following night.[34]

By the end of July, Count Leonetto Cipriani had also crossed Richard's Bridge. He described his visit at the bridge this way: "At noon we were at the bridge, property of four Canadian brothers. Alone except for the help from the Indians, they had been able to erect a bridge of twelve arches, entirely of cedar, with piers formed of huge tree trunks and filled with gravel. Though the toll could be considered moderate, three dollars per wagon And four for every hundred head [of livestock], the bridge assured them a good income."

The good Count was unaware that the rapidly dropping level of the Platte River had also dropped Richard's toll by more than half. Cipriani was most likely amused by the vast number of Indian lodges surrounding the bridge and assumed that they had assisted in its construction. More likely they were some of Richard's many Indian friends and family partaking of his well-known generosity. As Francis Parkman and Edwin Bryant had both noted, away from the trading table, John Richard, as well many other traders, were very willing to share most anything they possessed, the quirk in Richard's nature that acquired him his Sioux name, Always-Has-Plenty-of-Meat.[35]

⬦⬦⬦

William K. Sloan was a Scottish-born emigrant who was raised by his uncle, first in Pittsburgh and then in Illinois, following his father's death. In 1853 Captain Stewart, a fellow Scotsman, recruited Sloan to accompany him with a train of freight wagons to his farm near Salt Lake City. On September 8, 1853, they departed Fort Laramie on what they knew would be the roughest leg of their journey. The grass along the trail was cropped short from the heavy traffic of the season, and the hard gravelly road caused their oxen continuous problems with lameness. When they arrived at Richard's Bridge the train was in poor condition. Sloan wrote: "…a hundred and twenty miles west from [Fort] Laramie we again crossed the north fork of the Platte but on a bridge the only one we had seen since starting, this bridge was built by a Canadian Frenchman named John Richard the winter and spring preceding, and certainly was a good investment, the bridge cost not over $5,000.00 dollars and his receipts that season were over $40,000.00 from the bridge alone." John Richard was indeed having a good year at the bridge.[36]

The fact that both Cipriani and Sloan mistook John Richard for a Canadian is not unusual. Prior to the Louisiana Purchase, the Hudson's Bay Company and other smaller trading companies of Canada primarily controlled the trapping and trading business in North America. Following the purchase, many former employees of these companies remained in what then became the Louisiana Territory of the United States. Their loyalty to the region and their Indian friends and clientele was evidently deeper than their loyalty to Canada. Although most of those Canadians had long since passed on, many of their descendants still remained in the western United States. The fact that Richard was born in Missouri had little influence. If you spoke French or had a French accent in western America, you must be Canadian. This same misconception still held true well into the twentieth century.

John Richard was not afraid to barter for the toll across his bridge, especially if a traveler had something he wanted. It has been said that his modest log cabin at the bridge was the most elaborately furnished home between St. Louis and San Francisco. When emigrant William Sloan arrived at the bridge, he soon learned the practice of bartering: "There were quite a number of mountaineers located about the place and all very thirsty, from some of the men they ascertained that we had a five gallon keg of whiskey aboard the train, they must have it, price was no object. Stewart finally agreed to let them have it, in consideration of our crossing the bridge free, which was equivalent to $125.00 for the whiskey."

John Richard, well experienced in the pricing of whiskey, was undoubtedly controlling a seething rage at Stewart's asking price, but after all, it was a seller's market. While bartering for whiskey he was probably eyeing Stewart's dilapidated livestock. Richard merely waited for the next stage of the barter to recoup his loss. Sloan reported: "…we had several head of oxen too lame to travel farther, and it was necessary for us either to leave them on the road or sell them which we did to Richard at $2.50 per head, paying him $100.00 per head for fresh and fat ones to take their place." Little did Sloan seem to realize that these one-hundred-dollar oxen had been two-and-a-half-dollar oxen just a short time before.[37]

John Richard had well learned the value of healthy animals to the emigrants while trading near Fort Laramie. He had brought to the bridge all the livestock he could acquire prior to the emigrant season and had likely seen a substantial income from trading them throughout the year. The concept of this business was simple. He turned the trail-weary animals out on the rich grassy range and mountain spring water of Reshaw Creek (which is now known as Elk Horn Creek) where they soon recovered from the strenuous work, poor feed, and alkali water of the trail. Furthermore, the grazing along Reshaw Creek was convenient to Richard's location at the bridge.[38]

The goal of a successful trader is to make the customer believe that the customer cleverly took advantage of the poor unsuspecting trader, all the while turning the tables. William Sloan felt that he and his associates had made a cagey trade. In his estimation, the whiskey trade was little short of robbery and what they had given up on the oxen was of little consequence. In reality, Sloan and friends had profited by about twenty-five times their purchase price on the whiskey trade, which is certainly a nice margin, but Richard gained forty times his investment on the oxen, which substantially compensated him for his loss on the whiskey. John Richard may have had very little education, but he fully understood the value of the goods and services that he dealt in, and most assuredly was an extremely shrewd businessman at the bargaining table.

John Richard was finally back in his element in 1853. Little had changed in his methods since his days with Sibille & Adams; only his customers had changed. Instead of dealing primarily with Indians who were naïve to the ways of eastern finance, he now dealt mostly with easterners that were naïve to the ways of the West. With all the finesse of a less than scrupulous used car dealer, "Honest John Richard" owned a toll bridge and an "only driven on Sundays" used livestock business. His greatest success in life had occurred the past year. The bridge, with the cooperation of the spring waters of the North Platte, was off to a booming start. On November 2, 1853, J. Soule Bowman reported to the *Missouri Republican* that at a point 150 miles above Fort Laramie: "Here a substantial bridge has been erected over the river at which emigrants can cross their stock in safety, and at a fair price."

Although Bowman's distance may have been off by a few miles and the price may have varied with the rise and fall of the river, Bowman passed on to the public the first published statement by any non-interested party who had actually seen the bridge. Other bridges had been advertised as "substantial," but had washed away before the emigrants could get there to use them. Here was a bridge that had withstood the spring floods and would be there for those who would make the trip across the trail the next year.[39]

Notes to Chapter Five:

1. Jones, p. 9; when Mary Richard gave birth to Black Moon's daughter, John Richard accepted her and raised her as his own. They named her Mary, after her mother. Gilbert, 8; J. B. Doyle left Pueblo with Barclay's corn on January 26, 1847, and returned on March 5. Hammond, p. 145–146.

2. William Guerrier, who would later become a partner of Richard's, left Pueblo on March 7, 1847, with fifteen mules and one horse for the Platte. Hammond, p. 146.

3. The identities of the two traders that accompanied Richard to the east are not certain; Joseph Bissonette, Charles Bordeaux, and Charles Branham are among the likely candidates. *St. Louis Daily Union,* June 12, 1847, and *St. Louis Reveille,* June 13, 1847, cited in, Barry, p. 686; Alexander Barclay arrived in Westport on June 13, and St. Louis on June 20. He did not mention seeing Richard while he was there. Barclay was ill while there and either arrived after Richard's departure or missed seeing him due to his illness. Regardless, Barclay seems to have mentioned the other meetings they had, but not this instance. Consequently, Richard's movements in St. Louis are unknown. Hammond, p. 149.

4. It is not my intention to make William Empey look illiterate through his misspelling or improper English. On the contrary, William Empey was well educated for that time. My aim in quoting this diary verbatim is to express the character and emotion of the man who wrote his daily thoughts on those pages so long ago, just as Mr. Morgan left them untainted for his readers. Morgan, Dale L., "The Mormon Ferry on the North Platte," *Annals of Wyoming,* vol. 21, p. 130–132.

5. Although the Mormons certainly would accept cash for their ferrying fee, they preferred to trade for nonperishable staples, such as sugar or flour. They knew these items could be used in the winter to come, regardless of where the trail might take them. The further advantage of this barter was that goods received were valued at eastern prices rather than the inflated prices of the trading posts along the trail. The end result was considerably more food for their money. Cannon Creek was supposedly so named because an earlier group of explorers had cached a cannon there before continuing westward. Documentation to substantiate this lore has not been found, so as with many tales of the West, we may never know how true this story is. We do know that what was then called Cannon Creek is now called Casper Creek. The city of Casper, the fort, and the creek are all named after Caspar Collins who spelled his first name with an "ar." When renaming the fort after Collins in 1865, the military made an error and misspelled the name with an "er," This spelling was carried over to the city. When the museum was established at the fort in 1936, those in charge chose to use the correct spelling of Collins's first name. Hence, the fort is spelled Fort *Caspar* while most other placenames are spelled *Casper.* The result of this minor variation has created a source of confusion for years. Morgan, *Annals of Wyoming,* vol. 21, p. 132, 146; interview with Richard Young, curator, Fort Caspar Museum.

6. Morgan, *Annals of Wyoming,* vol. 21, p. 133–135; Glass, Jefferson, *Discussions with Tom Empey, 1996–1998,* (Unpublished Notes, Jefferson Glass's personal

collection); Ben Kern is a modern day wagon master who has led numerous wagon-train reenactments across the Oregon, California, Mormon, and Bozeman trails in recent years. He has used a replica ferry of similar construction for his wagons and says that they are a quite stable and suitable craft. Moulton, Candy, and Kern, Ben, *Wagon Wheels*, (High Plains Press, Glendo, Wyoming, 1996), p. 153.

7. Morgan, *Annals of Wyoming*, vol. 21, p. 135, 154–155.

8. The Hill Ferry was located near the area presently known as North Casper. It was about half a mile west of today's Bryan Stock Trail. The Mormon Ferry's second location was in today's Reshaw Park in Evansville, Wyoming. Its exact location was about one hundred yards west of the present bridge to the Oregon Trail Veterans' Cemetery. The various locations of the Mormon Ferry around modern-day Casper, Wyoming are very confusing. Over its years of operation it was moved many times. It was moved twice during its first year of operation. The locations quoted in this chapter have been thoroughly researched and are as accurate as can reasonably be determined. Morgan, *Annals of Wyoming*, vol. 21, p. 135–139, 154–155; Glass, *Discussions with Tom Empey; Frontier Times* and *New Oregon Trail Reader*, (Town of Evansville, Wyoming, Summer 1966), vol. 1, no. 1.

9. Morgan, *Annals of Wyoming*, vol. 21, p. 135, 140–145.

10. Lecompte, "Archibald Charles Metcalf," in *Mountain Men*, 4:221–223; Lecompte, *Pueblo-Hardscrabble-Greenhorn*, p. 61, 204–205; Hammond, p. 151–153; McDermott, "John Baptiste Richard" in *Mountain Men*, 2:296; Barry, p. 832; this Robidoux should not be confused with the brothers, Joseph and Gelecore, who had the trading post at Robidoux Pass, near Scott's Bluff. The Robidoux family was quite large and many of the men were married to women of various Indian tribes. At this writing no one is known to have conquered the immense task of sorting out the genealogy of this family. Hanson, p. 58–59.

11. Lecompte, "Archibald Charles Metcalf," in *Mountain Men*, 4:223; *St. Joseph Gazette*, May 4, 1849 and *The Daily Reveille*, St. Louis, May 26, 1849. Barry, p. 832; Lecompte, *Pueblo-Hardscrabble-Greenhorn*, p. 223.

12. Lt. Gunnison was in charge of Stansbury's Rifle Regiment which preceded the main party by a few days. Hyde, p. 51; McDermott, "Joseph Bissonette" in *Mountain Men*, 4:53; McDermott, James Bordeaux" 5:71 in *Mountain Men*; Jones, p. 9, 40; Hammond, p. 177.

13. Hyde, p. 51.

14. Lecompte, "Archibald Charles Metcalf," in *Mountain Men*, 4:223–224; Cragin, "Luz Trujillo Metcalf Ledoux," Notebook VII, p. 2/8; Hyde, p. 51; Cragin, F. W., "Interview of Jesse Nelson," (Unpublished Notebooks, Cragin

Papers, Colorado Springs Pioneers Museum, Colorado Springs, Colorado), Notebook VIII, p. 14/73.

15. Hammond, p. 177.

16. McDermott, "Joseph Bissonette" in *Mountain Men*, 4:50; Jones, p. 9, 12, and 42; Cragin, "Tom Autobees," Notebook I, p. 2/9–2/10.

17. Throughout this text, the author will refer to this bridge as the Parkerton Bridge. The community known as Parkerton did not exist until many years after this bridge was gone, but for the sake of differentiating this bridge from later bridges on the North Platte River, this name will be used. McDermott, "John Baptiste Richard" in *Mountain Men*, 2:295–296; Franzwa, Gregory M., *Maps of the Oregon Trail*, (The Patrice Press, Gerald, Missouri, 1982), p. 117.

18. McDermott, "John Baptiste Richard" in *Mountain Men*, 2:296; Barry, p. 988.

19. McDermott, "John Baptiste Richard" in *Mountain Men*, 2:297; Barry, p. 987; Jones, p. 9.

20. Jones, p. 11.

21. Jones, p. 12 and 42; Cragin, F. W., "Interview of William T. Eubank on August 18, 1908, at Denver, Colorado," (Unpublished Notebooks, Cragin Papers, Colorado Springs Pioneer Museum, Colorado Springs, Colorado), Notebook I, p. 5/25 & 6/26; McAllister, Rev. J.: Henderson, Paul, editor, "Rev. J. McAllister Diary," *Annals of Wyoming*, (October 1960), vol. 32, no. 2, p. 225.

22. Ricker, "Magloire Mosseau," tablet 28, p. 15–20.

23. Barry, p. 1127.

24. Jones, Brian, p. 12 and 43; Monroe.

25. McDermott, "Joseph Bissonette" in *Mountain Men*, 4:54; The exact location of Richard's Bridge was discovered by Thomas Nicholas, then the Attorney for the Town of Evansville, Wyoming in the 1960s. A few years later, the Town erected a replica of the south approach to the bridge. After the replica fell into disrepair the Town reconstructed this replica. The bridge is located in Reshaw Park, about one hundred yards west of the current bridge to the Oregon Trail Veterans' Cemetery. Nicholas, Tom, "Timbers From Old Reshaw Bridge Found," *Casper Star Tribune*, October 9, 1966, p. 4.

26. Murray, Robert A., *Trading Posts, Forts and Bridges of the Casper Area: Bison Hunters to Black Gold*, (Wyoming Historical Press, Casper, Wyoming, 1986), p. 10.

27. The Bissonette mentioned was Joseph Bissonette, Richard's long time associate and business partner. Kenceleur was William Kenceleur. He was born in 1804 in eastern Canada. A carpenter by trade, he lived in Missouri for many years and moved with his family to Rulo, Nebraska, in 1855. Along with Eli Plant he was considered one of the early pioneers of Rulo. By 1860 several of John Richard's sisters had also moved to Rulo and lived two houses away from

William Kenceleur's family. Bissonette and Kenceleur appear to have both been partners in the bridge from its conception, but the wording of the advertisement suggests that they also had a separate partnership in a trading post in addition to that of Richard's. Census of Rulo, Richardson County, Nebraska, 1860; Edwards, Lewis C., *Who's Who in Nebraska*, 1940 (NEGenWeb Project: Richardson County); Barry, p. 1140; McDermott, "John Baptiste Richard" in *Mountain Men*, 2:298; Jones, p. 11.

28. Joseph McKnight is often called Joe or Joseph Knight. His true name seems to have been McKnight, but some have apparently dropped the "Mc" in an Americanization of the name. He was born in Canada July 19, 1829. His family moved to the United States three or four years later. In 1848 he moved to Minnesota, then to Fort Benton the following year. After two years there he moved again, this time to St. Louis, and in the fall of 1852 he was headed for Fort Laramie. It seems likely that he may have joined either John Richard's sheep herding expedition that fall or Bissonette's wagon train. He appears to have been involved in the construction of Richard's Bridge, and it has been suggested that McKnight may have even designed Richard's Bridge. Coutant C. G., (Unpublished Notebooks, "Coutant Collection," Wyoming State Archives, Cheyenne, Wyoming), box 4, folder 53, book 36; Joseph McKnight, Indian Depredation Claim #8081, RG 123, cited by McDermott, John D., *Frontier Crossroads, The History of Fort Caspar and the Upper Platte Crossing*, (City of Casper, Wyoming, 1997) p. 7–8, and 114.

29. Murray, John, *Journal*, (Unpublished Manuscript, Special Collections, Washington State Historical Society), T–177, box 1, folder 12, p. 66–67.

30. This man Major, was quite likely Alexander Majors, later a partner in the freight and express company of Russell, Majors and Waddell. Barry, p. 1148–1149; Jones, p. 11; *John Hunton Papers*, Wyoming State Archives, cited by McDermott, "John Baptiste Richard" in *Mountain Men*, 2:299.

31. Sarah Sutton diary, cited in McDermott, "John Baptiste Richard" in *Mountain Men*, 2:299; Myer, Nathaniel: Ham, Edward B., editor, "Journey Into Southern Oregon: Diary of a Pennsylvania Dutchman," *Oregon Historical Society Magazine*.

32. Bradway, J. R., *Diary*, (Unpublished Manuscript, Library of the State Historical Society of Wisconsin), p. 43.

33. *Ibid.*; Murray, John, p. 66–68; Brown, William Richard, *William Richard Brown: Diary*, (Barbara Wills, granddaughter, Editor and Publisher, Mokelumne Hill, California, 1985), p. 44.

34. Portions of the diary of Dr. John Smith were hand-copied by Susan Badger Doyle, Ph.D. for the author in 1996. Smith, Dr. John, *Diary 1853*, (Unpublished Manuscript, Huntington Library).

35. The four Canadian brothers mentioned by Cipriani were most likely John and Peter Richard, Joseph Bissonette and Charles Bordeaux. Joseph Richard by all accounts was still living in Pueblo. Cipriani, Count Leonetto, *California and Overland Diaries*, (Champoeg Press, 1962), p. 89; McDermott, *Frontier Crossroads*, p. 7.

36. Sloan, William K., "Autobiography of William K. Sloan," *Annals of Wyoming*, (July 1926), vol. 4, no. 1, p. 245–246.

37. *Ibid.*

38. John Richard was well known along the trail for several years prior, for usually having good stock to sell to the emigrants. He advertised it in eastern newspapers. He was undoubtedly one of the pioneers in this method of refreshing the animals, but the practice was not uncommon. As for the location of his range, we can only ascertain that it was along what was then called Reshaw Creek and that this is why the creek acquired that name. Sgt. Isaac Pennock mentions the creek in two separate areas of his diary. Although his distances vary in accuracy, his descriptions of this and other nearby drainage's indicate it to be what is now called Elk Horn Creek: "This fight along Reshaw Creek, four miles from Lower [B]ridge." "…three miles from [lower] Bridge, passed Reshaw Creek 7 miles from upper bridge." Pennock, Sgt. Isaac "Jake," "Diary of Jake Pennock, (1865)," *Annals of Wyoming*, (July, 1951), vol. 23, no. 2, p. 12, 22; Magloire Mosseau also confirms the location of Reshaw Creek. He states the order of available water in the vicinity on the south side of the river as; "Deer Creek, Cottonwood Springs, Muddy Creek, Richard (Reshaw) Creek, Willow Creek, Fort Caspar." Ricker, "Magloire Mosseau," tablet 28, p. 47–48.

39. Bowman, J. Soule, *Missouri Republican*, November 2, 1853. Cited by Jones, p. 11.

Baptiste "Little Bat" Garnier was raised almost as a son of John Richard. Later he was a scout and interpreter for the military. (*Wyoming State Archives, Department of State Parks and Cultural Resources*)

6

⇨ From Little Bat to Big Bat ⇦

Baptiste "Little Bat" Garnier and Baptiste "Big Bat" Pourier were both prominent scouts and interpreters during the Indian Wars of the late nineteenth century. These two men were both strongly influenced by John Richard in their early years. It must be presumed that much of their wilderness cunning and wit was learned from this savvy frontiersman. A series of events and circumstances led up to the two Bats acquiring their respective nicknames and becoming associated with John Richard: the Grattan Massacre, the Battle of Ash Hollow, and one of the most compelling tales of the western migration, that of the Mormon Handcart Companies.

During the spring of 1854, Peter Garnier was working at Richard's Bridge. His Indian wife gave birth to a son, the first known child to be born in the little settlement that was beginning to form near the south end of the bridge. This new arrival was named Baptiste, possibly after John Baptiste Richard, but everyone called the boy Bat. John Richard was very fond of the boy. Young Bat, nearly from infancy, was not enthused with his older sisters and instead attached himself to John Richard's sons. The admiration seemingly was mutual, and Bat grew up virtually as a brother to the Richard boys.[1]

During the off season John Richard had decided to invest some of his profits from the previous year in his family. He took his two eldest sons to St. Charles, Missouri, where he enrolled John Jr. in school. While there, John Richard Jr. stayed with his uncle and aunt, Alexis and Susanne (Richard) St. Louis.[2]

⇨ ⇦

The toll business at Richard's Bridge was not as lucrative in 1854 as it had been the previous year. The normally high waters of the spring never came. Almost a year to the day after Richard had charged Sarah Sutton's wagon train five hundred dollars to cross, he charged Thomas

Reber's entire wagon train only thirty-eight dollars to use the bridge. He had lowered his tolls in hope of attracting the emigrants to visit his blacksmith's shop and trading post, which we can presume did a moderate business, but the boom of the previous year never came. Possibly also due to the dryness of the season, the Sioux were antagonistic to the settlers along the trail. Traffic was only moderate in comparison to previous years.[3]

⬦⬦

August 1854 brought the first significant conflict between Indians and whites along the North Platte River. The circumstances of the affair are unfortunate. Due to a combination of poor judgments by several individuals involved, a catastrophe developed. Shortly before arriving at Fort Laramie, a Mormon wagon train had a withering ox that was too lame to pull a heavy wagon. It lagged along behind the train on the trail. A Miniconjou warrior, High Forehead, saw the straggler. The scarcity of grass for game during this dry season was compounded by the emigrant traffic and livestock grazing along the trail. Probably both hungry and aggravated by the circumstances, High Forehead shot the ox and took it to a nearby Brule village, where he was staying. The highest ranking man of the Brule Sioux, Conquering Bear, headed the village. The owner of the ox promptly complained to the authorities at Fort Laramie about the loss of the animal. In his complaint he may have claimed this particular ox was the most valuable animal ever to walk the trail, as this was usually the attitude when someone felt an Indian had wronged him in those days. Regardless of the accusation made, the action taken by the Army was both naïve and irresponsible.

On August 19, 1854, young Lieutenant John L. Grattan was sent with some thirty troops and two cannons to confront Conquering Bear. This recent graduate's only experience with Indians was at West Point. There they avidly taught that Indians could be scared into submission, a method that has been called by many "Pacification by Force." This aggressive show was intended to intimidate the chief; thus he would become meek. Conquering Bear, however, had not received his name or his status because of a placid personality. Considering this and Grattan's total lack of experience in dealing with Indians under even the most pleasant circumstances, his parlay with the chief actually began fairly well. Grattan began, with reasonable calm, by telling the chief that one of the members of his village had stolen an ox from a passing wagon train and that he would have to return it. Conquering Bear, likely still picking his teeth, told him simply that the ox was not there. The old chief did his best to evade the subject. This, unfortunately, only tried Grattan's thin patience and his temper began to flare. Eventually Conquering Bear told Grattan that the ox could not be returned because the entire village had feasted on it the previous evening.

Grattan was enraged and demanded that the culprit of this crime be turned over to him to be taken to the fort and hanged for stealing the ox. Conquering Bear told him that he could not do this because this man was a Miniconjou Sioux, a guest in his village, and not a Brule; furthermore the man had not violated any accepted tribal law. In an attempt to reconcile the problem, Conquering Bear offered to repay the Mormon by allowing him to take his pick of any of the Indian's own fine string of ponies. Grattan flatly refused this, though it actually was quite a generous offer and probably should have been considered. The chief could not offer more and as the discussion continued, Grattan lost what little poise he had previously demonstrated. In frustration he fired upon the chief, probably believing another old myth learned in the east: when the chief was gone the rest would run away in disorganized fear. Nothing could have been further from the true result of his actions. The skirmish that followed ended with the death of Grattan and all of his men, though one man managed to escape back to Fort Laramie before dying from his wounds. Twenty-seven arrows had struck Grattan himself, his body only identifiable by his pocket-watch. What had begun with a lame ox, probably worth only John Richard's rate of $2.50, resulted in the death of an Army officer and his entire patrol and one of the most well-respected chiefs of the Sioux Nation.

Following what would soon be known as the Grattan Massacre, the seriously wounded Conquering Bear was taken the short distance to James Bordeaux's Trading Post where he died. Bordeaux had evidently been given the responsibility of dispensing a portion of the Indian's annuity goods, which he stored at the trading post. Following the death of their chief, the Brule band then ransacked Bordeaux's post and, in addition to their annuities, took nearly everything that Bordeaux owned. If this had not been bad enough for Bordeaux, the Army then ordered him to bury the dead at the village, which he did and reportedly without

This never-before-published photograph shows Baptiste "Big Bat" Pourier in his later years. *(Courtesy Valerie Purrier)*

ever receiving compensation. Jefferson Davis, then Secretary of War, considered the Grattan Massacre "the result of a deliberately formed plan" by the Sioux to rob the annuity goods from Bordeaux's Trading Post. Such was the way of thinking of some eastern politicians in 1854.

One more aspect of the events of this battle should be mentioned, even in this condensed account. The Mormons, or Latter Day Saints, prior to and following this incident, normally shared extremely good relations with nearly every tribe of Indians they had dealings with. There are two distinct possibilities to explain the owner of the ox's actions. First, he may have been unaware of his Church's policies regarding dealings with Native Americans. Second and far more likely, he may have thought that the government would simply compensate him for his losses without further retaliation against the Indians.[4]

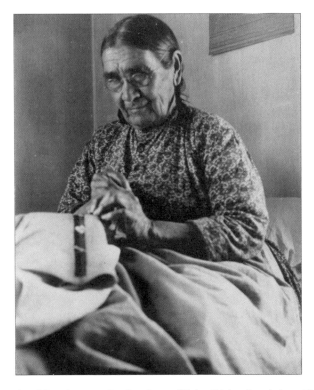

Josephine Richard Pourier was the daughter of John Richard and the wife of Baptiste "Big Bat" Pourier. This photograph was taken in 1935 when she was 83 years old. (*Department of Special Collections and University Archives, Marquette University Libraries by McNamara, Reverend Stephen E., S.J.*)

Immediately prior to the Grattan Massacre, Joseph Bissonette had been running Fort La Bonte in partnership with James Adams.[5] This trading post was located on La Bonte Creek near present-day Douglas, Wyoming. Following the battle he moved his family back to Bitter Cottonwood Creek, in much closer proximity to Fort Laramie. Although tensions were rising among the Sioux following this event, this action seems peculiar for Bissonette. He not only had a Sioux wife and several children with her, but he was extremely experienced in dealing with even the most difficult of circumstances with this tribe. For this reason it seems the only possible explanation for this sudden retreat would be if he too was dispensing annuities and feared that he might also be subjected to the same revenge from the tribes that had been rendered to

Bordeaux. James Adams evidently did not share Bissonette's fears; he stayed to continue the operation of Fort La Bonte.[6]

On November 29, 1854, Major William Hoffman, in command of Fort Laramie, reported one thousand lodges of Sioux were camped on the headwaters of the Running Water (Niobrara River) and planned a war against the whites throughout the winter. Although Indian Agent A. D. Vaughn at Fort Pierre filed a similar report, it was not the season that the Sioux would normally go to war, and they did not stage any attacks until the following spring.[7]

❖ ❖

About this time John Richard contracted Joseph McKnight to make some significant repairs on the bridge during the off-season. Richard then assembled his entourage and headed for the Green River to trade for horses through the winter. It is known that John Richard was loosely associated with the legendary mountain man Jim Bridger in years to come, and it seems likely that this expedition of Richard's may have been in some way affiliated with Bridger's operations in that same area. Richard and his men spent the entire winter collecting a sizeable herd of mixed horses and mustangs. Although many of these animals were somewhat tamed, the crew spent any available time breaking them to harness. After a long and hard winter's work the men finally returned to the Platte in the spring of 1855 with a large herd of replacement stock for the arriving emigrant season.[8]

Joseph Merivale was one of the many men on this horse-hunting expedition. He described their return to the bridge in this way. "We burned off the old grass to let the new grass grow, one night five Crow Indians came in and told us that they saw a party of Blackfeet, that night the ponies were all stolen; I followed them the next morning with two Oglalas, Torn Belly and Black Hills…on the best of a few tired-out mounts that the Indians had left, we followed them about 25 miles to the north but did not overtake them." All that they had spent months working for had been lost overnight.[9]

❖ ❖

Joseph Bissonette's fears were confirmed, though not directly, in March 1855. Miniconjous ambushed John Provo, a Bissonette employee, while en route to Powder River to trade with the Crows. The long-time enmity of this branch of the Sioux with the Crows may have been the reason behind the attack, but Bissonette felt it was vengeance for the murder of Conquering Bear. All of Provo's livestock was stolen and his trade goods destroyed. Although Provo apparently survived the ordeal, the financial loss was a blow to Bissonette. In April a trader near Independence Rock had his livestock stolen, and the Richard's former post at Ash Point, now belonging to Ward & Guerrier, was also raided.[10]

John Richard too suffered more losses at the bridge. The emigrant traffic came grinding to a near halt due to the various marauding bands of Sioux along the trail. Before long the Army put a stop to all trade with the Indians in the vicinity. Trading was virtually Richard's last remaining source of income, now it too was gone for the year.

The commander of Fort Laramie, Major William Hoffman, realized the importance of Richard's Bridge to the emigrants as well as mail and freighting operations. He requested a detachment of troops be sent to protect it from potential Indian depredations. His request was approved. On October 28, Lieutenant James Deshler, with twenty-one enlisted men and two non-commissioned officers were sent "to the Bridge 125 miles above this Post and [to] establish ... there with a view to prevent depredations of Indians, and to give protection to the mails and persons traveling on the road." The orders went on to say: "When you arrive at the bridge you will keep your party at all times on the alert, exercise day and night the greatest vigilance. It will parade under arms for inspection every evening at Sunset. During the night the sentinels will call the half hours."

John Richard and his family were ordered to Fort Laramie (for their own protection) and, though disgruntled, they obeyed. The partners at Sweetwater Bridge and Devil's Gate were given their choice of going to Fort Laramie or Green River. Magloire Mosseau chose Fort Laramie. All the others, who had Shoshone wives, opted for Green River. Lieutenant Deshler, following his orders, set up camp on a low hill southwest of the bridge. This location had a commanding view of both sides of the river. But the problem with the site was that the openness and high-ground posture subjected his men, camped in Sibley tents, to the severe winds for which the area is famous. Conditions only worsened as winter approached.[11]

Following the Grattan Massacre, Jefferson Davis had appointed General William S. Harney to organize a campaign to teach the Sioux a lesson. Little Thunder, the successor of Conquering Bear, was camped

This photograph, taken at Fort Laramie by Alexander Gardner in 1868, is another with conflicting identifications. The first two people to the right of the horse are sometimes identified as Peter Richard and Mrs. Peter Richard (Red Sack aka Lucy) but may also be Leon Pallardie and Mrs. Moran. John Richard Jr. may be one of the three men standing on the right, perhaps the man holding the rifle. The seated man farthest to the right may be Little Bat Garnier, though he would have been only fourteen years old. (*Mokler Collection, Casper College Western History Center. Photo presented to A.J. Mokler by H.C. Bretney*)

on Blue Water Creek with his village of 250 Brules, mostly women and children, on September 3, 1855. General Harney, "the Butcher" as the Sioux called him, surrounded the Brules there and laid siege to their camp. When the smoke lifted, eighty-five "warriors" were dead, and seventy-five women and children were captured. This massacre at Blue Water Creek was somewhat in the proximity of Ash Hollow. Since the soldiers were the victors, it was dubbed a battle. Due to the recorder of the incident's ignorance of the local geography, it is usually referred to as The Battle of Ash Hollow.[12]

In December Lieutenant John Mendenhall was sent from Fort Laramie to relieve Lieutenant Deshler at the bridge. Major Hoffman took the opportunity to offer John Richard the chance to return, with the stipulation that he refrain from doing business with any Indians there. Richard tried to have this condition repealed, arguing that Indians were the only potential customers at his trading post during this season. His plea fell on deaf ears, and he refused the offer to return. The next month Lieutenant Robert Clinton Hill took command of the detachment at Richard's Bridge. His post return report for that month is the only known reference to the post being called "Fort Clay," presumably in honor of former Secretary of State Henry Clay.[13]

In March 1856, Captain Henry Heth was sent to take charge of the operations at the bridge. John Richard and his family returned with him, without restrictions. By this time the detachment had grown to a full company complete with three officers and a bugler. A mountain howitzer was added to increase their strength. In February the encampment had acquired the name of "Camp Davis" in honor of Jefferson Davis, which it remained until disbanded. Among the civilians employed by Camp Davis was the well-known Nick Janis, as interpreter. John Richard was once again in his height of glory. The water was high, emigrant trade was good, and he was obviously enjoying a fair amount of trade from the soldiers of the 10th Infantry at Camp Davis, only a few hundred yards from his trading post.[14]

⟨ジ⟩ ⟨ジ⟩

Soon after Heth's arrival at the bridge, the first confrontation between the United States Government and the Northern Cheyenne arose. While a band Cheyenne were camped near the bridge, a young warrior, Little Wolf, found a group of stray horses belonging to Charles Antoine, one of John Richard's employees. In an attempt to regain his missing horses without further development, Antoine offered a reward for them. The warrior offered to return all but the best horse. Antoine then reported the matter to Captain Heth who sent for the chief of the Cheyenne band. The chief agreed to send the warrior with his cavvy to Camp Davis. Antoine identified his four horses, and Heth told the young Indian that he would receive five dollars each as a reward for finding them. The warrior said that it would be too difficult to separate them from the herd then and that he would bring the horses in question back the following morning. This was acceptable to all parties.

Later that evening, however, Heth learned that the warrior still intended to keep Antoine's best horse and to shoot anyone who tried to take him. Heth then sent Lieutenant Nathan Dudley and his men to bring back the Indian, the horses, and the reward. Upon the accomplishment of this task, Heth ordered that Little Wolf be sent to Richard's blacksmith's shop and put in irons. During the process, the warrior escaped and was wounded. Dudley was then sent back to the village to take two Indian hostages.

The following day one of the hostages was released with instructions to return with Little Wolf or, if the warrior had died from his wounds, to bring in Little Wolf's father.

In the meantime, Little Wolf and his father had killed Peter Garnier, who had been returning from Richard's pastures on Reshaw Creek, in retaliation for Heth's actions. Following the attack Garnier had been scalped and his body mutilated. Heth's remaining prisoner, Wolf Fire (or Fire Wolf), was sent to Fort Laramie in irons. The prisoner was successfully transported to the Fort, but died there while incarcerated.[15]

By this time Magloire Mosseau had also moved to the vicinity of Richard's Bridge. A number of people had collected at the bridge forming a small community. Richard employed many of these people, but not all; some lived there for convenience and safety from Indians. Mosseau established a ranch of sorts some five or six miles above the bridge on the north bank of the river. At times he had up to 200 cattle and 120 horses and mules. Some diaries of this period mention a trading post, mostly dealing in livestock, near the top of the hill about five miles beyond the bridge. This was presumably Mosseau's operation. The date of his departure from this area is not certain, but apparently around 1864 he moved on to the South Pass area.[16]

Following Peter Garnier's death, Mrs. Garnier prepared to move her son and three daughters to Fort Laramie. John Richard could not bear to see Little Bat go. After some deliberation, an agreement was made and Bat stayed on at the bridge as an extended member of the Richard family. The terms of this arrangement are lost to history, but Baptiste Garnier spent the next several years as much a son to John Richard as any of his own boys. Little Bat learned both sides of his mixed heritage and became one of the most outstanding scouts and hunters the United States military ever employed.[17]

⋘∘⋙

On July 4, 1856, the trading company of Todd & Gordon arrived at the bridge with a train of freight wagons headed for points west. Todd & Gordon broke out their whiskey, and Captain Heth furloughed his men to celebrate Independence Day. J. Robert Brown, who kept colorful account of his trip west, was in the employ of a similar company that arrived the following day and remained there a few days for repairs. The following entries from his journal give quite an explicit description of the frontier military camp and life at Richard's Bridge:

"*Saturday, July 5, 1856*—We soon came in sight of the bridge across the Platte.... Just before we got to the buildings, a soldier came out to meet us with his gun and an order from Capt. Heath [Heth] to Yates & Maunder [Brown's employers] not to sell any liquor to any one. There are several very good log buildings here; these are used as a store, dwelling houses for the traders, blacksmith shop, etc. There are about thirty lodges belonging to the Crows and Sioux, the soldiers live in lodges also; there are only fifty-eight of them here now; many are deserting at every opportunity.[18] Todd & Gordon arrived here yesterday morning, and the Capt. giving his men the holiday, they had a real drunken spree off Todd & Gordon's whisky, of which they sold a large quantity.

"The brothers Richards (pro. Reshaw) own the post and the bridge here, and are coining money from it; they have made over $200,000 apiece, but that demon, gambling, keeps them down. They appear to be very clever men. They are from Florisant, and have asked me hundreds of questions about their old stamping ground. They knew grandpa Hume, and Lewis and George very well, and talk very familiar of them; they praise to the highest "old uncle Johnny," as they call him. We were to stop here and get our tire reset on two wagons. There are a number of men here returning from California. They speak in the highest terms of the country. They are amusing themselves by betting with the soldiers. One bet I could but notice: A soldier offered to bet $200 that he could take Colt's Dragoon Pistol and hit a hat five times out of six shots at a distance of 200 yards, this hat to be thrown up into the air by another man and he to hit it while in motion. The Californian took him up. The soldier went up to raise the money among his companions, but he did not return. Capt. Heath did not wish him to show his dexterity to every one that pleased to call for it, so we did not get to see this great trial of skill. At the battle of Ash Hollow last fall, this same soldier shot an Indian who was trying to escape. Gen. Harney ordered him to shoot, although the Indian was on horseback and running with might and main, at a distance of 309 yards. Gen. Harney pronounced it the best shot on record with the Colt [and who would argue with the man called *The Butcher*]. I helped the U. S. gunsmith to fix my pistol, but he was so tipsy that he could not work. There is the most bustle and stir here for the small number of men that I have seen since I left home. This is quite a busy place. Wood is very scarce here, and we could hardly get enough to bake our bread. Capt. Heath sent down a guard to watch Yates and his wagons, to keep him from selling whisky to the soldiers. Yates is very much vexed and put out about this, and calls it "taking away the liberties of an American citizen on his own soil!" Good, I say. I went to bed very late, and then could not sleep, for a squaw was crying and moaning for her *dead dog* until long past midnight. She was two hundred yards from camp, and her moans are very annoying. The Indians moan the same for a favorite dog, horse or other pet, as they do for a human being.

"*Sunday, July 6, 1856*—Morning cool and balmy. Indians all up early, white folks up late; they had a grand spree among themselves last night. After breakfast, I agreed to help the blacksmith work on the wagon. Whistling Bill and Theodore were sent up the river about three miles to guard the cattle. The Indians are coming in from all directions; there are three tribes represented among these, Crows, Sioux, Shoshones or Snakes; some are dressed very gaudily; there were four or five young chiefs whom I admired very much, they were so well dressed in their wild romantic Indian costume—beads, feathers, brass rings and steel, buckskin and buffalo robes, were all displayed to advantage. They had some very fine horses, of which they seemed very proud. One of these young chiefs had a small white horse which he had painted red; he and his horse presented a laughable picture. Naked little Indians, male and female, running all around here; some of these little fellows are models of form. Other little Indians are dressed as white children, and exhibit some taste.

"Yates has been trading with the Indians this morning, giving them lead, coffee, sugar, etc., for their buckskins. A train of

California emigrants passed over the bridge. Capt. Heath sent his Lieutenant and six men and a little wagon to our camp, rolled out Yates's whisky and put it in this little wagon, and rolled it off up to camp Davis, to put the disorderly article in limbo. Todd & Gordon had to take their whisky wagon up there, too. The Captain did this so that he could have his eye on the whisky affairs. The whole thing appeared to me a most ludicrous farce; for, by treating the guard to a horn or two, Yates could have sold as much whisky as he could have measured out, just as if there were no guard present. As long as there was whisky here, there were soldiers around our wagons begging, soliciting, and offering almost any price for it, but they were invariably refused. The whole of this whisky matter has been a source of sport for me. I got my pistol repaired to-day for one dollar.

"My stock of dogs were increased to-day to nine. I gave one to an Indian chief; it happened to be a female, and he then made signs that he wanted a male, too. I gave him one, and he went on his way rejoicing. I was visited by a number of Indians, young and old, and gave all of the little pups away but one, which Yates claimed. Yates gave that to "Richard 3d" [Peter S.?]. Yates and Maunder have sold $1500 worth of goods to the Richards at a fair profit. This has been an active, exciting day to me; I have been busy, and had some fun.

"*Monday, July 7, 1856*—After breakfast I again helped the blacksmith finish the wagons. He could have finished them yesterday, if he had worked as he ought, but by some means he got hold of some whisky, and consequently could not work. I worked very hard, and did not take time to see what was going on around me. Yates and Billy replaced the goods in three wagons, having sold one to the Richards. Yates went up to the "whisky prison", to get some, and found the barrel had been tapped and some taken out; he did not know how much. Capt. Heath denied this, and Yates asserted it as strongly. We could not hear their words at the camp, but could see their gestures. They had quite a quarrel over their little whisky. The Capt. finally compromised by agreeing to pay Yates $10. The joke is, that Capt. Heath and his Lieutenant had personally watched the barrels all night, besides having a regular guard over them; and how this liquor was stolen will remain a mystery to all except the perpetrators.

"Todd and Gordon again hitched up and left us, saying they were going to beat us into Salt Lake, or kill all their oxen. Yates says they "sha'nt". The soldiers have been here again begging for whisky. One soldier said he would give $3 for one drink. When Yates told him that he would have to charge them that, the fellow took out the money, when Yates said, "I will treat you if it costs me all I am worth", and he did. There are not so many Indians about to-day as there were yesterday. After the Crows left yesterday, the Sioux went out and drove in all their horses and stood guard over them all night. A few days ago, Capt. Heath heard that the Crows and the Snakes were about to have a battle. He sent for their chiefs, and in council told them these words: "You may fight if you wish, but if you, Mr. Crow, fire the first gun, I will help the Snakes whip you; and Mr. Snake, if you begin the fight, I will help the Crows whip you." This was talking plain Indian, and they took the hint and profited by it, and no fight came off; but the grudge is not out, for I saw several Indians with the war paint on their faces.

"I went up to the Captain's camp to get some beans. I had to wait until they were done drilling the Company, when the Captain invited me into his lodge. I conversed with him and his Lieutenant for some time, and found them very sociable and agreeable. Captain asked $10 per bushel for beans [which happened to be the exact amount he had had to pay Yates for the missing whisky]; this was more than Yates said to give, so I returned without them. As soon as I got back, we started; crossed the bridge, which is an excellent one, built entirely of wood. At the north end of this bridge is an excellent coal mine. We traveled over a very hilly and sandy road, and camped near the river. Soon after dark two men came up from Camp Davis, and drank some more whisky with Yates. He sold them what was left in one of the barrels, which was then hidden in the brush. They went away, and we to bed."[19]

◈◈

Joseph McKnight, who then lived at Richard's Bridge and had worked for Richard for several years, married John Richard's stepdaughter, Mary, about this time. Her Indian name was Eagle Wing Feather, and she was the daughter of Mary Gardiner (Richard) and Black Moon. Joseph Bissonette had by this time either sold his share in the bridge to the Richard brothers or at least become somewhat of a silent partner in the operation of it. Early on it is believed that he and William Kenceleur had operated a trading post separate from that of Richard's at the bridge in addition to his Fort La Bonte operation. By this time however, he had been back in the Fort Laramie vicinity for some time. During the few months that he had spent the previous winter at the fort itself, he became acquainted with the new Indian Agent there, Major Thomas S. Twiss. In September of 1856, Twiss appointed Bissonette as the official interpreter for the agency.[20]

By the fall of that year the Army decided that since depredations by the Indians had been minimal along the Platte for several months, and appraising the fact that the trading post had grown into a sizeable civilian community there, it was decided that Camp Davis should be abandoned. Likely, with the problems they had encountered previously with the enlisted men at the post, the true opinion was that all the men would desert if condemned to spend another winter at the camp. Whatever the reasoning behind the evacuation, in November 1856, Captain Charles S. Lovell, then in command of the camp, was ordered to pack up his 10th Infantry Company and return to Fort Laramie.[21]

⊰⊱»⊰⊱

One of the most written about endeavors of all the western migration is that of the Mormon Handcart Companies. The success of the vast majority of these expeditions is not only extraordinary, but also remarkable. John Richard probably connected with many of the handcart pioneers at his bridge and trading post, but he literally saved the lives of a few of the men.

In 1856 two companies departed for Salt Lake City far too late in the season, a costly and fatal mistake for many of those involved. These were the Edward Martin and James Willie Handcart Companies.[22]

When Brigham Young received word in Salt Lake City that these last two companies were snowed in and in serious trouble between Richard's Bridge and South Pass, he immediately organized a rescue party. Among the rescuers was Daniel Webster Jones. Like many people of that era, Jones felt that he was a part of history being made and kept a daily record of the facts as they happened. Though many first-hand accounts were recorded of this rescue and some differences exist regarding the details, Jones's story seems to be one of the most accurate.

The Willie Company had progressed furthest and met the rescuers first. Seeing the dire condition of these emigrants, the rescuers determined that a small advance party should be sent with utmost haste to the remaining emigrants who lagged behind. Joseph A. Young, Abe Garr, and Daniel Jones were selected for this mission.

Taking the best horses and a mule packed with provisions, they set out immediately. At nightfall they were forced to camp after finding no sign of the lagging emigrants. After traveling an additional twelve miles the following day, Joseph Young spotted a man's boot-track in the snow. Pushing their horses to pick up the pace, the advance party soon sighted the camp of Martin's Handcart Company and Ben Horgett's wagon train. Horgett himself was absent and had evidently returned to Richard's Bridge for help. Yet another wagon train was behind them, so after offering what assistance they could, the trio held a meeting with those in charge. They informed the emigrants that they should strive to make as much headway toward Salt Lake as possible and that they would soon meet the main rescue party ahead on the trail. The emigrant groups decided to depart the camp where snow had held them captive for nine days on the following morning.

Without further hesitation, the trio continued on in search of John Hunt's wagon train. Late in the day they sighted the camp of Hunt's wagons some fifteen miles further down the road. When Young, Garr, and Jones arrived at Hunt's camp they were apparently mistaken for mountaineers and kindly ignored as they rode in. Young, somewhat put out by the cold reception, told his partners that it seemed they were not needed there. Too late to proceed further that day, they made camp a short distance from the wagons. A short time later a passerby from Hunt's camp recognized Joseph Young and made a mad dash back to his own camp to report the identities of the strangers. They were soon escorted to the main camp in a flurry of apologies. Before they were settled in among the wagons, John Hunt, Ben Horgett, and two others rode in from Richard's Bridge. The men determined that the wagon train must move on, regardless of the conditions, the next day. They had already lost a number of oxen to the storm and would only lose more if they stayed longer.

The following morning Joseph Young, evidently accompanied by Hunt and Horgett, departed for Richard's Bridge, leaving Garr and Jones in charge of getting the train moving. The teamsters did not share Garr and Jones's feeling of urgency. Instead of going out to bring in their oxen that had scattered in search of forage over the past few days, they argued as to who should be harnessed with this chore. It began to snow again, and Garr's patience wore thin. The two rescuers saddled up and prepared to depart. About this time an opening in the clouds far to the west allowed a distant glimpse of bright sunlight. Garr turned to the teamsters with this statement, "Do you see that hole? You had better get out of here before that closes up, for it is your opening to the valley [Salt Lake]. We are going." With that Garr and Jones left the camp headed west to try to overtake Martin's outfit.

Hunt's train was packed and moving at first light the following day. Garr and Jones passed through the camp of Martin and Horgett. The handcarts had long since departed, but Horgett's wagons were just getting started. Garr and Jones caught up with the handcarts on Prospect Hill. To Jones the first sight of the struggling ascent almost sickened him. There were men tugging at their carts, some loaded with their sick wives or children, women trying to hold their exhausted husbands erect and help pull the cart at the same time, and small children trudging through mud and snow that reached to their waists. Garr and Jones spared no energy in helping the carts to the bitter cold camp at the top of the hill and then without rest returned to help the wagons make the climb. To Jones's amazement several emaciated emigrants in their miserable camp that night sang thanks to their Lord for allowing them to make it up the dreadful hill. Many of the party died that night. Jones did not feel much like a hero.

Before daylight Joseph Young rode in and, as soon as the handcarts were again moving, the trio left what supplies they had remaining and advanced west to intercept the rest of the rescue party. They met this group at Devil's Gate Fort, the one-time trading post built by Lajeunesse, Papin, and the Perats that was now used as a Mormon way station.

The winter storm continued to rage and many more lives were lost at the emergency encampment made in a cove in the mountain across the river, two miles above the fort. Several days later, after the storm had subsided, the wagons were unloaded of everything not absolutely essential to immediate survival. The decimated survivors were then loaded into the wagons and with a record-breaking pace the party plunged through the lingering snow to Salt Lake.

The story of the Mormon handcart disaster ends there in most tellings. It was not, however, the end of the story for Daniel Jones and several other members of the rescue party who were left behind at Devil's Gate Fort. Some twelve hundred emigrants had been forced to cache their personal belonging at the fort, and Jones and his companions were left there to protect the goods. Those who remained behind were left with enough food to get by for a few weeks when a relief party would arrive to assume their duties. In the spring a wagon train would be dispatched to retrieve the belongings that occupied nearly every nook and cranny of the fort.

What no one considered was that this early storm that had entrapped the emigrants was only the beginning of a series of storms that would halt all traffic along the trail for months to come. It was not long before Daniel Jones and his companions realized the reality of their situation; help would not arrive soon. They began hunting wild game to supplement their food supply and rationing all that they had. Soon their hunting trips took them farther and farther from the fort, as game became more and more scarce. As their livestock became weak from lack of forage, they began systematically butchering those in the worst condition. Early in December they received a message from church leader, Brigham Young, via a last-ditch effort to send mail east that somehow succeeded in traversing South Pass. The message briefly stated that no further attempt would be made to send a relief party until spring. They were on their own.

Before the couriers' departure Brother Little, one of the messengers, surveyed their supplies. Noting the hides that were hanging nearby from their previous butchering, he offered some advice. "Save those hides, they are better than nothing at all to eat." It proved good advice. A few days later Jesse Jones of the Magraw Mail Company arrived at the fort with his westbound coaches. They refitted the coaches to a pack train and continued on to the west. Nearly a month later they returned to Devil's Gate, all nearly frozen to death. They had never made it even to South Pass. Just as hungry as the men at the fort, they continued on to Richard's Bridge, some fifty miles back down the road, where they wintered. Daniel Jones told the men that it was of no use, three of his own men had gone to the bridge previously to procure supplies. John Richard and his men had nothing to eat there either, except the wild game they hunted.

By February, Daniel Jones and his partners had been living off boiled rawhide for several weeks. Jesse Jones had carried a message to Richard that the men at Devil's Gate would pay highly for any meat that could be brought to them. John Richard sent out his two best hunters, Maxim and Eli Plant,[23] to perform the task. After two weeks of hunting, the two men returned to the bridge empty-handed and nearly starved themselves. By March the men at Devil's Gate Fort were destitute, few strong enough to venture out hunting. They had eaten the last of their rawhide the previous morning. The only possible food left at the fort was an old packsaddle that they were contemplating soaking and eating.

Daniel Jones made another unsuccessful hunting trip then decided to attempt to walk in the deep snow to Richard's Bridge for help. This he thought would take two to three days, if he survived. That would mean four to five days of strenuous exercise without food for him, and six to eight more days without food for the rest of the men. It was their only chance of living through the ordeal so he would take that chance or die trying.

He had trudged but a few miles when he met some men from Richard's Bridge bringing beef. John Richard had believed the unfortunate men at Devil's Gate Fort had long ago starved to death. But then he heard from some Indians that he was wrong, but not far from it. Under the extreme circumstances Richard had butchered several of his oxen and sent them by pack train to Devil's Gate. Later reflecting on his physical condition at that time, Daniel Jones concluded that he would not have survived the trip to the bridge. Undoubtedly, John Richard's compassion for human kind plus the word of some unknown Indians had saved his life as well as that of all the men at Devil's Gate Fort.[24]

⊰⊱

Late that spring, John Richard loaded up his younger sons and his winter's trade of buffalo robes and headed to St. Charles. When they arrived there, he enrolled Louis in school. His eldest son, John Richard Jr., was still attending school there, living with Richard's sister Susanne. During this time Baptiste Pourier met John Richard Jr. They attended the same school, and John Jr. also worked as a clerk in a store that the Pourier family frequented. Baptiste Pourier was awed by the tales of the beautiful western frontier told by this handsome, mixed-blood young man. The two boys quickly became friends. Baptiste heard immediately of the arrival of his friend's father from the west. While at his sister's home in St. Charles, John Richard was approached by Baptiste Pourier. The fourteen-year-old Pourier asked Richard if he wanted to hire a man. "Yes, I want to hire a man," replied Richard, "but not a boy."

Pourier responded, "I can do a man's work!" Evidently John Richard was impressed by the young Pourier's spunk and hired him on the spot.[25]

Bat then raced home to tell his mother that he had hired on with Mr. Richard and was going west. His mother cried and pleaded with him not to go, but Bat eventually talked her into allowing it. Richard then sent Pourier and another young man, Henry Boshmere, up the river on the *Minnehaha* to Fort Leavenworth. Here the buckskin clad John Baker, brother of mountain man Jim Baker, boarded the riverboat and asked in a roar over the crowd if any Richard men were aboard. Bat reluctantly answered the brash call with, "Yes, there are two." Baker then beckoned them ashore where he installed the boys in a room at a hotel. There, they waited several days for John Richard's arrival. After Richard's outfit was eventually assembled at the fort, they traveled twenty-five miles to the place where Richard's oxen and wagons had been left. The next day they yoked the oxen and headed for Leavenworth City, where they spent the next several days purchasing and loading goods, reloading every item at least twice, as it seemed to Pourier.

Eventually the men had all of the wagons loaded and in order, but it was June when they departed for the Wild West. The sluggish trudging of oxen soon dissolved Bat's mental image of galloping horseback across the western horizon. He was, however, immediately given a man's responsibility of driving one of the teams as he walked beside them.

After what seemed a lifetime on the trail, John Richard and his new pledge arrived at the bridge in an October snowstorm. Here Baptiste Pourier met the three-year-old Baptiste Garnier. In no time at all everyone was calling them Big Bat and Little Bat, to differentiate them. Those boyhood nicknames stuck their entire lives. "Big Bat's" first assignment at Richard's Bridge was to assist with unloading the goods from the wagons into one of Richard's warehouses. Then the crew was sent to the mountain to secure firewood for the winter. The wood camp was about six miles from the bridge, and every other day the ox train made the trip to the camp and returned with a load of timber. It took a full month to stockpile enough wood to last the winter.

By the time this job was completed the snow was knee deep at the bridge. Big Bat was then assigned to assist a pack train that was leaving to trade with Red Cloud at his village on Wind Creek. Richard's trader, John Floreseur, Big Bat, and another man loaded eight packhorses with goods and headed out through the snow. A little over a week later the trio arrived at Red Cloud's camp where Bat was given the task of caring for the horses. He took his assignment very seriously and checked on the animals several times each day as they grazed freely in the surrounding area. The young Baptiste Pourier quickly absorbed his new surroundings and learned the language of many of the Indians. In a few years he was one of the Army's premier scouts, a job he often used to supplement the income he earned as a trader, the profession of his mentor, John Richard.[26]

Notes to Chapter Six:

1. Nothing seems to be known about Peter Garnier or where he came from. Jones, p. 15 & 42; Vaughn, J. W., *The Reynolds Campaign on Powder River*, (University of Oklahoma Press, Norman, Oklahoma, 1961) p. 142.

2. Some sources state that John's sister, Susanne Richard, never married. Gilbert, p. 4. Although Susanne never had children of her own, she and her husband were very involved in the lives of many of their nieces and nephews. In addition to helping some of her brothers' children attend school, she and her husband also raised some of her sister Mary's children. Susanne married Alexis St. Louis, son of Jean Baptiste St. Louis and Marie Angelique Heineman, in Portage des Sioux, St. Charles County, Missouri, on August 2, 1843. Alexis was born in 1828 in Ottawa, Canada. Monroe; By 1860 Alexis and Susanne had moved from St. Charles to Rulo, Nebraska. Census of Rulo, Richardson County, Nebraska Territory, 1860.

3. Reber, Thomas: Tewsbury, Albert M., editor, *The Journal of Thomas Reber*, (MA Thesis, Claremont College).

4. If Lt. Grattan had possessed any understanding of the social structure of the Sioux Nation, he may have accepted Conquering Bear's predicament for what it was and his and many other lives may have been spared. Regardless,

American Indian policy of that era was poor at best. Utley, Robert M., and Washburn, Wilcomb E., *The American Heritage History of the Indian Wars*, (American Heritage Publishing Co., Inc./Bonanza Books, New York, 1982) p. 205; Ambrose, Stephen E., *Crazy Horse and Custer: The Parallel Lives of Two American Warriors*, (Doubleday & Co., Garden City, New York, 1975), p. 55–60; McDermott, "James Bordeaux" in *Mountain Men*, 5:73–74; McDermott, *Frontier Crossroads*, p. 9; Jones, p. 13, 42; Susan Bordeaux Bettelyoun claimed to have witnessed her father bury Lt. Grattan and his patrol when she was a young girl. She further stated that her father's trading post "was not molested" by the Indians. Since she was not born until 1857, it must be assumed that she had mistaken the details of this conflict with that of the Horse Creek fight of 1865. Bettelyoun, p. 4, 54.

5. James Adams was a brother to David Adams, former partner and friend of John Richard, discussed extensively in earlier chapters.

6. Ruxton, George Frederick: Bishop, L. C., editor, *La Bonte: Hunter, Free Trapper, Trail Blazer and Mountain Man of the Old West, 1825–1848*, (Earl T. Bower & L. C. Bishop, Publishers, 1950) p. 9, 17; McDermott, "James Bordeaux" in *Mountain Men*, 5:55; Hanson, p. 103.

7. Hyde, p. 51.

8. Murray, Robert A., p. 10.

9. Merivale, Joseph, deposition, November 2, 1886, file 8081–123, Indian Claims Files, National Archives. Cited by Murray, Robert A., p. 10–11; John Richard lost seventy-five horses to the raiding party. Hyde, p. 51.

10. McDermott, "James Bordeaux" in *Mountain Men*, 5:55; Hyde, p. 51.

11. Nicholas, Thomas A., "Platte Bridge and the Oregon Trail in the Civil War Period: 1855–1870," *Casper Star Tribune*, February 19, 1961, p. 14, 16–17; Nicholas, Thomas A., "A New Look at Richard's Upper Platte Bridge and Trading Post at Evansville, Wyoming," *Casper Star Tribune*, 1963, p. 12–13, 16; McDermott, *Frontier Crossroads*, p. 10; Ricker, "Magloire Mosseau," tablet 28, p. 16–20.

12. Utley and Washburn, p. 205–206.

13. Nicholas, *Platte Bridge and the Oregon Trail*, p. 14; McDermott, *Frontier Crossroads*, p. 10–11.

14. McDermott, *Frontier Crossroads*, p. 12; Murray, Robert A., p. 13.

15. McDermott, *Frontier Crossroads*, p. 12–13; Chalfant, William Y., *Cheyennes and Horse Soldiers*, (University of Oklahoma Press, Norman and London, 1989), p. 34–36; Susan Bordeaux Bettelyoun relates a story of "Trapper" Garnier being killed and scalped by Cheyennes in 1857. This could be Peter Garnier, if so Bettelyoun has mistaken the year. Once again this story reported by her is hearsay, as she was born that same year. Bettelyoun, p. 69; J. W.

Vaughn relates yet another story of Peter Garnier's death, stating that he was mistakenly killed one Saturday when he was bringing home a deer he had shot, carrying it on his back. Vaughn, p. 142.

16. Ricker, "Magloire Mosseau," tablet 28, p. 21–24, 51.

17. Jones, Brian, p. 42; Vaughn, p. 142; Dean, Julie, "Transition Years, 1880–1890: Chapter Three, Fort Robinson Illustrated," *Nebraskaland Magazine*, (Nebraska Game and Parks Commission, Jan.–Feb., 1986), vol. 64, no. 1, p. 42–44.

18. The deserters referred to by Brown were 1st Sgt. Edward Lovejoy and Sgt. Fred Meredith. Both departed shortly after the murder of Peter Garnier. McDermott, *Frontier Crossroads*, p. 13.

19. The preceding quotations are all directly from this journal. Portions of the text are irrelevant to this story, but it was felt that the character of the document would be lost if only the pertinent phrases were quoted out of context. Great thanks to Yale University for permission to quote. Brown, J. Robert, *J. Robert Brown's Journal*, (Western Americana Collection, Beinecke Rare Book and Manuscript Library, Yale University Library, New Haven, Connecticut), p. 51–54.

20. Bettelyoun, p. 41, 148; Barry, p. 1140; McDermott, "James Bordeaux" in *Mountain Men*, 5:55.

21. Murray, Robert A., p. 14.

22. These last two handcart companies of 1856 did not depart from Iowa until late in July. Bryans, Bill, *Deer Creek: Frontier Crossroads in Pre-territorial Wyoming*, (Glenrock Historical Commission, Glenrock, Wyoming, 1990), p. 34–36. Jones, Daniel W., *Forty Years Among the Indians*, (Westernlore Press, Los Angeles, California, 1960), p. 64.

23. Eli Plant had recently married Susan LeClair, the bicultural daughter of a former trader in the Sibille & Adams Company. They had also recently homesteaded in Rulo, Nebraska, during the summer of 1855 along with William Kenceleur, a carpenter by trade and a partner in the construction of Richard's Bridge. Census of Rulo, Richardson County, Nebraska Territory, 1860; Article in the *Rulo Register*, November 18, 1909, cited by Stewart Monroe. Monroe; Edwards.

24. Jones, Daniel W., p. 64–88.

25. In recalling the sons of John Richard, Susan Bordeaux Bettelyoun had this to say, "John [Jr.] was sent to St. Louis to school. The boys all were highly educated, but education did not help John [Jr.], nor did his Free Masonry." Bettelyoun, p. 40; Baptiste Gene Pourier was born July 16, 1843, to Joseph Pourier and Mary Aubuchon in St. Charles, Missouri. Bat's father had been a fur trapper and trader in what are now Colorado, Wyoming, Montana,

and the Dakotas; particularly in the area of the White River. His father had died when Bat was only two years old. Bat had two older brothers: Joseph, who died at age twenty-one, and John, who died about the time of Bat's birth. He also had a sister, Elizabeth, who was older than he and a younger brother, Louis, who also presumably died young. After his father's death, Bat's mother married a man named Neville. They had a daughter, Marie and a son, Emile, with whom Bat remained close. Gilbert, p. 2–4; Ricker, Judge Eli S., "Interview of Baptiste Pourier, Wounded Knee Creek, January 7, 1906," (Unpublished Manuscript, Nebraska State Historical Society Library, Lincoln, Nebraska), tablet 15, p. 75–77; Monroe.

26. Wind Creek is a tributary of Antelope Creek, which in turn feeds the Cheyenne River through South Fork and Dry Creek. Some sources have mistaken the name for Wind River, which is well over one hundred miles west of the location of Red Cloud's camp. Gilbert, p. 5–12; Ricker, "Baptiste Pourier," tablet 15, p. 77–83.

7
⋙ TURBULENCE 𝕒𝕟𝕕 TRIUMPH ⋙

OVER THE NEXT months John Richard's abilities and character would again be tested. The vast migrations of the Mormons provided a fairly large percentage of his business. Many members of the church had become Richard's customers and friends, even though he was far from being a follower of their beliefs. His business relationships and acts of kindness toward the Mormons left him open to suspicion by the military during the Utah Expedition. By the time Richard overcame this suspicion and regained his standing with the United States Army, another season had passed. Before long, however, gold was discovered in Colorado. The Richard brothers were not far from the center of the bustle of the next gold rush.

By the time John Richard arrived back at the bridge in 1857, Joseph Bissonette had established a new trading post at Deer Creek, within the present town of Glenrock, Wyoming. Soon after this move, Major Thomas Twiss also moved the Upper Platte Agency from Fort Laramie to Deer Creek, and the newly formed Brigham Young Express and Carrying Company had also begun plans for a supply station there. By June a group of "express missionaries" had begun construction of a mail station a short distance up Deer Creek from the trading post. By July 1, however, the Y.X. Company, as it was most often called, had lost its mail contract and all construction came to a halt.[1]

Rumor had circulated Washington D.C. that Brigham Young intended for Utah to declare independence from the United States. With this in mind, the mail contract was therefore cancelled on the basis that the company had failed to make its first delivery on time. The irony of this claim is that the Y.X. Company had not even received notification that they had been awarded the contract until after the first scheduled delivery was due. The Magraw Mail Company was some three months late delivering the contract to the Y.X. due to the extraordinarily disastrous winter, the same

117

storm that waylaid Jesse Jones at Richard's Bridge. The Y.X. protested the cancellation, but received no satisfaction. Had the delay actually been the reason for the contract cancellation, they perhaps would have had a chance for reinstatement. Continual disagreements between the Mormons at Salt Lake and territorial officials escalated the ill feelings of the United States toward the Mormons.[2]

To add to the antagonism, the Mormon colonists at Salt Lake City were quite negative toward businesses owned by non-Mormons. To discourage outsiders, they attempted to control nearly all commerce in the region. In the process of trying to maintain this somewhat totalitarian approach to business, Brigham Young and his followers created many enemies. W.M.F. Magraw, owner of the Magraw Mail Company, was among those that felt the bite of Young's economic politics. Perhaps in response to the Y.X. bid for the mail contract, Magraw voiced his contempt in a letter to Washington in October 1856.[3]

There is little question today that the Indian Agent Major Twiss was at the very least a rather dubious character. Twiss worked closely with both Richard and Bissonette, and by 1860, rumors had it that his pet bear got more of the government's annuities than the Indians for whom they were intended. In 1857, however, Twiss was evidently highly regarded by his superiors. His motives are subject to speculation, but on July 13, 1857, he wrote a powerful letter to John W. Denver, Commissioner of Indian Affairs in Washington, alleging that the Mormons had encroached on Sioux lands without authorization and urged President Buchanan to intervene. With seemingly no response to this letter, Twiss followed it up with additional letters on September 15, 1857, and November 7, 1857. These letters advised his superiors in both St. Louis and Washington that there was an enormous plot by the Mormons to recruit vast numbers of Indians from several tribes to revolt against the United States Government.[4]

In May 1857, the Buchanan administration had made the decision to intervene militarily in Utah. What they were actually planning to intervene in has yet to be discovered, but the Twiss letters were used as evidence of the rebellion before Congress in February 1858. The United States Government had begun moving troops west to take action against the Mormon's alleged anti-government movement. Colonel Albert Sidney Johnston was in command of the expedition whose mission as published in the *New York Times* on March 9, 1857, was to re-establish United States control of the Utah Territory.[5]

At first this movement of troops toward the Utah Territory was based on questionable information, but news of the "Mountain Meadows Massacre" soon stifled any doubt of the serious problems in the West. The Francher wagon train, headed for California in 1857, was made up primarily of Arkansas farmers looking for a better life. Among them, however, were a few antagonistic Missourians who still held bitter resentments toward the Mormons stemming from troubles along the Mississippi River with the Saints more than a decade earlier. While crossing southern Utah late that summer, the wagon train stopped near Cedar City to replenish supplies. When the locals refused to sell their winter stores of food so late in the season, some of these Missouri men vandalized Mormon property and threatened to return from California with an avenging army to wipe the Mormons from the face of the earth. Both in anger and fear, the Mormons convinced a local band of Indians to attack the wagon train on September 11, 1857, while they were camped at Mountain Meadows, a short distance from Cedar City. The Indians succeeded in killing seven of the emigrants, then laid siege to the wagon train for another five days without further result. The Mormons then contacted the emigrants and told them the Indians had been subdued and that they were safe to proceed on their journey with an escort of militiamen.

Believing the locals, the party hastily loaded their arms in a wagon and quickly began their departure from the meadows. When they passed through a narrow passage they were ambushed by a contingent of Mormons and Indians including their escort of militiamen. In all, 120 emigrants were murdered and mutilated. The only survivors were seventeen children. Aghast at the result of their actions and fearing punishment from the Church and the United States Government, the local Mormons blamed the Indians for the massacre, stating that their own militia had tried to save the emigrants but had arrived on the scene too late. Although the true culprits of the Mountain Meadows Massacre were soon known, only a few were ever punished. When news reached the East of the most violent religious atrocity in American history, the animosity that many had felt toward the Mormons became a bitter hatred. Any question that there were problems in Utah vanished.[6]

<Ξ>·<Ξ>

Long before the Mountain Meadows Massacre, the Mormons stationed along the Platte began a mass exodus toward Utah in advance of the U.S. military. They abandoned their stations and burned them, along with any provisions that they could not take with them. The Mormons' rapid departure undoubtedly provided a little extra business for John Richard, but not nearly the volume that was lost with the halt of the church's normal migration traffic.

The newly-established company of Russell, Majors and Waddell had the contract to transport a large portion of the supplies for Johnston's Army. This large supply train trailed several days behind Johnston. On October 5, 1857, a mounted detachment of the Nauvoo Legion under the command of Major Lot Smith waylaid three units of this train and ordered the teamsters to abandon all the wagons except for enough to transport themselves to Fort Bridger. The Mormons then burned the remaining wagons and the provisions they carried. The freighters estimated their losses in livestock and equipment at seventy-two thousand dollars, for which they were never reimbursed by the government. Traders like Richard undoubtedly reaped the benefits of the Mormons' action since it forced Johnston to secure supplies from local traders.[7]

<Ξ>·<Ξ>

About the time of the Mountain Meadows Massacre, Captain John Wolcott Phelps, leading artillery troops west to Utah, reached Deer Creek. Captain Phelps was highly educated and a prolific writer. An extensive portion of his daily diary was reproduced in Hafen's *Utah Expedition*.

A few miles from Richard's Bridge, Phelps had to deal with an overturned wagon in his company. The driver, a young mixed-blood Cherokee, was unhurt, "except for his pride as a teamster." This, it seems was damage enough for this proud young man who displayed "great energy and force of character."

Phelps was overwhelmed by the extensive damage caused by previous emigration along the trail. The forage along the Platte had been eaten literally to the dirt. He felt any grass remaining would not have been edible because every square inch of the ground was "wholly consumed by tattoo."[8] Phelps's troops soon arrived at "the bridge," as he reports was the only name for Richard's Bridge at that time. He remarked on Richard's ingenuity in creating the structure, although low water that fall allowed him and his troops to ford the river just above the bridge. He also noted the presence of the small coal mine on the north bank of the river.

John Richard was still in St. Louis when Phelps passed through, but even without his presence, the trading post did a booming business with the troops. The company camped a few miles beyond the bridge on the north bank of the Platte and spent the following day at rest, which Phelps explains is not at all like it sounds. Rest, he states, means not moving. In fact it is a grueling day of labor, greasing wagon wheels, shoeing livestock, and making all of the numerous repairs necessary to proceed the following day. Captain Phelps did, however, manage to catch up with his correspondence that day and read a copy of the Mormon's *Deseret News* that had been picked up at Richard's Trading Post. Phelps also met an English engineer, a Mr. Finley, that day. Finley was headed east to Fort Laramie and was with "Magraw," though he had previously been traveling with the 10th Infantry. It can be assumed that Finley and Magraw carried the captain's letters east with them.[9]

⋘∗⋙

About a month after Captain Phelps's departure, John Richard and Baptiste Pourier arrived back at Richard's Bridge. Bissonette's Trading Post at Deer Creek was well established. It included a store, blacksmith's shop, and the first official United States Post Office in the region.[10] On November 30, 1857, F. W. Lander presented a preliminary engineering report on the western wagon road to the Secretary of the Interior. Unfortunately Lander's report was not presented to Congress until early in 1859. Had this report been acted upon soon after its writing, America's westward migration may have developed in a considerably different manner. The following paragraphs are excerpts from that report regarding Richard's Bridge:

> "…I was guided by the following conclusion, viz: A large sum of money had been appropriated to build a practicable wagon road over a route where a practicable wagon road had existed for the last ten years. Want of grass, danger of loss of stock by deleterious and poisonous waters, extreme tolls levied by traders' bridges, and the circuitous route pursued, were difficulties to be overcome or obliviated…

> "A preliminary reconnaissance, made by [t]he chief engineer, has established the fact that several days' travel can be saved upon the

rear division between Fort Kearney and the South Pass. The emigration can also be divided on this division, much sandy road avoided, and many of the traders' bridges rendered free by the expenditure of the sum of $40,000 . . .

"In the last instance, it is proposed that the work is to be done during the summer of 1859, and after the division from the South Pass to City of Rocks is completed the bridges of the rear division to be rendered free by the proceeds of the sale of the stock of the expedition when the work is over. This proposal to postpone the purchase of the traders' bridges until 1859 must be qualified by the presumption of the fact that the present tolls will be an exorbitant tax on government transportation during 1858, if large military operations are carried on in Utah Territory.

"The arrival of Assistant Engineer Mullowny will bring intelligence of a new route, by which it is proposed to avoid the bridge over the north fork of the Platte. The price of fifteen thousand dollars ($15,000) is asked for the bridge by the owner, and the passage of it yearly costs the emigration from four to ten thousand dollars. The bridge is offered for sale in apprehension of the building of a free bridge by the wagon road expedition. The owner, Mr. John Richard, is a reliable mountain trader. He proposes either to give bonds to keep the bridge in good repair for six years, and to renew it if destroyed within that time, or to receive only one sixth part of the purchase money yearly. The same arrangement could undoubtedly be made in relation to the bridge at [Fort] Laramie. In view of the large military operations now going on in the country, the War Department might properly join their funds with those of the wagon road in the purchase of the Richard bridge…"[11]

⋘⋅⋙

In the meantime the military was flexing its muscle along the very road that was under consideration. On November 13, 1857, Major J. Lynde at Fort Laramie issued an order to search Richard's establishments at the bridge for arms and ammunition that, based on information received by Colonel Johnston, were allegedly cached there by Grosbeck's Mormon wagon train. Lieutenant J. S. Marmaduke carried out that order on December 3. This search was carried on both at Richard's Bridge and

Bissonette's operations at Deer Creek. As a result some twenty to thirty rifles were confiscated by Marmaduke and returned to Fort Laramie. Richard and Bissonette profusely protested this action stating that the rifles taken were their personal property. Richard went on to say that the rifles were not only needed for trade purposes, but for his organization's own protection. Indian Agent Twiss even testified that Colonel Johnston's information had been false. John Richard traveled to Camp Scott, in the Utah Territory, to plead his case to Johnston himself. When Johnston refused to listen to reason, Richard demanded that the Government reimburse him three thousand dollars for the rifles. All was to no avail, and Richard returned to the bridge empty handed.[12]

John Richard then went to Independence, Missouri, for supplies and to attain additional help to run his operations during the coming season. While there he met F. W. Lander who was preparing for his Central Pacific Wagon Road expedition: "The sutler at Fort Laramie, S. E. [Seth] Ward, was contracted to bring the expedition's supplies forward to that fort. John Richards, a mountain trader who owned a bridge across the Platte, was in Independence engaging carpenters for repair work. He assured the road engineer that beef cattle and oxen for mountain work would be available at his post, 830 miles up the Platte, in exchange for some of the expedition's mules." Whether this trade ever took place is unknown, but Richard, with his keen sense for business quickly recognized his opportunity to trade some of the oxen and cattle for the more highly valued mules which he would, in turn, trade with the emigrants.[13]

John Richard's relations with Colonel Johnston's Army were not all bad. He apparently sold to the Quartermaster at Camp Scott a fair amount of merchandise after the loss of the supplies carried by Russell, Majors and Waddell. In the spring of 1858 he drove some one hundred head of livestock to Camp Scott for the same purpose. Within a few days of this delivery, the order was received at Fort Laramie to return Richard's confiscated rifles to him.[14]

❦ ❦

By early June the United States Government had made the decision to re-establish a post at Richard's Bridge. The purpose this time was to protect and assist the numerous trains of supplies that were traveling west to support the troops in Utah. Captain Joseph Roberts was in command of the two companies of artillery that arrived there in July. More than one hundred men were stationed at the new "Post at Platte Bridge" including some two dozen civilian teamsters. The new post was set up just south of the former Camp Davis. Officially it was named "Post at Platte Bridge," but unofficially it was referred to as "Camp Payne" in honor of Lieutenant Colonel M. M. Payne of the 4th Artillery. The soldiers stationed there satirically revamped this name into "Camp Pain" shortly after Private John Morgan died in the post hospital there that August.

One of the junior officers at Camp Payne was 1st Lieutenant Joseph Claypoole Clark Jr., who was a talented artist and during his stay there drew "a well and neatly executed topographical sketch of the post and its vicinity." This sketch, unfortunately, has eluded historians' searches.[15]

⊰⊱ ⊰⊱

Rumors of the presence of gold in the Rocky Mountains had been circulating for several years, but most seekers of the precious metal had concentrated their efforts in the Sierra Nevada Mountains of California. Early in 1858, however, new information, perhaps contributed by local Indians, prompted two expeditions into the Pike's Peak region of present-day Colorado. In May, one of these groups left Lawrence, Kansas, in search of the alluring yellow metal. Shortly after this group's arrival in the country, members of the Lawrence Company were successfully panning gold from Cherry Creek at present-day Denver, Colorado. Within days, John Richard had received word of the strike through his own information network. He then traveled to Fort Laramie where he and a group of his cronies set off for the South Platte to confirm the story.

⊰⊱ ⊰⊱

After John Floureseur had completed a sizable trade with Red Cloud the previous winter, he had sent Baptiste Pourier and another laborer to Richard's Bridge with eight packhorses heavily loaded with 160 buffalo robes to exchange for trade goods. On their way to the bridge, Bat met Charles Carbonneau who was then operating a small ranch on Deer Creek. Carbonneau offered Bat twenty-five dollars per month to tend his horses and haul firewood for the winter. Pourier accepted and Carbonneau lent him a horse to ride to the bridge to obtain his belongings before reporting to the ranch. John Richard was apparently not upset at Pourier's resignation and paid him what he had earned. Big Bat left for Deer Creek on Carbonneau's horse the next morning and remained there through the winter.

Red Cloud led a group of Oglala Sioux who traded with Richard and his partners. (*Wyoming State Archives, Department of State Parks and Cultural Resources*)

News of the Colorado gold strike had also passed through Deer Creek. In April of 1858, Carbonneau departed for Cherry Creek, a tributary to the South Platte River, to reap the bounties of the boom. Joseph Bissonette, Ben Claymore, and Cuddifield joined him. Oxen pulled all of the wagons. Bat's cousin John Aubuchon drove one of the two wagons belonging to Joseph Bissonette. Bat herded horses and cattle on the month-long journey to Auraria, later to become Denver and Aurora, Colorado. Upon their arrival, Bat hauled logs for the construction of trading houses at the fledgling mining town. Shortly after their arrival, Pourier ran into another cousin, Alexander Woods, who invited Bat to join him in a prospecting venture. Bat quit Carbonneau and went with Woods to the gold-mining camp of California Gulch, near present-day Leadville, Colorado, where the two spent the summer.[16]

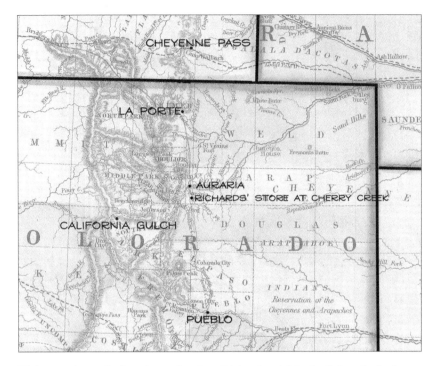

This map shows the locations of various Richard activities in Colorado during the time of the California Gulch gold rush. (*Map based on W.H. Gamble's "Map of Kansas, Nebraska and Colorado Showing also The Eastern portion of Idaho." Philadelphia: S. Augustus Mitchell Jr., 1863.*)

⋘⋙

By the end of August word of the gold strike had reached St. Louis, and John Richard was one of the first men to have reported it. He had arrived in Kansas City on August 28, with reports of a very rich gold find which, even with limited prospecting, was producing amazing results. He said two men with poor equipment had washed out six hundred dollars in gold in less than a week. On September 1, 1858, the *Missouri Republican* reported that John Richard, Charles Martin,[17] and William Rencleleur [Kenceleur] had recently arrived at Rulo, Nebraska Territory, with news that gold had been discovered on Cherry Creek. By the time John Richard, Elmore King, and C.C. Carpenter arrived in St. Louis, the mayhem of the famous Pike's Peak Gold Rush had already begun.[18]

Before year's end, John Richard and his brother Joseph had opened the first store at Cherry Creek to supply miners with numerous necessities. Joseph Richard also started a ranch on Clear Creek, some five miles outside of the town. Peter Richard opened a trading post at Cheyenne Pass, which he ran in conjunction with his brothers' operations at Cherry Creek and Richard's Bridge. John Richard did not give up his bridge operation to solely concentrate his efforts in the gold fields; instead he used both to his advantage.

The miners when arriving at Cherry Creek were often too busy or too broke to care for the livestock that brought them there. Consequently, most of these animals were simply turned loose on the prairie to fend for themselves. For those who could afford it, care and grazing were offered for a fee at Joseph Richard's nearby ranch. For the rest, John Richard offered to purchase their livestock at a minimal price.

All sources of wild game were soon driven from the area by the vast influx of miners and a shortage of meat developed. John Richard was the man to take advantage of this situation. He had established large herds of both oxen and beef cattle in the north. The horses and mules he acquired in Colorado were herded to Richard's Bridge, where he received top dollar from the emigrants for them. Once there, his drovers gathered a herd of cattle to take back to Joseph's Clear Creek ranch to sell for meat. John Richard made money at both ends of the trail.[19]

⟨⟩⟨⟩

Late that summer, Hiram B. "Hi" Kelly and Tom Maxwell, his brother-in-law, started for Salt Lake with a mule train. They were in the employ of the Ford & Smith Freight Company, who had contracted with a Mr. Kincade to deliver a sizable shipment of goods. Due to their late start and the poor condition of their animals, they were forced to delay this expedition in September. They spent the winter at Fort Laramie and grazed their mules in Goshen's Hole, eventually concluding their journey the following spring. During this extended layover Hi Kelly may have first become acquainted with the Richard family. Undoubtedly he became familiar with other personalities at the post, which influenced his later exploits in the region.[20]

⟨⟩⟨⟩

Evidently Alexander Woods had sent a letter from the mining camp to Baptiste Pourier's mother, Mary Pourier, in St. Charles to let her know that Bat was alive and well. Soon thereafter, Woods received a letter from Mrs. Pourier begging him to send her son home. Woods loaned Bat a horse and made arrangements for him to accompany another man to St. Charles.

When Bat and his newly appointed guardian arrived in Denver from California Gulch, they ran into John Richard. Richard had purchased a shipment of flour in Taos or Pueblo, but one of his teamsters had abandoned him. Richard convinced Pourier to change his destination by offering him forty-five dollars per month to drive a wagon to the bridge and work there through the winter. Bat handed over his horse, and once again joined Richard.

Baptiste Pourier spent that winter hauling hay for John Richard. By spring he had purchased his own horse and saddle and returned to Denver. About the same time, the wagon train of F. M. Baker arrived at the bridge. Baker recorded the day like this: "Started on again, soaking with rain, and reached a ranch at Platte Bridge, an eight-span wooden structure. Crossed over and paid two dollars per team of four horses. Rain slackened, and after awhile stopped for dinner. At the ranch two companies of troops were stationed. Quite a number of Indians hung around. A young-looking squaw came along with her ponies and papooses. She had on a clean calico dress, mostly of a pink color. Her children looked clean…. She tied a long strap around the second pony's neck, then started her own pony with agility, and throwing over her shoulders her clean white blanket, she was off in a moment, her nest of papooses next, her little boy following, then a mare and colt."[21]

❦◦❦

Shortly after Baker's visit to the bridge an incident occurred near the post that the garrison should have taken more seriously. On April 26, 1859, an Indian fatally stabbed a Frenchman named LaBeau in the chest. The Officer of the Day searched the village and examined several Indians in an effort to discover the assailant. He eventually arrested three men, but later released them for lack of evidence. Perhaps this was not the true reason that the investigation was so quickly dropped. Camp Payne was preparing to abandon the Post at Platte Bridge, which they did a few days later. President Buchanan, through Thomas L. Kane and peace commissioners Ben McCulloch and Lazarus W. Powell, had negotiated an agreement with the Mormons, and Brigham Young had officially been pardoned nearly a year before. The Mormon War, or Utah Expedition as it is now called, was over, and once again the military no longer felt the need to protect the bridge.[22]

⟨⟩⟨⟩

John Richard left Denver for St. Charles to retrieve his son John Jr. and, by June 1859, they were back at the bridge on the Platte. He arrived there in time to greet most of the emigrant traffic and witness the birth of his second daughter, Rose. Several diarists mention the bridge and trading post that year. Hammet Hubbard Case crossed Richard's Bridge on June 12 and called it a stout timber bridge. He also referred to the fifteen or twenty "comfortable" log homes that stood nearby. J. A. Wilkinson crossed the bridge the same day. He surmised that the construction of such a structure over such a swift river as the Platte must have been quite a costly project. He also ventured into the trading post where he was amused by the efficiency of Richard's clerks, bartering with the Indians through sign language.[23]

Others were not so well entertained by John Richard and his employees. About this time another enterprising individual offered the first competition to Richard's Bridge in several years. At a point a few miles upstream from the bridge, a true ferry was put into operation. Details of the ownership of this ferry are sketchy. Previous ferries were steered across the river and landed at some point downstream to be towed back upstream with oxen. This new ferry included guide ropes spanned the river and with pulleys attached to .

John Richard was furious about this challenge to his monopoly and reportedly bought out this new entrepreneur for three hundred dollars. Then Richard towed the ferry to the north bank of the Platte and tied it off there. A short time later a large wagon train bound for California arrived at Richard's Bridge, and the wagon captain began negotiating with Richard for the toll. When Richard would go no lower than two-and-a-half dollars per wagon, the captain told him his wagons would continue on to the ferry. To this Richard responded that the ferry no longer existed, and, after a heated argument, Richard informed the captain that the price would be five dollars per wagon when they returned. The captain refused to believe him and led his train on to the ferry crossing. When they arrived there, they found the ferry tied up where Richard had left it so they put it into operation.

When the emigrant train failed to return, Richard ascertained what had happened and gathered together a group of well-armed men. They then crossed the bridge and proceeded to a vantage point on the north bank at the ferry crossing. When they arrived at the top of a steep hill overlooking the ferry, Richard could see that all but a few of the wagons were already across. Leaving the majority of his small army at the top of the hill, Richard and three of his best men descended the hill and confronted George Morris, who was in charge of the operation on the north side of the river. Attacking Morris with a fusillade of profanities, Richard proclaimed that he would enlist his Indian friends to waylay the wagon train and most assuredly there would be no survivors. Morris soon grew tired of Richard's verbal abuse, and Richard in his blinded fury did not notice Morris draw his pistol. With John Richard at gunpoint, Morris told him that he had heard enough, and if he had anything more to say to tell it to the captain who was still on the south bank.

Richard, with his three men, then boarded the ferry and crossed to the south side of the river, where he immediately laid into the captain with a barrage of indignations and profanities. He was just warming up with his repeat performance, when he heard the ominous click of a rifle being cocked behind him. The silence was deafening as John Richard measured the circumstances in his mind. His men atop the hill on the far side of the river were out of range. If he was killed, those men could easily annihilate a large portion of this wagon train, but none of his men was in a position to deal with the man who held the rifle at his back. As calmly as possible, Richard ordered his three men back to the bridge and the foursome proceeded along the south bank. When the men had covered a safe distance, he turned and hollered back to the captain that five hundred Sioux would be on their tail by sundown. The wagon train continued to California and arrived there without further malice or molestation.[24]

Another diarist stated that John Richard, in quite a drunken state, drove his carriage through an emigrant train causing a stampede which killed two men. The fact that John Richard did drink his own whiskey and go a little wild at times makes this report believable. Whether this event occurred as an aftermath to the previous one is not known. There are no other accounts to substantiate this event. The diarist did not claim to have witnessed the event, so the second-hand story may have been exaggerated in telling, as was often the case in the wild frontier.

During this same year John Richard also opened a "sub-post," located near Red Buttes Crossing about ten miles west of Richard's Bridge.[25]

⬦⬦⬦

When Baptiste Pourier returned to Denver he again went to work for his cousin Alexander Woods. The next fall he quit Woods and went to work for Joseph Richard hauling lumber to town for the new store Richard was building. When this job was finished Big Bat stayed on with Joseph and moved to his ranch to tend cattle and horses. By this time Joseph Richard was one of the most prominent businessmen in Denver. He was a member of the staff of the Union Day School, the first school in the area, which opened October 31, 1859. He operated not only a ranch and store, but also a first-rate saloon and hotel. This mountain man turned businessman located on what became Blake Street. The Richards had built their first store there before anything resembling a street existed along Cherry Creek. John and his brothers first had built a huge log building in which they carried the largest stock of Indian goods ever in Denver. During this time John Richard employed over twenty Indian women at the bridge making buckskin clothing, moccasins, and other Indian items that were sold to miners in Colorado. This enterprise was undoubtedly the first operation that could be classified as an industry in what is now Wyoming.[26]

⬦⬦⬦

Peter Richard was enjoying his own success at Cheyenne Pass. He had purchased eighteen thousand pounds of bacon in St. Louis to sell from his trading post to the miners. At his inflated boomtown prices, he brought in nine thousand dollars from sales of the bacon alone. The 1860 Denver census records show that though Joseph and Peter were the primary operators of the Colorado businesses, John still owned the controlling interests. The census reported the estimated "value of personal estate" and showed Jno. [John] Richard, aged 50, at $25,000; Peter Richard, aged 40, at $1,400; and Joseph Richard, aged 35 [37], at $10,000. All were wealthy for that period when a skilled laborer earned around twenty to thirty dollars per month in the eastern United States. William H. H. Larimer, a notable pioneer in Denver, commented on the spectacle of John and Joe Richard's families preparing for a vacation.

"They had a large band of paint ponies which they would drive in and saddle for the whole family to go visiting someone for a week or two."[27]

◇◆◇

While business boomed for his brothers in Colorado, John Richard spent the fall of 1859 at the bridge. On October 11, Captain William F. Raynolds left his camp for the Platte Bridge in advance of his topographical expedition with Dr. Ferdinand V. Hayden and Mr. Wilson.

Prior to his departure, he asked well-known guide Jim Bridger if there was any danger of missing the Platte road when they came to it. Bridger only laughed. When Raynolds first saw the famous thoroughfare, he realized for the first time the significance of the migration, and the humor Jim Bridger had seen that morning in his ignorance. Raynolds found the volume of traffic on the road astonishing, even this late in the season. He was further amazed that about the same amount of traffic traveled eastbound as west and that he was seldom out of sight of a vehicle "upon this great highway." He even passed a group of ladies traveling in an ambulance "bound for the States."

The Raynolds Expedition had traveled from Fort Pierre to the Black Hills and then southwesterly. The captain intersected the Oregon Trail near Red Buttes. After arriving there he and his companions headed east on the road at a rapid pace and soon covered the eighteen miles to Richard's Bridge and Trading Post. When he arrived at the trading post, John Richard informed him that Lieutenant H. E. Maynadier's party was not far behind his own. Raynolds questioned how Richard could possibly know that, and Richard answered that an Indian informant had seen them on Powder River. John Richard also gave Raynolds a four-month-old letter and told him that there was more correspondence waiting for him at the post office at Deer Creek, Bissonette's Trading Post.

At the request of Raynolds, Richard sent a man to Deer Creek for his mail, and Raynolds sent a message to Fort Laramie to send their supplies to the bridge. While the captain was enjoying Richard's well-known western hospitality and the luxury of eating dinner from a table while sitting down, the majority of the Raynolds military contingent arrived and immediately began sampling the wares at Richard's two saloons. Before returning to their camp at Red Buttes, Raynolds's escort had imbibed enough alcohol to turn the camp "into bedlam." The commander of the escort considered Raynolds's title of captain simply honorary as

Raynolds was an engineer not a military man, so consequently he considered that Raynolds had no authority over them. The expedition, in all reality, suffered a mutiny by the escort.

Without military support Captain Raynolds, accompanied by Jim Bridger, then performed a reconnaissance of Carson's Creek in search of a suitable location to spend the winter. When Raynolds and Bridger returned to camp, they found that the escort had in fact abandoned them. To their surprise, however, Lieutenant Maynadier had arrived in advance of his own party, who also soon joined them. Also that day a man arrived from Richard's Bridge with the mail for both parties from Deer Creek. The arrival of the mail and Maynadier uplifted Raynolds's spirits. Carson's Creek had proven to be an unsuitable location for their winter quarters, and the next several days were spent exploring other possible alternatives.[28]

Raynolds had exhausted nearly all options when Major Thomas Twiss, the Indian Agent for the Upper Platte Agency at Deer Creek, offered a solution. When the Mormons had abandoned their Y. X. relay station at Deer Creek a few years earlier, they left several unfinished dwellings at the site. With winter drawing near, these cabins offered the quickest available shelter. Captain Raynolds took Twiss up on his offer and soon his expedition was afforded some protection from the elements.

The completion and repair of the houses could not have been more timely. By mid-November, with several of the men still living in tents, the thermometer had already dipped to sub-zero on more than one occasion. Captain Raynolds and his party spent most of the winter transcribing page upon page of survey notes from the previous summer's work into useful maps and documentation.[29]

⋘⋙

Several weeks prior to Raynolds's arrival at Deer Creek, a group of Lutheran missionaries had arrived there en route to the Crow Indian country when multiple delays had set them far behind schedule. They knew they would not have time to reach the Powder River Basin before winter's arrival. Two of the original six missionaries returned to the East while the remaining four took advantage of the same offer from Twiss to take over one of the old Mormon dwellings. When Raynolds arrived, the Lutherans offered what assistance they could to their new neighbors. They were greatly repaid for their kindness before winter's end. The missionaries had intended to grow vegetables to supplement their meager supplies, but they had arrived far too late to attempt gardening and were desperately short of food. Captain Raynolds and his topographers shared some of their food and helped them attain credit for supplies from Bissonette's Trading Post.

When Christmas Eve arrived the missionaries made the trek some three miles through the snow to a wooded area to cut a Christmas tree in the tradition of their native Germany. By the time they returned and had decorated it, the evening had passed into night. Hope of celebrating the holiday with their neighbors faded when Braeuninger, one of the missionaries, discovered both the Twiss and Bissonette families already fast asleep, unaware that it was Christmas Eve. Undaunted, he rousted a nearby Indian village and acquired a few volunteers for the celebration. He then went to the engineers' dwellings and managed to wake Raynolds and a few of his men. Raynolds played the flute and Braeuninger the violin to entertain the guests while the rest of the missionaries excitedly distributed their meager feast of bread and coffee.

On Christmas Day Raynolds, with his flute and some of his officers, returned to the missionaries' cabin with some dried fruit and other food. Together they sang and played every American and German hymn or carol that any could recall. The celebration was likely an event that none would soon forget, a fleeting moment of escape from winter's harsh realities for lonely men far from home.[30]

Notes to Chapter Seven:

1. *The Brigham Young Express and Carrying Company* was most commonly known as the B.Y.X. Carrying Company or simply the Y.X. Company. Many historians believe that Young used the initials to divert attention from himself and mollify eastern adversaries. Bryans, p. 36–42; Jones, Brian, p. 14.

2. Bryans, p. 42; McDermott, *Frontier Crossroads*, p. 15.

3. MacKinnon, William, Correspondence with the author, 2001 (Jefferson Glass's collection).

4. Little evidence substantiates Twiss's possible motives for writing the three letters. Possibly his motive was to halt the construction of the Y.X. station at Deer Creek, which might have drawn attention to Twiss's illegal use and distribution of the Indian annuities. Hyde, p. 89–90; MacKinnon.

5. *New York Times,* March 9, 1857, cited by McDermott, *Frontier Crossroads*, p. 15–16.

6. Lewis, Jon E., *The Mammoth Book of the West: The Making of the American West,* (Carroll & Graf Publishers, New York, 1996), p. 110–111; Milner, Clyde A. II, O'Connor, Carol A., Sandweiss, Martha A., editors, *The Oxford History of the American West,* (Oxford University Press, New York, 1994), p. 364, 416.

7. McDermott, *Frontier Crossroads*, p. 15–16; MacKinnon; The trio of Russell, Majors and Waddell had all been in business in the region for many years and in different combinations of partnerships. This particular partnership was formed under this name in 1856. It must also be noted that the losses claimed by Russell, Majors and Waddell of $72,000 was only for their livestock and equipment. Losses to the military from the goods that they carried would have been considerably higher. William T. Eubank was an early freighter on both the Platte and Santa Fe Trails. When speaking of John Richard he said, "They charged immigrants $5 a wagon; to the big [outfits] they asked as toll only an order on the company (Jones & Cartwright or Major, Russell & Waddell). This was an old plainsman [Jones]. Jones & Brown began about 1840, long before Majors & Russell began about 1857 [1856]; and Jones & Cartwright began 1858. This Jones was John S. Jones." Cragin, "William T. Eubank," notebook I, p. 5/25 & 6/26.

8. Phelps's use of the word "tattoo" probably indicates the soil was totally drummed down by repeated hoofprints.

9. Phelps, Captain John Wolcott, *Diaries of John W. Phelps*, (Unpublished Manuscripts, Rare Books and Manuscripts, New York Public Library, New York). The "Mr. Finley" mentioned was William Porter Finlay, who although described as English was a native of Belfast, Ireland. "Magraw" surely must have been W.M.F. Magraw, owner of the Magraw Mail Company. MacKinnon.

10. Vaughn, p. 80; McDermott, "Joseph Bissonette" in *Mountain Men*, 4:56.

11. Lander, F. W., *Preliminary Report of F. W. Lander, Report of the Secretary of the Interior, 35th Congress, Feb. 23, 1859,* (National Archives).

12. Jones, Brian, p. 15; McDermott, "John Baptiste Richard" in *Mountain Men*, 2:300; McDermott, *Frontier Crossroads*, p. 15–16.

13. Jackson, W. Turrentine, *Wagon Roads West*, (Yale University Press, London and New Haven, 1952), p. 207; Ben Kern, experienced modern-day wagonmaster and co-author of the book *Wagon Wheels* has provided much insight regarding wagon train travel, both then and now. The use of mules to pull wagons on such a journey was by far preferred over oxen or horses. In addition to their natural hardiness, mules tend to be more adaptable to the constant changes in feed and water that occur on such a long journey than other draft animals. Kern, Ben, conversations with the author, 1997–2002.

14. Jones, Brian, p. 15; McDermott, "John Baptiste Richard" in *Mountain Men*, 2:300; McDermott, *Frontier Crossroads*, p. 16.

15. McDermott, *Frontier Crossroads*, p. 16–17; Murray, Robert A., p. 15.

16. Ricker, "Baptiste Pourier," tablet 15, p. 82–85; "Baptiste (Big Bat) Pourier reportedly hauled the first load of logs to Denver." West, Elliott, *The Contested Plains: Indians, Goldseekers, & the Rush to Colorado*, (University of Kansas Press, Lawrence, 1998), p. 185.

17. Charles Martin was born in Canada in 1818. He was listed as one of the founders of Rulo, Nebraska, along with William Kenceleur and Eli Plant in the summer of 1855. He also appeared on the 1860 census there. His early exploits in Colorado must have been very lucrative. His occupation was listed as "gentleman" and his personal and real estate value at $11,000. Edwards; Census of Rulo, Richardson County, Nebraska Territory, 1860.

18. Articles from the *Missouri Republican* August 31, 1858, and September 1, 1858, cited by Brian Jones. Jones, Brian, p. 15–16, 42; McDermott, "John Baptiste Richard" in *Mountain Men*, 2:300; McDermott, *Frontier Crossroads*, p. 16; Barry, p. 1140; C. C. Carpenter was a member of the Lawrence Company. Jones, Brian, p. 15; the William Rencleleur mentioned is undoubtedly William Kenceleur, who had earlier been a partner in Richard's Bridge and Joseph Bissonette's trading posts. According to the 1860 census, William Kenceleur was born in Canada in 1804. He had three children by a previous marriage ranging from eleven to seventeen years old and a young nineteen-year-old wife, Zella, who was the mother of their six-month-old daughter, Melissa. William's occupation is listed as carpenter and the value of the family estate at $5,120. Census of Rulo, Richardson County, Nebraska Territory, 1860.

19. Jones, Brian, p. 16; McDermott, *Frontier Crossroads*, p. 16; Hafen, LeRoy, *Reports From Colorado*, vol. XIII, p. 206.

20. Hiram Kelly was born in Missouri, October 14, 1834. At the age of fifteen he and his father, Hiram S. Kelly, joined in the California Gold Rush, traveling west on the Platte River route. From 1854 to 1857 he worked as a teamster on the Santa Fe Trail for various freight and mail companies. Kelly's brother-in-law, Tom Maxwell, may have been the same man who in partnership with Quinn, had been attacked by Apaches at Raton Pass in 1848. There were several Maxwells involved in the freight business on the Santa Fe Trail and in the Taos area during that period. Another Maxwell of that region was a partner of Kit Carson in a large cattle ranch in the Taos area. Both Kelly and Maxwell were presumably previously acquainted with Seth Ward. Ward, who was then the post sutler at Fort Laramie, had in earlier years also traded in the Pueblo and Santa Fe regions. When Kelly and Maxwell arrived in Salt Lake the next spring, their portion of the freight was sent on to Camp Floyd, some forty miles to the south. There they made arrangements to sell their

mules to the Army and returned with the other freighters to Missouri. The deal they had made with the Army fell through, however, and the next fall the mules were delivered to them in Missouri, where Kelly and Maxwell sold them at auction. Ricker, "Magloire Mosseau," tablet 28, p. 79; Briston, Dave and Dubois, William R. III, "Highlights in the Life of "Hi" Kelly", *Bits and Pieces: Your Own Western History Magazine*, (Mabel E. Brown, publisher, Newcastle, Wyoming, 1969), vol. 5, no. 9, p. 1; Bartlett, I. S., editor, *History of Wyoming*, (S. J. Clarke Publishing Company, 1918), vol. III, p. 140.

21. Ricker, "Baptiste Pourier," tablet 15, p. 85–87. Baker, Hozial H., editor, *Overland Journey to Carson Valley & California*, (The Book Club of California, 1973), p. 34–35. Perhaps the most important contribution of this diary is the description of the Indian girl. Baker uses the word "clean" three times in this description. The fact is that the Plains Indians were extremely clean people, bathing and washing their clothing far more often than most whites in that era. Portrayals of these people as a dirty race are a gross inaccuracy.

22. McDermott, *Frontier Crossroads*, p. 20; MacKinnon.

23. Jones, Brian, p. 42–44; The diaries of Hammet Hubbard Case and J. A. Wilkinson are both cited by McDermott, *Frontier Crossroads*, p. 20.

24. The author has pinpointed the location of this ferry, just south of the present-day Casper Event's Center and the National Historic Trails Center. The owner of this ferry may have been Magloire Mosseau. Although he does not mention embarking in such an enterprise, the location was in the immediate vicinity of the ranch he operated there at the time. Ricker, "Magloire Mosseau," tablet 28, p. 21–24, 51; William H. Carmichael traveled to California on this wagon train in 1859. In the 1890s he resided in Wheatland, Wyoming, and related this story to Coutant in an interview. Coutant, C. G., *The History of Wyoming from the Earliest Known Discoveries*, (C. G. Coutant, publisher, Chaplin, Spafford & Mathison, printers, Laramie, Wyoming, 1899), p. 365–367.

25. McDermott, *Frontier Crossroads*, p. 21.

26. Ricker, "Baptiste Pourier," tablet 15, p. 87–90; Hafen, *Reports From Colorado*, vol. XIII, p. 200; Gilbert, p. 14–15.

27. Hafen, *Reports From Colorado*, vol. XIII, p. 206; 1860 Denver census records are cited by Jones, Brian, p. 40; Gilbert, p. 14.

28. Raynolds, Captain William F., *Report on the Exploration of the Yellowstone River*, (United States Army Corps of Engineers, 1868), p. 70–72; the Carson's Creek in Raynolds's description is what is now known as Bates Creek. John C. Frémont named it Carson's Creek on one of his early expeditions for his guide, the legendary mountain man Kit Carson. The origin of the name of Bates Creek varies. One source states that it was named for the trapper Bates, who stumbled off the Laramie Plains into what is now called Bates Hole. After becoming entangled in a mass of brush, he was forced to halt until daylight.

When he awoke he reportedly looked around him and said, "Well, Bates has sure got hisself into a hell of a hole this time." A less colorful, but more likely, origin is that it was named for Captain Alfred Bates following a skirmish he and his troops had there with Indians in 1874. By the early 1880s settlers knew the creek as Bates Creek. Scott, George C., *These God Forsaken Dobie Hills: Land Law and the Settlement of Bates Hole, Wyoming 1880–1940*, (Unpublished Manuscript, MA Thesis, University of Wyoming, Laramie, Wyoming, 1978, copy in Special Collections, Goodstein Foundation Library, Casper College, Casper, Wyoming) p. 1–2; Urbanek, Mae, *Wyoming Place Names*, (Johnson Publishing Company, Boulder, Colorado, 1967), p. 17.

29. Raynolds, p. 72–73.

30. Bryans, p. 88–91.

8
❦ Stages, Freighters, ᴀɴᴅ the Pony Express ❦

WHILE THE MEN at Deer Creek reflected on far away friends and family that Christmas of 1860, so likely did John Richard reminisce on days gone by. His time as "King of the North Platte River" was drawing to a close. Louis Guinard, whose bridge across the Sweetwater River had washed out the previous spring, contracted with Joseph McKnight to build a new bridge across the Platte a few miles above Richard's. Richard would lose the monopoly that he'd held for eight years with his bridge on the Upper Platte. A rumor that Guinard had been a partner in Richard's Bridge early on cannot be substantiated. If so, the animosity Guinard created with his new bridge may have been caused by a much older enmity between the two men. Furthermore, McKnight, married to John Richard's stepdaughter and long an employee of Richard, would be building the competing bridge for Guinard.

Perhaps the newly attained "promised land" of the Colorado gold fields was an omen that it was time for a change at John Richard's Bridge and Trading Post. Richard's interests in Colorado required his frequent absence from the North Platte operations, but his involvement did not diminish. These absences, however, may have cost him influence in some new ventures pending along the Platte.[1]

The well-known freight company of Russell, Majors and Waddell was the instigator of one of the most famous, but shortest lived, ventures in U.S. history—the Pony Express. The company invested thousands of dollars establishing nearly two hundred relay stations along the proposed route in 1859 and 1860. Joseph Bissonette's Deer Creek operation was one of the selected sites, as well as Fort La Bonte, where he may have still been a partner. John Richard's Red Buttes Trading Post was also on the list, but Louis Guinard's new bridge was chosen over Richard's Bridge for the crossing of the Platte and became, consequently, the relay station.[2]

❦ ❦

William Russell had spent several months lobbying that the Platte River route for mail service to California was far superior to the much longer southern route of the Overland Mail Company. In April 1860, the inaugural run of the Pony Express was set into motion. Some riders suffered delays, but other men made up time with heroic rides. Thus began the romantic tales of the perilous adventures of the Pony Express riders. By July, the successful demonstration plus Russell's political efforts had paid off, and the Pony Express received federal approval. Much to Russell's dismay, while the North Platte route was approved, in March 1861, the contract was awarded to the Overland Mail Company. The Overland was not prepared to undertake the operation and was forced to subcontract Russell and his partners to fulfill their obligations.[3]

Among the many contract mail carriers prior to the Pony Express were several stage lines, including one run by Russell, Majors and Waddell. In 1859 they had acquired the former Salt Lake Stage and Mail Line which became the Leavenworth and Pikes Peak Express. The new owners once again renamed it. It now became the Central Overland, California, and Pikes Peak Express or COC & PP. The freighters quickly learned that a stage line was considerably more difficult to operate profitably than their freight operations had been and joked that the initials actually stood for "Clean Out of Cash and Poor Pay." The Pony Express endeavor was an effort to lift their newly acquired stage line out of the red. The subcontract for carrying the mail for Ben Holladay's Overland Mail Company had produced little profit for the stage line.[4]

The COC & PP continued to operate at a loss through 1860. In August of that year they carried a rather famous passenger, world traveler Sir Richard F. Burton. Burton was observing the West, with a planned stay at Salt Lake before continuing on to California. At Deer Creek Station, he met Joseph Bissonette on August 16 and commented that the station was well stocked and the prices competitive with others he had seen along the way. Little Muddy Creek Station he found was poorly stocked: "—whiskey forming the only positive item."[5]

Burton's observations shed considerable light on John Richard, his bridge, and the community that surrounded it. Burton's experience as a connoisseur of diversified cultures and human behavior prompted him to see life from a different perspective than other diarists of the era. Even in late August he noted the necessity of the bridge for crossing the Platte's raging currents. Enjoying a glass of whiskey in Richard's "indispensable store,—the *tete-de-pont*," he was surprised to have it served "on ice," the first he had seen in weeks. It is surprising that Burton, who had spent a considerable amount of time in France, should misspell Richard, as "Regshaw."[6]

Burton and Richard conversed in enough detail for Burton to ascertain that Richard had "gained and lost more fortunes than a Wall Street professional 'lame-duck.'" Burton noted the coal vein on the north bank of the river and concluded that it could prove to be one of Richard's most valuable assets. The settlement adjoining Richard's Bridge had also grown to the point that Burton referred to it as a "town." Nearby, the now-vacant Post at Platte Bridge had deteriorated to "a few stumps of crumbling wall, broken floorings, and depressions in the ground."

The "town" Burton referred to consisted of at least the following buildings: two saloons, two trading posts, two blacksmith shops, one large warehouse, one ice-house, one lodging house, one eatery, one livery, and fifteen to twenty homes. The population fluctuated from about sixty to one hundred civilian residents, in addition to the various military and Indian encampments. Richard also maintained a grazing camp near the foot of what is now Casper Mountain. He employed carpenters and an accountant, in addition to his clerks, traders, hunters, teamsters, herders, laborers and various other workers.[7]

After enjoying John Richard's amenities, Burton's coach continued on the short distance to Guinard's Bridge where he spent the night at the COC & PP station. There he met Louis Guinard and his Shoshone wife who operated the stage station. He was unimpressed by their hospitality and accommodations and disgusted by the meal he received, wishing he had eaten at Richard's. Burton commented: "It was impossible to touch the squaw's supper; the tin cans that contained the coffee were slippery with grease, and the bacon looked as if it had been dressed side by side with 'boyaux' [guts]. I lighted my pipe, and air-cane in hand, sallied forth to look at the country."[8]

⌧ ⌧

As the Pony Express riders rushed past John Richard's settlement to his competitor's door, it must have seemed to him that time itself was passing him by. Richard was now in his early fifties and was considered an old man by the standards of the day. Joseph McKnight had left the North Platte for the gold fields of Colorado after completing the construction of Guinard's Bridge. Evidently with the money he earned from Guinard, he had accumulated the capital to start a successful trading post at Thompson or Thompson's Creek, near what would later become Fort Collins, Colorado. He remained there selling supplies to the miners and trading with the Indians for the next four years.[9]

⋖⧊⧓ ⧳⧊⧓

Hiram Kelly was enjoying the benefits of the excitement in Colorado too. He left Missouri in partnership with "Hi" Harrison and Sid Barnes, with three freight wagons loaded with nails and headed for Denver. They arrived in Denver on March 10, 1860, and quickly sold their cargo at twenty-five cents per pound. Kelly then headed for California Gulch (now Leadville) with another load of freight and then went to work in one of the mines there for six dollars per day. After a month, he and several other free-spirited men went to the hills to try their own luck with pickaxe and pan. When winter began to approach the high mountain boomtown, he lost heart and returned to Denver. He stayed the winter in a hotel on the corner of Blake and Sixteenth Streets, later the site of the Inter-Ocean Hotel. Most likely this earlier hotel was built and owned by the Richard brothers.

When the snow melted Kelly returned to Fort Laramie in search of his next venture. The garrison there was looking for a contractor to supply them with hay. Kelly had just passed over some 150 miles of freshly sprouting spring grass while en route from Denver, and soon he had contracted to supply one hundred tons of hay at twenty-nine dollars per ton. The hay was cut by hand with a scythe along Fox and Chugwater Creeks, then hauled about forty miles to Fort Laramie.[10]

⋖⧊⧓ ⧳⧊⧓

News came to the Platte that construction had begun on the transcontinental telegraph. In 1861 Thomas Twiss resigned as Indian Agent for the Upper Platte Agency, and the agency was moved back to Fort Laramie. Twiss and his Indian family remained at Deer Creek. Red Cloud was waging war against the Crow to the north, an act which Richard and Bissonette did not discourage because it greatly increased their sales of arms and ammunition. The telegraph was completed in October of that year, and Deer Creek Station was selected as the headquarters for that portion of the system. A young telegrapher named Oscar Collister was assigned the duties of operator there, which included maintaining the line for forty miles in each direction. He also ran the post office there for Bissonette, who along with Twiss, were soon his good friends.[11]

⊰⊱ ⊰⊱

When he was eighteen, John Richard Jr. returned from school in Missouri. He soon met with one of his old friends, Yellow Bear, now a sub-chief. John was accepted back among his friends and before long they called him Skinny White Man as they had before his long absence. Yellow Bear was impressed with the young man's education, and they talked of how John would be able to help the Sioux. Shortly after this meeting, Yellow Bear announced that Skinny White Man would marry his two sisters. This was probably an effort to solidify John's connection to his band. When young John heard of this engagement, he laughed it off and said that Yellow Bear's beautiful young daughter was more suited to his tastes but that he was not ready to marry anyone. Word got back to Yellow Bear somewhat differently, and it was misconstrued as a proposal to his daughter.

A few days later Yellow Bear delivered his daughter to John's mother, Mary, who was greatly surprised. John explained to his mother it was all a misunderstanding, but she knew Yellow Bear would consider it a terrible insult if John refused the honor of marrying his daughter. Fearing repercussions, Mary convinced her son that he had no choice but to marry the girl. Young John, however, was not willing to accept the responsibility of a wife, so he left his new bride with his mother.[12]

⊰⊱ ⊰⊱

Another new resident to the area was a young man whom Oscar Collister remembered as Brenon. This Missourian set up camp near Richard's Bridge, presumably with the intention of beginning a farming operation there. By this time the Civil War was well underway, and though most men in the West kept their opinions on the politics of the East to themselves, Brenon was not closemouthed about his strong beliefs in the secessionists' cause. Collister took an immediate liking to Brenon, but being very pro-Union himself, soon made it clear that if they were to be friends they must keep their politics to themselves. Brenon made regular trips to Deer Creek to send and collect mail. On one occasion, Collister, while repairing the telegraph line to the west, stopped to visit and consequently spent the night at Brenon's camp.

Shortly after Collister's visit, Brenon was found murdered along the trail between Twiss's old agency and Deer Creek Station. Collister thought it odd that neither Bissonette nor Richard, who both were acquainted with Brenon's father in Missouri, notified him of this tragedy. Collister, in his capacity as postmaster, decided to write to Brenon's family and inform them of their loss.

When he mentioned to Bissonette that he had written Brenon's family, Bissonette was perceivably irritated. After a considerable amount of badgering, Bissonette apologized to Collister and told him that it was just as well that Collister had been the one to tell them. He said that Brenon's father was an old and dear friend, and the young man had been honorably buried near the old agency. With that said Bissonette started to leave Collister's cabin, but was obviously still greatly disturbed. He turned finally and told Collister that his son, Joseph Bissonette Jr., and John Richard Jr. had murdered Brenon.

With this knowledge Collister was beside himself. In short order he received a letter from Brenon's father asking that Collister find out who killed his son and have them brought to justice. Mr. Brenon suggested that Collister enlist the help of his two good friends, Joseph Bissonette and John Richard, in apprehending the fugitives. Meanwhile John Richard Sr. had come to Collister and, in a drunken and tearful oratory, confirmed the culprits involved in the horrific murder. He put no restriction on this information and upon receipt of Mister Brenon's letter, Collister replied. He named the two mixed-blood young men as the murderers, but reminded Brenon that no law was recognized in the vicinity, and there was no one to enforce it if there had been.

Collister then lived out the winter without seeing the younger Bissonette or Richard and assumed he was done with the unpleasant affair. The following spring, however, two letters arrived from Mister Brenon, addressed to the elder John Richard and Joseph Bissonette. Collister was tempted to destroy the letters, but with much anxiety he delivered Bissonette's himself and asked Wheelock, a stock-tender for Richard, to deliver the one to his boss. John Richard Jr. and Joseph Bissonette Jr. were staying at John Richard's grazing camp on Deer Creek. When Collister accompanied stock-tender Wheelock to the camp the next day, he saw young Bissonette and Richard for the first time since Brenon's murder. When they arrived, John Richard Sr., who obviously had been drinking, invited Collister and Wheelock into the cabin. While Collister was not particularly inclined, he and Wheelock shared a drink with Richard in the cabin. John Richard was cordial and gave no indication of deceit.

When the two men left Richard's cabin they noticed the younger Richard and Bissonette, both armed, preparing to leave the camp also. Collister and Wheelock made a hasty gathering of the mules they had come for and rapidly retreated to Deer Creek Station. Oscar Collister lived the next several days in mortal fear. He regretted that he had ever written to Brenon's family and that he told Joseph Bissonette about it. He wished he had never learned the identity of the murderers. Life became even more precious to him when he heard that the two killers had followed him and Wheelock back to the station from Richard's grazing camp. The thought of them waiting in ambush weighed heavily on him at every moment.

After learning of Collister's letters to Brenon, John Richard arranged a meeting with Joseph Bissonette to discuss their two son's plight. The men agreed that if the wild boys wished to be renegades they should be treated as such. When a band of Red Cloud's warriors arrived on the Platte to replenish their ammunition, the two boys rode off with them to join the chief's siege on the Crow. The closest law enforcement was the Army at Fort Laramie, which was short-handed at the time due to the Civil War, so the Brenon matter eventually faded into the myriad of unresolved crimes on the western frontier.

Thus also began the notorious career of John Richard Jr., a renegade that no amount of education would change. So too began the years of heartbreak for his father whose wish had been that his children have a better education and consequently a better life than he had.[13]

⊰⊱ ⊰⊱

While John Richard and Joseph Bissonette were searching for solutions for their family problems, Hiram Kelly was working for the notorious Jack Slade of Ben Holladay's Overland Stage Line. Kelly initially began as the operator of the Horseshoe Creek Station, but soon was the messenger for their operations between Julesburg and South Pass. In addition to his other duties he herded bull teams to and from the various stations bringing food, hay, and firewood.[14]

In the spring of 1862, Big Bat Pourier, in the company of Joseph Richard and his family, was returning to Richard's Bridge from Denver. Joseph Richard had fallen on hard times after suffering severe financial losses both from the legendary Denver fire and raids on his livestock by Utes. He had become a heavy drinker, but before all sense had left him he decided to return to the North Platte.

On their way, they stopped over at Thompson, and there he reconnected with Joseph McKnight. McKnight offered his home and potential employment to Joseph Richard, and Richard accepted. But even with the new hope offered by McKnight, Joseph Richard never substantially recovered from the emotional devastation.

Also at Thompson was John Richard Jr., whom Baptiste Pourier had presumably not seen since leaving St. Charles. Resuming their old friendship, Pourier and John Jr. together returned to Richard's Bridge, where John Richard Sr. engaged them to trade in the Indian camps through the winter. By this time John Jr.'s wife had given up on him and returned to her parents. Yellow Bear was both insulted and humiliated and John Richard Jr. had, by his own disregard, created a lifelong bitterness. When next the two men met, Yellow Bear spat at Richard's feet in disgust. It was soon common knowledge in the area that Yellow Bear wanted the younger Richard dead, and John Jr. often heard while among the Indians, "Whoever kills Skinny White Man will have tongue to eat." Buffalo tongue was the ultimate of delicacies among the Sioux.[15]

~

That same winter Little Bat Garnier's mother and two sisters were burned to death in a fire at Fort Laramie. Following the deaths, Garnier and his surviving sister went to live with Elias W. Whitcomb near Fort D. A. Russell near present-day Cheyenne, Wyoming. Twenty-nine-year-old bachelor Whitcomb adored the orphaned children and raised them as his own. Little Bat, after living his life thus far at Richard's Bridge, loved the outdoors. Whitcomb, as had John Richard, nurtured the boy's natural instinct as a hunter. He bought Little Bat a small caliber rifle to hunt rabbits and sage grouse, and Garnier, soon an expert shot, then graduated to a larger caliber and larger game. By the age of fourteen, he had gone to Fort Laramie where his prowess soon won him the job of professional hunter for the fort.[16]

Elias Whitcomb, with his wife Kate, raised Little Bat Garnier after the death of Little Bat's mother. Whitcomb was also a trader in early Wyoming. (*Wyoming State Archives, Department of State Parks and Cultural Resources*)

⬧⬧⬧

With the completion of the Overland Telegraph in October 1861, the Pony Express was soon out of business. While Richard lost some business at his Red Buttes Trading Post due to the ending of the Pony Express, he continued to contract grazing for the stage line horses. Shortly after the completion of the telegraph, the U.S. Army was given the task of keeping depredations to the line and stations to a minimum. This required the establishment of a series of small military posts along the North Platte River. In May 1862, a post at Deer Creek Station was established as well as a new post near the bridges on the Platte. This time the site chosen was not Richard's Bridge, but Guinard's Bridge; the new post was called Platte Bridge Station. Although John Richard did not reap as much business from the Army as he would have if the soldiers had been stationed closer, he still benefited from their presence. Richard soon was supplying both hay and livestock to the new post.[17]

That year H. M. Judson was a member of a westward-bound wagon train that traveled on Child's Route along the north bank of the Platte River. On the morning of July 8, 1862, near La Prele Creek, Judson and his train received news that a California-bound wagon train had been attacked recently by Indians, resulting in the deaths of fifteen men and the theft of 135 head of livestock. They took this news seriously and maintained a vigilant eye for trouble. Late that afternoon they passed Deer Creek. "The buildings look commodious & comfortable for adobe houses — Here also is a Tel. Station & usually a ferry—It is now out of order." Judson also commented that the road on the south side of the river was nearly "within hailing distance" and that they saw several wagon trains on both sides of the river.[18]

On July 9 Judson and his wagon train passed "a Frenchmans Lodge" in the proximity of the present day Converse/Natrona county line. The Frenchman confirmed the news of the attack on the California wagon train, but not the killing of the fifteen men. He told them to "keep a sharp look & you will not be molested." Later that day they arrived at Richard's Bridge. Rather than continuing to travel along the north bank of the river where the road was sandy, Judson and his group crossed Richard's Bridge to the south bank and later crossed back to the north bank at Guinard's Bridge. They paid the toll-man the price of "50 cents pr team for both bridges."[19]

Judson described Richard's Bridge as follows: "The bridge is a very good one—has seven piers & the abutments—built entirely of hewn logs obtained from the beautiful mountain about three miles from our camp." He went on to say that the toll-man, presumably John Richard, frightened them with tales of Indian depredations. He told them that the Indians would make every effort to steal their horses and mules, but had little use for cattle. He went on to tell them that the Army was totally unable to control these attacks on settlers and that a patrol of some thirty soldiers had completely vanished and were presumed dead. The tale continued that the Indians had literally dared the soldiers to fight, but they would not. Scared half to death, Judson and his companions continued on to camp a short distance from the upper bridge where the Army post was now located. The next morning Judson's fears were somewhat relieved when the stock-tender from the stage station visited their camp,

Kate Whitcomb, of Oglala ancestry, became the wife of Elias Whitcomb in 1865. She and Whitcomb raised the Garnier children as well as their own. (*Wyoming State Archives, Department of State Parks and Cultural Resources*)

searching for a stray mule. He told Judson that the Indian stories were exaggerated and that the stages were operating on a regular schedule.[20]

Colonel William O. Collins was in command of the 11th Ohio Volunteers stationed at various points along the Platte and Sweetwater Rivers. Among his responsibilities was procuring hay and firewood for these outposts. Colonel Collins contracted with Joseph Bissonette for fifty tons of hay to be delivered to Deer Creek Station at twenty dollars per ton. With John Richard he contracted 105 tons of hay to be delivered to Three Crossings, Sweetwater Station, and Platte Bridge Station for the same rate. Both agreements were monumental tasks when you consider the method of harvesting and transporting such vast amounts of hay. Joseph Bissonette made his delivery to the Deer Creek Station and left plenty of grass standing in the Deer Creek valley. John Richard made his deliveries of thirty tons of hay to each of the posts at Three Crossings and Sweetwater Station, but fell short of the forty-five tons needed at Platte Bridge Station.

Due to heavy grazing by the Army's horses along nearby tributaries, the grass available had been diminished significantly. John Richard could only produce thirty-one-and-a-half tons for Platte Bridge Station. Before Richard could arrange to get the hay elsewhere, the Army offered Bissonette thirty dollars per ton for an additional fifteen tons for Platte Bridge Station. Unaware of Richard's predicament, Bissonette agreed.

The Army refused to pay Richard, not even for the hay he'd delivered, since he had not met his contract in full. Meanwhile partly to prove his good faith to the Army, Richard delivered fifty dollars belonging to a soldier at Platte Bridge to Fort Laramie to be sent home to the soldier's wife. While there he pled with Colonel Collins for payment, but evidently without results. He returned to Richard's Bridge to prepare for his winter trading season among the Indians.[21]

With the completion of the transcontinental telegraph the Overland Stage changed its route from the North Platte to what became known as the Overland or Cherokee Trail. This new route wound its way through Denver to what is now Laramie, Wyoming, then on west to Fort Bridger. With this move Hiram Kelly contracted the construction of the new stage stop at Virginia Dale, Colorado. There he built the station, barns, and corrals. He then went on to construct several other stations along this new route.

Upon completion, he returned to Fort Laramie where he, in partnership with E. W. Whitcomb, again secured the hay contract for the fort. One grueling hot summer day Kelly became fed up with the strenuous work and threw his scythe into a patch of willows. He told Whitcomb that they were never going to get rich working like dogs for someone else's benefit and that he was through. Whitcomb spat back that they were never going to get rich if they were afraid of doing a little work and that this was only the beginning of bigger and better things to come. Kelly retrieved his scythe and the two men returned to their task.[22]

In March 1863, John and Peter Richard along with part of their families moved from Richard's Bridge to Richeau Creek, a tributary to Chugwater Creek. There he established a horse and cattle ranch. John Richard should certainly be considered among the first ranchers in Wyoming, if not the very first. As early as 1845 he was trading livestock with emigrants and later with freighters and the government. This ranch on Richeau Creek, which appears to be his first traditional ranching operation, was established at what had previously been one of his grazing camps. Richeau Creek is an intermittent stream that is often completely dry most of the year. The valley it occupies does, however, contain numerous springs that help to maintain the natural forage along its floor. Near one of these springs, John Richard constructed a dugout cabin and enlarged the spring to form a small stockpond. The depression left by the cabin and the improved spring are still quite visible today.[23]

❧ ❧

About this same time fifteen-year-old John Russell arrived in the Fort Laramie area. John, who preferred to be called Jack, was the epitome of the cliché of the runaway boy who went west seeking adventure and fortune. At first convenience, he donned the buckskin garb of the mountain men he idolized and was seldom again seen in conventional clothing. In short order, he received the nickname "Buckskin Jack." The name stuck and as he acquired some notoriety as a scout in later years, he was always known as Buckskin Jack Russell.[24]

❧ ❧

When John Richard and his family left the bridge, he sent his son Louis Richard, Baptiste Pourier, and an Indian with a wagonload of buffalo robes to Fort Collins to trade for provisions, probably at Joseph McKnight's trading post there or through his brother Joseph Richard. The Richards probably hoped that either of these men would give them a better deal than their competitors.

The route these men took was a critical aspect of this journey and may have historic importance. Instead of traveling to Fort Laramie and then south on the Old Trappers' Trail, the men headed west to Carson's Creek, then southeast along the western foothills of the Laramie Mountain Range. This route may have been more popular during that era than has previously been suspected. At what point the trio struck the Overland Trail is unknown, but before reaching the pass near Virginia Dale, they were struck by a blizzard. In an effort get across the mountains before the passes were choked closed with snow, they attempted crossing at Cheyenne Pass. With greatest effort they managed to clear the summit, but the deepening snows halted their movement soon after. At the fork of Pole Creek, where it enters Crow Creek near the former site of Camp Wolbach, they were snowbound. There they were held for five days, without food, and with minimal shelter, before the storm passed.

When the weather finally lifted, Big Bat assessed the situation. They were all tired, cold, weak, and hungry. The wagon was deeply buried in snow, but the mules seemed to be in fairly good shape. Bat knew that John Richard Sr. had a horse camp on Chugwater Creek somewhere to the northeast that was run by an Indian named Rocky Bear, Mary Richard's half-brother. Leaving the wagon, they mounted the mules and headed off cross-country in search of the horse camp. After traveling some twenty miles without finding Rocky Bear's camp, they discovered a bull belonging to Elias Whitcomb. The men made quick work of slaughtering the bull for meat, and they all ate far too much after going so long without food. Louis Richard became violently ill, and Bat, though sick, managed to keep the meat down. After recovering from the consequences of gorging themselves, they continued on to Rocky Bear's camp which they found another five or six miles ahead. "Rocky Bear doled out the victuals to them in sparing quantities." After they began to recover they notified Richard of their whereabouts and paid Whitcomb forty-five dollars for his bull. In a few days, Buckskin Jack Russell joined Bat and Louis, and they returned to the pass for the wagon.[25]

<&>

John Richard's reason for leaving the bridge has never really been proven. The new Indian Agent J. Loree revoked Joseph Bissonette's trade license because he believed him to be trading liquor with the Indians, which was likely. This too may have been John Richard's plight, although some believe the notorious whiskey smuggler had given up this line of trade by this time. He seems to have planned to leave Pourier and his sons at the bridge to conduct his business with the Army and to quietly carry on what trade they could with the Indians. In the meantime he started a legitimate livestock business on Richeau Creek, perhaps an attempt to clean the slate and regain his trade license in the future. In later years family stories recounted that in 1863 John Richard Sr. staked his son John Jr. to eighteen hundred dollars to establish himself in business in Denver. It appears, however, that John Richard Jr. stayed at Richard's Bridge trading with the Indians, later joined by Baptiste Pourier, through the spring of 1864.[26]

Some believe that John Richard totally quit trading liquor with the tribes. He had learned through his years of experience that the difficulties it caused far outweighed the advantages. Although he may have been able to make a good deal when trading whiskey, when the Indians were drunk they did not hunt and soon they had nothing left to trade. According to descendants of John Richard interviewed by Hila Gilbert for her book on Baptiste Pourier, John Richard Sr. totally abandoned trading whiskey with the Indians in favor of stocking sugar, coffee, tobacco, and good quality Mexican blankets, beads, and cloth, which were more profitable. Gilbert repeated a familiar family story about John and Mary Richard hauling a wagonload of goods to the bridge, including whiskey for his saloons there. As a band of Indians approached them on the trail that cold day, Richard told his wife that if the Indians became unreasonable she should break open the kegs and let the whiskey pour on the ground. When Richard refused to sell whiskey to the band, they jumped on the wagons and began pulling the tarps to locate it. Mary grabbed an axe and smashed the kegs open, then pushed them off of the wagon as Richard put the whip to the horses for a rapid escape. As they sped from the scene, Mary saw the Indians trying to lick whiskey from the ice of the frozen stream where the kegs had landed.[27]

⋘∘⋙

About the same time Big Bat Pourier and Louis Richard left Richard's Bridge for Fort Collins, the 11th Ohio Volunteer Cavalry was assigned to Platte Bridge Station. Ben Arnold (birthname Connor) was among the volunteers arriving there and recalled two toll bridges: "Richaud's and North Platte, the latter built by Joseph [Mc]Knight." Arnold and a Kentuckian named Bill Lock guarded the horse camp for the station. The mail route was via the Overland Trail, and the telegraph was out of order most of the winter. Arnold complained that there was no way to receive any news. Days became weeks and soon they lost track of the dates. Christmas and New Year's came and went, and the two men did not even know they had passed. As spring began to break, Arnold and Lock could occasionally take turns making a trip to the post for a change of scenery and conversation: "Two traders, brothers by the name of Bernard [Guinard], had a store near the bridge from which they supplied some necessities to the travelers at what would now be considered fabulous prices. They also owned the bridge and collected a toll of $10 for each wagon that crossed it. As the water was swift and the crossing difficult, few had the temerity to attempt to ford the stream in order to avoid paying the bridge toll."[28]

⋘⋙ ⋘⋙

After John and Peter Richard moved to Richeau Creek, Peter's fifteen-year-old daughter, Elizabeth, returned from St. Louis. Peter had sent his only daughter to an exclusive girl's school there to learn culture and charm, traits he felt a young lady should possess. The beautiful "Lizzie," as her friends knew her, soon caught the eye of thirty-year-old Hiram B. Kelly who was living in a sod shanty on his homestead on Chugwater Creek. The couple soon fell in love and took advantage of an available parson at Fort Laramie to marry them. Unlike many of the families of mixed ethnicity of that era who adopted the Indian way of life, the Kellys lived in a style more traditional to white families. It was said that Mrs. Kelly was a handsome woman and performed her domestic duties in a manner that would reflect credit upon any New England housewife. Hi Kelly was obviously proud to have this lovely woman for his wife and later built what was considered a sumptuous mansion at the site of their humble soddy.[29]

⋘⋙ ⋘⋙

John Richard's premonition that he might regain his trade license if he stayed out of the limelight proved true. He and Joseph Bissonette recruited Colonel William Collins to their cause. Colonel Collins petitioned Indian Agent Loree claiming the men were reliable and that Loree was unjustified in revoking their trade licenses. In February 1864, both were reinstated. By that spring, depredations by the Sioux and Northern Cheyenne had again reached a peak. As a consequence, the Department of Indian Affairs again issued an order forbidding the sale of arms or ammunition to Indians. After just regaining their licenses to trade, Richard and Bissonette were hindered by this ruling.[30]

As John Richard made plans to return to his bridge and trading post, Joseph McKnight was making changes in his life also. Trade with the miners in Colorado was subsiding, and many miners moved to the recently discovered gold fields of Montana. McKnight had enjoyed a successful few years at Fort Collins but could see his opportunities there rapidly diminishing. He sold his trading post there to Joseph Richard and moved to St. Joseph, Missouri. Upon his arrival in St. Joseph, the bustle of hopeful

Montana gold hunters shed a new light on his future. McKnight had been trading with miners for the last few years and fully understood their lack of preparation when they were in "the rush" state of mind.

When these starry-eyed hopefuls arrived in Montana they often lacked many necessities, and some were even short of food. McKnight purchased two heavy freight wagons, found able-bodied drivers among the dozens of men searching for transportation west, and working with his old suppliers, acquired the perfect stock of merchandise. Within a few days he headed his freight wagons back in the same direction from which he had so recently come. Joseph McKnight had no intention of establishing a store or trading company in Montana. He established a clientele among the businessmen already located there by selling them the supplies he carried. He then compiled orders from them and returned for another load of merchandise.[31]

Notes to Chapter Eight:

1. William Eubank stated in his interview that John Richard and Louis Bernard (Guinard) had been partners in Richard's Bridge. Around 1855 they "got at outs, and the latter went and built a bridge about seventy-five miles further up the Platte [Sweetwater Bridge]." They were forever after enemies. Since Eubank was a freighter along the Platte and had associated with both men throughout this time frame, it must be assumed that he had first-hand knowledge of this partnership and their separation. Cragin, "William T. Eubank," notebook I, p. 5/25 & 6/26.

2. Bryans, p. 118–121; McDermott, *Frontier Crossroads*, p. 25.

3. McDermott, *Frontier Crossroads*, p. 25; Nevin, David, *The Expressmen: The Old West*, (Time-Life Books, New York, 1974), p. 88–98.

4. Bryans, p. 127–128.

5. Burton, Sir Richard F.: Brodie, Fawn M., editor, *The City of the Saints and Across the Rocky Mountains to California*, (Alfred A. Knopf, New York, 1963), p. 154–155; Bryans, p. 61.

6. *Tete-de-pont*, [French], work thrown up to defend the entrance of a bridge. *Webster's New School & Office Dictionary*, (The World Publishing Company, Cleveland & New York, 1943), p. 755; Burton, p. 155–156.

7. The exact location of Richard's grazing camp is unknown. A likely candidate for the site is in the NE quarter of the SE quarter of Sec. 35, T33N, R79W, 6th Principal Meridian. Surveyors, Downey & Grant in 1880 and William Owen in 1881/1882 recorded a cabin at that location. This site is near the

headwaters of a branch of Elkhorn Creek, which is believed to have then been called Reshaw Creek. Since there was no homestead patent applied for at this location until many years later, the cabin was presumably not regularly occupied at that time. Tract map T33N, R79W, 1883; Survey notes used to compile that map, 1880–1882. USGS survey records, Bureau of Land Management, Cheyenne, Wyoming.

8. Burton, p. 156.

9. Coutant, C. G., "Coutant Collection," box 4, folder 53, book 36.

10. Bartlett, vol. III, p. 140; Briston and Dubois, p. 1.

11. Collister, Oscar: Mrs. Charles Ellis editor, "Life of Oscar Collister, Wyoming Pioneer," *Annals of Wyoming*, (July 1930), vol. 7, no. 1, p. 347–352.

12. Gilbert, p. 17–18; Lt. Caspar W. Collins confirmed the approximate time of this marriage in a letter from Fort Laramie to his mother dated February 23, 1863. Service, Alex, *The Life and Letters of Caspar W. Collins*, (Casper: City of Casper, Wyoming, Publishers, 2000), p. 48–49.

13. Collister, Oscar, vol. 7, no. 1, p. 347–352. The author believes that the man Collister recalled some seventy years later as Brenon, was in fact John Branham, the eldest son of John Richard Sr.'s former partner and brother-in-law, Charles Branham. John Branham was born in 1845 and following the death of his mother, Mary Elizabeth (Richard) Branham, around 1855 he lived with his aunt and uncle in Rulo, Nebraska. The Branham family were abolitionists, but it appears that this rebellious teen, John Branham, was sent to live with or near his uncle, John Richard Sr., to keep him from joining the Confederacy. The statements that Brenon's father was a respected citizen in his hometown in Missouri and possibly a former mayor helps substantiate this connection. Charles B. Branham had at different times been a councilman, marshal, and sheriff. Monroe, Stewart, various letters dated 1999, (Jefferson Glass's personal collection). Susan Bordeaux Bettelyoun stated of John Richard Jr. that, "He took a cousin to the mountains and claimed his cousin was lost…Sam Terry, who was living then, said that he [John Richard Jr.] was one of the most bloodthirsty men he ever saw." Bettelyoun, p. 40.

14. Jack Slade was the notorious division superintendent of the Overland Stage Company. He had the dubious reputation of shooting any employee who did not fulfill his expectations. Bartlett, vol. III, p. 140; Briston and Dubois, p. 1–2.

15. Ricker, "Baptiste Pourier," tablet 15, p. 90–92; Vaughn, p. 142; Gilbert p. 17–18.

16. Elias W. Whitcomb was born December 28, 1833, in Oxford, Massachusetts. After living in Virginia he came west in 1859 and settled near Fort D. A. Russell. Coutant, C. G., "Coutant Collection," box 5, folder 48, book 16.

17. McDermott, "John Baptiste Richard" in *Mountain Men*, 2:302; Bryans, p. 124–125.

18. Judson, H. M., *Diary 1862*, (Unpublished Manuscript, Nebraska State Historical Society, Lincoln, Nebraska) p. 21–22; Franzwa, p. 246–247.

19. Some historians have said that John Richard purchased Guinard's Bridge about this time. Others state that John Richard Jr. and Louis Guinard were partners in a trading post and/or sutler's store at Guinard's Bridge. Neither transaction can be found recorded anywhere. Judson's reference to paying Richard the toll for both bridges would perhaps indicate his ownership of both bridges. One prominent fact undermines both of these theories: Louis Guinard and his brother continued to operate a store and Guinard's Bridge for at least the next few years. Murray, Robert, p. 20; Judson, p. 22–23.

20. Judson, p. 23.

21. Collins, Colonel William O., *Order book of Colonel William O. Collins, October 27, 1862 to April 8, 1863*, (Typescript from the original, Morgan Library, Colorado State University, Fort Collins, Colorado: Copy in Special Collections, Goodstein Foundation Library, Casper College, Casper, Wyoming) p. 1, 3–4, 13.

22. Virginia Dale was named in honor of Jack Slade's wife, Virginia Slade. Bartlett, vol. III, p. 140; Briston and Dubois, p. 3; Larson, Robert R., Platte County Extension Homemakers, editors, "Kelly, Hiram B.," *Wyoming: Platte County Heritage*, (Platte County Extension Homemakers Council, Wheatland, Wyoming, 1981), p. 268.

23. Ricker, "Baptiste Pourier," tablet 15, p. 92–93; Osgood, Ernest Staples, *The Day of the Cattleman*, (University of Minnesota, 1929, reprinted by University of Chicago Press, Chicago and London, 1970), p. 1–23; Richard lived and traded on Chugwater Creek off and on for many years. He eventually settled and had a ranch on Richeau Creek, a tributary of Chugwater Creek. Richeau Creek and the Richeau Hills are named for John Richard and in 1872 were spelled Richard on USGS maps. In later years they were changed to Richeau in an attempt to correct a misspelling. Little did those good-intentioned people realize that they were spelled correctly to begin with, but when local residents pronounced them Reshaw, they thought the maps were wrong. They knew that Reshaw was a slurred Americanization of a French name and did their best to correct it by spelling it Richeau. Grant, Duncan Paul, *Memoirs 1881–1975*, (Unpublished Manuscript, Robert Grant Family Collection, Grant Ranch, Richeau Creek Rd., Wheatland, Wyoming); USGS survey records, United States Bureau of Land Management, Department of the Interior, Cheyenne, Wyoming. Robert Grant guided the author to the location of Richard's dugout on October 4, 1998. The site, which had been identified to him by his father as a small boy, then still had remnants of timbers from the roof of the dugout. The location is on what is now known as the Lewis Ranch, owned and operated by the West family. The Wests have been most gracious in allowing me

supervised access to the site. Further history of the Richeau Creek valley can be found in the *Memoirs of Duncan Grant*, Robert Grant's father.

24. Jones, Brian, p. 17; McDermott, "John Baptiste Richard" in *Mountain Men*, 2:301; Magloire Alexis Mosseau claims the honor of naming Buckskin Jack because he always wore buckskin clothing. Born in Missouri in 1847 John Russell (Buckskin Jack) ran away from home and ended up in Denver in 1862. It is possible that he became acquainted with Joseph Richard in Denver and had accompanied him and Baptiste Pourier to Thompson, then Pourier and John Jr. to Richard's Bridge. Whatever the circumstances, Buckskin Jack was with the Richards at Richeau Creek.

25. Ricker, "Baptiste Pourier," tablet 15, p. 93–96; Little Bat Garnier was presumably still living with Whitcomb at this time. In February 1865, Whitcomb married Kate Steele. They had four children: Lizzie, Mildred, Charles, and one other. Coutant, "Coutant Collection," box 5, folder 48, book 16; Buckskin Jack Russell is confirmed working for John Richard Sr. on his Laramie River (Richeau Creek) ranch by Vaughn, p. 72; Rocky Bear and Black Tiger were half-brothers of Mary (Gardiner) Richard. Rocky Bear worked for his brother-in-law from time to time in various capacities. Gilbert, p. 11.

26. McDermott, "Joseph Bissonette" in *Mountain Men*, 4:58; Gilbert, p. 15–16.

27. Gilbert p. 16.

28. Arnold (Connor), Ben, *Rekindling Camp Fires: The Exploits of Ben Arnold (Connor)*, (Capital Book Company, Bismarck, North Dakota, 1926), p. 62–65.

29. Many sources have stated that Elizabeth (Richard) Kelly was the daughter of John Richard. She was in fact John Richard's niece. Larson, p. 268; Spring, Agnes Wright, *The Cheyenne and Black Hills Stage and Express Routes*, (The Arthur H. Clarke Company, Glendale, California, 1949), p. 105; Jones, Brian, p. 41; Briston and Dubois, p. 2; Bartlett, vol. III, p. 142.

30. McDermott, "Joseph Bissonette" in *Mountain Men*, 4:58; Jones, Brian, p. 17.

31. Joseph McKnight was successful in his St. Joseph headquartered freight business. He also claimed St. Joseph, Missouri, as his place of residence until 1869. Coutant, "Coutant Collection," box 4, folder 53, book 36.

9

⇜ ANOTHER MOTHER LODE ⇝

EVERYONE LIKES A good "Lost Gold Mine" story and perhaps the story of the Lost Cabin Mine is one of the best of them. Allen Hulburt resided in Janesville, Wisconsin, in 1849 when he heard the news of the big gold strike at Sutter's Mill in California. As with many, his dreams of quickly becoming rich overcame sanity and reason and, in October of that year, he joined the stampede and was off to find his fortune. Through the 1850s he prospected his way from California up the coast into what is now Washington. In 1863 he found himself tired, hungry, and broke in the town of Walla Walla. Along with two companions, Jones and Cox, he managed to put together an outfit to explore the eastern slope of the northern Rocky Mountains in a last-ditch search for gold.

The trio departed across the Mullen Trail and eventually wound up on the Yellowstone River. They built a raft and floated down the Yellowstone to the mouth of the Big Horn River where they camped on an island which provided them some security from marauders. They had traveled only by night in an effort to evade the tribes which were said to be antagonistic toward whites. Hulburt and his partners then proceeded up the Big Horn River and began exploring and prospecting its many tributaries. Not familiar with the country, these men soon found themselves in increasingly remote country, but had avoided confrontations with Indians.

As they entered the foothills of the Big Horn Mountains they began seeing signs of "color" in their pans of gravel. The further they trekked, the better the indications became, and the faster they traveled, but they kept to the ritual of moving camp only at night. They climbed higher and higher into the mountains, finally coming to a gulch that appeared to be the source of the gold they had found below. With further sampling and exploring, they found a rich streak of gold in the gravel that was like none they had ever seen before. They sunk a shaft to bedrock and found gold in every pan they washed. They decided to stay the winter in the gulch.

Hulburt, Jones, and Cox dammed the stream and built sluice boxes. They worked steadily and averaged over one hundred dollars a day each from the sluice boxes. When the stream froze, they were forced to halt their mining operation, and only then did they prepare for winter. They hastily erected a cabin and fortified it with a makeshift stockade. Of their six horses, five remained. One had drowned in the Yellowstone as they were swum behind the raft. They frantically cut what hay could be found, knowing the snow would soon be too deep for the horses to forage.

As soon as the water began to flow again in early spring, they were back at the sluice boxes working diligently. One day, Hulburt left Jones and Cox at the sluice boxes to return to the cabin for a tool. He had only covered a few yards when the quick report of two shots echoed through the gulch. Hulburt sneaked back to where he could view the site under cover and saw both his friends dead in the stream. He then caught a glimpse of movement in the trees. Petrified, he watched as Indians scalped and mutilated the bodies. The Indians then passed within a few feet of Hulburt's hiding place as they went down the trail to ransack the cabin.

The Indians then attempted to set fire to the cabin, but the green logs would not burn, so they took the horses and departed down the gulch. Hulburt remained hidden until he was certain they were gone for good. He then went to the cabin, quickly gathered what nuggets he could carry in a knapsack, and fled the gulch. He knew the Oregon Trail was to the south, so he began his course in that general bearing, again hiding in the daytime and moving at night. Though he did rest, he slept very little, keeping a vigilant eye out for danger.

After several nights of walking with little food, Allen Hulburt struck an open spot where he viewed vast prairie to the east. To the west were miles of lofty mountains.

Taking his chances with the open country, he veered his course eastward hoping to strike a trail to the Platte. In places he found remnants of a trail which made traveling easier. When daylight came he holed up away from the trail at a place with a good view to watch for possible friends or foes. On June 11, 1864, he came to Richard's Bridge after eighteen days of treacherous travel.[1]

<E><E

The route that Hulburt had traveled to Richard's Bridge, once he encountered the plains east of the Big Horn Mountains, was by no means a new one. As early as 1824 a group of mountain men had left Fort Henry, at the confluence of the Little Big Horn and Big Horn Rivers, and traveled overland to the North Platte River, striking the river near where Richard later built his bridge. The men—Hugh Glass, Marsh, Chapman, Moore, and Dutton—were from the Ashley/Henry fur trapping expedition. About a quarter of a mile below the bridge was a ford commonly called the Old Indian Ford, which had been used for many years by the nomadic tribes of the area. In 1860 topographer J.D. Hutton surveyed a portion of the trail from Deer Creek to the head of Salt Creek. In 1863 John M. Bozeman and John M. Jacobs, along with his daughter Emma, blazed a trail from the Montana gold fields to the North Platte by a similar route and attempted a return trip with a small wagon train that departed from the crossing at Deer Creek.[2]

Several substantial strikes of gold had been discovered in Montana by 1862. Getting to them was difficult. The only established route from the east was to take the Oregon Trail to Fort Hall, Idaho, then head north on the Montana Trail. A route which was both reasonably direct and safe that avoided Indians was in high demand. Bozeman and Jacobs left Bannack, Montana, in March 1863, with a mission to find such a route. They did not hold a monopoly on the idea of a shortcut to the gold fields; the legendary mountain man, Jim Bridger was also mulling over routes in his mind.

<E><E

While Allen Hulburt made his escape from Indians in the Big Horn Mountains, Jim Bridger embarked from Richard's Bridge with the first wagon train to cross what would be called the Bridger Trail to the Montana gold fields. Bridger had crossed most of this route in 1860, while guiding Captain William Raynolds on his expedition to the Yellowstone.

Bridger left the Oregon Trail near Red Buttes on May 20, 1864, with some three hundred men with sixty-two wagons and arrived at Virginia City, Montana in early July.

John Richard Jr., Big Bat Pourier, and Amede Bessette left Richard's Bridge with ten freight wagons loaded with goods to sell to miners a few days later. Prior to their departure John Richard Jr. had married Louise

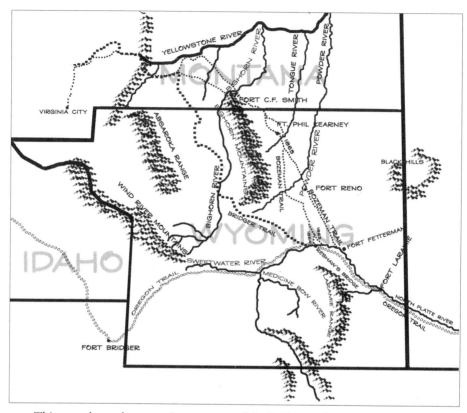

This map shows the approximate routes of the Bridger and Bozeman Trails, along with the forts that were important to the emigrants. *(Based on 1866 Johnson Map of Montana, Wyoming, Idaho, Nebraska, and Dakota)*

Merivale. She and her father Joseph also were on this wagon train. They overtook Bridger's train at the Stinking Water River, then accompanied his party on to Virginia City, Montana. They reached the Yellowstone River on the third of July and awoke on Independence Day to an inch of fresh snow on the ground.[3]

<Ξ>·<Ξ>

By early June, Joseph McKnight, who had started a new freighting business embarking from St. Joseph to supply miners in Montana, arrived at Fort Laramie with his wagons. There he met Robert Vaughn, the captain of a Montana-bound wagon train, and discussed the best route. McKnight's knowledge of the area impressed Vaughn, and McKnight agreed to guide Vaughn's group. Before they arrived at Richard's Bridge they added another group of wagons led by James Roberts also headed to Montana. By June 10, the party had grown to 129 wagons and some four hundred men. That day they departed Red Buttes under Mc-Knight's guidance following Bridger's trail to Alder Gulch, Montana.[4]

John Richard was conducting a booming business at the bridge with the hundreds of men headed for the Montana gold fields. When Allen Hulburt first walked into the trading post near starvation, Richard probably donned his doting humanitarian nature and nursed him, doling out small quantities of food and water until Hulburt could eat more. Picture the transformation that likely took place in Richard's demeanor when Hulburt offered to pay for his care from his knapsack full of gold nuggets. It is a wonder old John's heart withstood the shock. Remember Francis Parkman's remarks as to Richard's character: he was a generous and compassionate man until there was an opportunity to make money. Several pounds of gold nuggets was something John Richard had reason to really appreciate.

John Bozeman was probably already at Richard's Bridge recruiting gold-seekers for his shortcut to Montana when Hulburt arrived. Dozens of want-to-be-millionaires were stalled near Richard's, trying to decide which route to take, when up walked a man with more gold than any of the pilgrims had ever seen. He came from the approximate route Bozeman was promoting. The frenzy must have been something akin to a school of Amazon piranhas that just smelled fresh meat hit the water. When Hulburt told of his exploits of the past few months, it breathed new life into the trail-weary gold-seekers at the bridge. No one was more anxious to see Allen Hulburt's Lost Cabin Mine than Hulburt himself. Within a few days Hulburt was adequately recuperated to attempt the return. John Richard provided Hulburt with the best outfit available for a reasonable number of those nuggets.[5]

On June 16, 1864, Allen Hulburt departed Richard's Bridge for the Montana Territory. This was the first wagon train to embark on what would become known as the Bozeman Trail and complete the trek. The wagon train consisted of 124 wagons teamed by 438 people. Allen Hulburt was unarguably the guide, though Abram Voorhees had been elected by his peers as marshal for the trip west and was still officially in charge of the train. John M. Bozeman left Richard's Bridge with the second train to cross this route two days later. Although ten wagon trains left following Bridger's route in 1864, a total of only four wagon trains chose the shortcut over the Bozeman Trail.[6]

Hulburt's wagon train made good time for the first several days, following remnants of an old Indian trail and, for a time, they followed the trail left by Bozeman's 1863 expedition. When they arrived at Big Piney Creek, near the later location of Fort Phil Kearny, a suitable passage for the wagons was not as easily located. The wagon train halted there while Hulburt searched for a route through the hills.

Bozeman's wagons would have been at Hulburt's heels had they not experienced their own delays. They lost considerable time waiting for the small train of John T. Smith to catch up to them. When the wagon train led by Allen Hulburt intersected Wolf Creek, near present-day Sheridan, Wyoming, they headed up the creek about five miles to camp. Hulburt and some companions went into the Big Horn Mountains to try to locate the gulch and mine he'd left behind, while other members of the company went in pursuit of their own bonanzas. At this camp Bozeman's wagons overtook Hulburt's train and proceeded on to become the first wagon train to complete the journey across the Bozeman Trail to the Gallatin Valley of Montana.[7]

After a delay of several weeks while Hulburt searched without success for his lost mine, members of that wagon train grew increasingly agitated. Eventually Allen Hulburt confessed that he was unable to recognize any landmarks from the previous year. A few irate travelers did not accept his apology and proposed that Hulburt be lynched for leading them astray and possibly endangering their lives. As the accusations grew louder the camp began to take on the character of a mob, and Hulburt grew fearful for his life.

Before he was strung up from the nearest tree, however, one of the saner members of the party petitioned Hulburt's case. Gaining the crowd's attention with a drawn six-shooter, he argued that Allen Hulburt had done no wrong. He had offered to share the vast riches of his mine and had shown all of them the nuggets he had harvested. Furthermore, in good faith, he had spent every conceivable amount of his own energy and effort to locate the mine. With a final argument that no one had more to lose by his inability to find the mine than Hulburt himself, the mood was finally calmed. Allen Hulburt's life was spared and the wagon train resumed its trek across the now well-beaten path of the Bozeman

Trail. They arrived in Virginia City quite late in the season and the members of the train were soon dispersed throughout the "diggin's" of the Gallatin Valley.[8]

❦ ❦

Not long before Jim Bridger's wagon train arrived in Virginia City, a wagon train led by A. A. Townsend crossed Richard's Bridge and departed on their journey up the Bozeman Trail. The date was June 29, 1864. They had enlisted as guides Minton "Mitch" Bouyer and John Al Richard at the rate of four dollars per wagon, a total of six hundred dollars for the 150 wagons of this train. These guide's services included finding "a passable road, wood, grass, and water, and act[ing] as interpreters if Indians were encountered." Neither the Hulburt nor Bozeman wagon trains had encountered any trouble with Indians, but anyone with knowledge of the area knew that to cross the hunting grounds of Powder River country was an invitation for trouble. Bouyer and Richard would soon prove to be a valuable investment.[9]

Townsend's company was not as lucky as its predecessors. On July 8, 1864, a man named Mills lost a cow while the train was camped at their crossing of Powder River. While crossing the Dry Fork of Powder River, Bouyer and John Al Richard noticed a significant amount of Indian sign. At their suggestion, Townsend diverted his train up Soldier Creek to camp among a grove of large cottonwood trees. The following morning, Mr. Mills returned to their previous encampment to search for his missing cow while the rest of the party ate breakfast and prepared for the day's trek. As the wagons took their positions, awaiting the order to proceed, one man strolled a short distance ahead of the lead wagon. Suddenly he ran back yelling a warning that a large band of mounted Indians was approaching. Townsend immediately belched the order to corral the wagons and prepare for defense.

With the sudden commotion within the wagon train, the Indians realized that their approach had been observed. Bouyer and Richard were sent out to the advancing party for a parlay. In short order Bouyer returned to discuss the parlay with Townsend while Richard brought the Indians to within a few yards of the wagon train. Bouyer told Townsend that the Indians were hungry and he recommended that they provide a meager token meal. While food was being put together, Richard told Townsend and Bouyer that the Indians, Northern Cheyenne, claimed to be on their way to retrieve some stolen horses from the Crow and had asked to accompany the wagon train along the way. The two guides said the Cheyenne should not be trusted, so Townsend adamantly denied the request. The man who had sounded the warning reported that shortly before seeing the Indians, he was most certain that he had heard several shots fired in the distance. This information induced the men to be even more wary.

Behind the cover of the wagons, a group of men was formed to ride back and verify the welfare of Mills. Richard, hoping to create a diversion, went to the spot where the Indians were eating and resumed the conversation. The leader of the Indians, talking loudly enough for Bouyer to hear, told Richard to move the train out. Bouyer translated this to Townsend and told him to do nothing of the kind, reasoning that when the train started moving the Indians could easily stampede the livestock. Soon the Indians, who had remained mounted, saw the search party depart. They threw down their food and quickly cut off the party from the wagons.

This action set off a hand-to-hand running fight. Relying on the theory that offense makes the best defense, the search party turned toward the Indians in a full charge. T. J. Brundage and Asher Newby were in the lead. The charge slowed the Indians long enough for some of the men to get back to the wagons. After a short skirmish, Brundage and Newby, still mounted, began a dash to the wagons. As Brundage neared the wagons, he realized Newby was no longer with him. Turning, he saw Newby on the ground, wounded, and being helped by three men on foot. Brundage turned his horse and raced back to his comrades. Dismounting, Brundage and the others managed to throw Newby over the horse and make it back to the wagon train. All of the search party eventually escaped back to the relative safety of the wagon train.

By this time the wagon train was under siege from the Indians. The battle lasted most of the day until Townsend and his men finally repulsed the Indians. In the final tally the Townsend train had lost three men, plus Mr. Mills, who could not be found and was presumed dead. Asher Newby took an arrow in his back that had penetrated three inches and punctured his left lung. Blood gushed from his nose and his skin was ashen white. Two doctors on the train, a Frenchman and another named Hall, managed to extract the arrow and Newby eventually recovered.

After burying their dead, the Townsend wagon train resumed their journey and arrived in the Gallatin Valley without further troubles from Indians.[10]

⋘≫ ⋘≫

The fourth and final wagon train to cross the Bozeman Trail that year was captained by Cyrus C. Coffinbury. They crossed the North Platte on July 6, "on a toll bridge kept by one Reshaw—one of the ubiquitous Richard family. Here the Bozeman Trail began." They then spent several days camped on the north bank of the Platte, allowing their livestock to rest and debating the best course for their journey. The fate of the Townsend train—traveling only a few days ahead of them and with the advantage of two experienced guides—caused brave men to doubt their plan. Finally the members of the train voted to follow the Bozeman route regardless. They left camp on July 17, 1864, with sixty-eight wagons, divided into three or four companies.

On July 22, the Coffinbury train camped at the location of the Townsend fight a few days earlier. Coffinbury saw that Townsend had taken a detour from the earlier route of Hulburt and Bozeman. Trusting Townsend's experienced guides, Coffinbury followed in Townsend's tracks. When preparing their camp, member David Weaver noticed several iron-tipped arrows strewn about. He knew these valuable commodities were not often left carelessly on the prairie. Weaver watched another man remove something from a nearby tree which appeared at first to be a dead crow. It was a scalp, which was later determined to be that of Mr. Mills, the man who had gone looking for his missing cow. On the large cottonwood tree they found an inscription which confirmed their location: "Captain Townsend had a fight here with Indians July 9, 1864."

The next day the travelers discovered the opened graves of three men. At first they thought that wolves had dug up the bodies, but the corpses had been stripped of clothing and burial blankets, indicating that graverobbers had been the culprits. The evidence of the battle kept Coffinbury and the emigrants on constant alert, but they arrived at their destination unscathed. Ironically, the only wagon train that year to hire experienced guides and interpreters was also the only one to need them.

When the Coffinbury train arrived in Virginia City, the man with the scalp boastfully showed it about the town. When some women from the Townsend train saw it, it created quite a ruckus. Mr. Mills's brother was summoned to the braggart and exclaimed in shock, "That's my brother's hair!" However, no one seems to remember what became of the hair of Mr. Mills.[11]

⊰⊱

Following their arrival in Virginia City with his wagons of supplies, John Richard Jr. sold his goods to the local miners and merchants. He and his wife, along with Baptiste Pourier, then went to Jefferson's Fork where they stayed at the Slade Ranch, formerly owned by the notorious Jack Slade, for several weeks resting from their journey. Soon Joseph McKnight arrived at the ranch on his return from the gold diggings; then he and Pourier returned to Richard's Bridge to work for John Richard Sr. through the next spring. John Richard Jr. and his bride, Louise, accompanied them to Bozeman, where they built a home and remained for the next few years.[12]

⊰⊱

After leading the first wagon train across the Bridger Trail, Jim Bridger returned to the Platte and led the last wagon train of 1864 up the trail also. Departing from Red Buttes on September 18, he guided Major John Owen and Samuel Anderson with ten wagons and twenty-five men to Montana. Though they departed late in the season, they managed to complete their journey with few troubles.

However the emigrant activity on the Bozeman Trail aggravated the tribes that hunted along Powder River and soon other white/Indian encounters led it to become known as the Bloody Bozeman. This year also marked the beginning and end of Richard's Bridge as the primary departure point for the Bozeman Trail because the trailhead was moved first to Deer Creek and then to Fort Fetterman.

The following year Jim Bridger guided General Patrick E. Connor's Powder River Expedition up Sage Creek and cut off another forty miles of the shortest route.[13]

⊰⊱

While John Richard was enjoying the bustle occurring at Richard's Bridge, Joseph Richard's business in Colorado was mediocre at best. Joseph celebrated the Fourth of July with John and Jim Baker, by having several dozen drinks together. The Baker brothers were not only notorious mountain men, but notorious drinkers as well. "Jim and John Baker could drink liquor heavily without any appreciable effect on them." Joseph Richard had acquired his own considerable tolerance of alcohol but he was evidently far from the league of the Baker men. The three drank all the night long on the Fourth, and Joseph Richard died on July 5, 1864, quite possibly from alcohol poisoning (though this phenomenon had yet to be identified by medical practitioners of the time). Jim and John Baker buried Joseph near the trading post and personally carried the news of his death to his brothers John and Peter. John Richard was seriously shaken by the death of his youngest brother and fell into depression for some time. He reportedly never again returned to Colorado.[14]

The events of the month of August could not have helped John Richard's depressed mood. Depredations by Indians along the Oregon Trail were on the rise, and military authorities at Fort Laramie had again ordered sanctions against sale of arms and ammunition to them. Early in August, John Richard and all of his family at the bridge were arrested and taken to Fort Laramie. Although the specifics of the arrests have been lost, it likely resulted from the illegal sale of weapons that ended with an Indian named Grass being wounded.

Indian Agent J. Loree spoke with Black Tiger and sent a letter to Colonel William Collins on August 10, 1864, in Fort Laramie: "The bearer, Black Tiger, brother-in-law to John Richard, says that he an[d] family were taken prisoners with eight ponies at the time the Indian, Grass, was wounded. He was not there and had nothing to do with it."[15]

Those arrested were John Richard and his family, Black Tiger, half-brother of Mary Richard, and his family, Stone Belly with six persons, Milk with five persons, and Rocky Bear. Louis Richard was then operating the store and trading post at Platte Bridge Station, located at Guinard's Bridge, so Louis was not arrested. Upon discovery of the arrests, Louis packed up all of his family's belongings at Richard's Bridge and moved them back to the trading post at Guinard's. Whatever the charges were against John Richard and his family, they were soon dropped and all were allowed to return to the bridge. The depredations, however, did not stop. That fall Joseph Bissonette lost fifty horses to a marauding band of Sioux.[16]

To further the tensions building between the Sioux and the white men along the Platte, one of the largest tragedies to occur between a military organization and Indians was about to take place in southeastern

Colorado. In mid-November scout Moses E. "California Joe" Milner led Colonel John N. Chivington and his 3rd Colorado Volunteers to Black Kettle's village of Southern Cheyenne camped on Sand Creek. Black Kettle flew an American flag from his teepee to display that the camp was not hostile. At dawn on November 29, 1864, Colonel Chivington and his men laid siege to the village. The carnage left two hundred Indians dead, mostly women and children. Black Kettle and the other survivors, which included a few Oglala Sioux and Northern Cheyenne, fled north to the headwaters of Powder River. There they found refuge with the Sioux and Northern Cheyenne who typically wintered there. They pleaded that vengeance be taken on the wagon trains and settlements along the Platte road for the massacre at Sand Creek.[17]

Notes to Chapter Nine:

1. Allen Hulburt is often called Hurlbut or other similar names. This book uses the name that Charles K. Bucknum used in an 1897 article. Mr. Bucknum had been in the west for many years at the time he wrote the article and lived in Casper, Wyoming. He is believed to have met Hulburt in Virginia City, Montana, a short time after this event. Bucknum's telling of this tale is not only the most believable, but appears to be the most authentic account that has been recorded to date. "The most reliable and authentic account of the Lost Cabin Mine is found in an article written by Charles K. Bucknum," wrote Alfred James Mokler. The article cited here was reprinted by Mokler. Mokler, Alfred James, *History of Natrona County Wyoming, 1888–1922*, (R. R. Donnelley & Sons Company, The Lakeside Press, Chicago, 1923, reprinted by Mountain States Lithograph, under the direction of Kathleen Hemry, 1989), p. 89–91; Doyle, Susan Badger, "The Bozeman Trail, 1863–1868," *Annals of Wyoming*, (Spring, 1998), vol. 70, no. 2, p. 6.

2. Myers, p. 173–180; Pennock, p. 8; This popular Indian ford and camping area was still used by Indian hunting parties as late as the 1930s. Anderson, Kevin, and Glass, Jefferson, *Oral History of William Trevor Evans*, (Unpublished cassette and typescript, Special Collections, Goodstein Foundation Library, Casper College, Casper, Wyoming, 1998); Johnson, Dorothy M., *The Bloody Bozeman*, (McGraw-Hill Book Co., New York and Toronto, 1971), p. 3; In 1863 Bozeman and Jacobs led a train of forty-six wagons and eighty-nine men from Deer Creek to a point near present day Buffalo, Wyoming. There they met a party of Sioux and Northern Cheyenne who forced them to turn back to the Oregon Trail. This aborted attempt at the "shortcut" cost the party over two hundred miles. Doyle, p. 3–5.

3. Lowe, James A., *The Bridger Trail, An Alternative Route to the Gold Fields of Montana Territory in 1864*, (The Arthur H. Clark Company, Spokane, Washington, 1999). p. 21, 93–118; Louise Merivale was the daughter of Joseph Merivale. Her father was a Mexican, sometimes noted as Jose Miraval, presumably from Taos or Pueblo, who had worked for John Richard Sr. at Richard's Bridge since as early as 1854. Ricker, "Baptiste Pourier," tablet 15, p. 97–100.

4. Lowe, p. 94, 97–98, 139–140.

5. Mokler, p. 91.

6. Bridger, John Richard Jr., Jacobs, Allensworth, McKnight, Todd, McMinn, Rollins, Stafford, and a second Bridger train all departed over the Bridger Trail in 1864. The Jacobs who led the third train across Bridger's route was none other than John M. Jacobs, who had helped explore the Bozeman Trail, and attempted a crossing with a wagon train the previous year. Lowe, p. 93–114; Hulburt, Bozeman, Townsend, and Coffinbury chose the Bozeman Trail. Doyle, p. 7.

7. As Susan Badger Doyle mentioned, had it not been for this pursuit of Hulburt's Lost Cabin Mine by the members of that train, they would most assuredly have been the first to arrive at their destination. Doyle, p. 6–7.

8. Allen Hulburt never did find his mine in the Big Horn Mountains, but was later credited with being the first to discover gold along Prickly Pear Creek in Montana. Several other experienced miners have searched for the Lost Cabin Mine, and one Colorado miner, Jack McDonald, reportedly found it after more than a year of searching the Big Horn Mountains. McDonald excitedly returned to Colorado, planning to go back to the lost mine the next year. There he became ill and before drawing his last breath told his friend Bart Beckley of his discovery. Following McDonald's death, Beckley made his own expedition into the area, but even after finding many of the landmarks McDonald had described to him, a year of exploration turned up nothing. Many others followed these men, trying to locate the legendary mine, without success. There have been rumors that the Fremont and Natrona County businessman J. B. Okie discovered the mine in his early days as a sheepherder in the Big Horn Mountains and consequently gained the capital to begin amassing his vast holdings in central Wyoming. Many of those who believe this rumor base this on the fact that Okie named his community Lost Cabin. However, John Signor had operated a road-ranch called Lost Cabin in the vicinity (which incidentally happened to be along the Bridger Trail), reportedly named simply to incite curiosity. J. B. Okie acquired the ranch and merely kept the name. The Lost Cabin Mine truly is a mystery of legendary proportions and, more than likely, will remain that way. Mokler, p. 91–93; Doyle, p. 6; Hendry, Mary Helen, *Tales of Old Lost Cabin, and Parts There-*

about, (Mary Helen Hendry, author and publisher, Lysite, Wyoming, 1989), p. 1–2, 25–28.

9. Two primary sources provide the identities of the guides hired by this train. Both are cited by Johnson in *The Bloody Bozeman*. Benjamin William Ryan stated that the guides were Raphael Gogeor and John Boyer. David Weaver said the guides were Michael Boulier and John Richards. The latter seems the most accurate. Mitch Bouyer is another individual whose true identity may never be known. His name began appearing in the areas along the North Platte River and in Montana as a guide, trader, or scout in the 1860s. His first name shows up as Michael, Minton, or Mitch and his last name as Boyer, Bouyer, Bovier, or Boulier. John Bouyer, who is often thought to be one in the same, was, in fact, a half-brother of Mitch. The John Richard that acted as the other guide to this wagon train must have been John Al Richard, the eldest son of John Richard's brother Peter Richard. Both John Richard Sr. and John Richard Jr. are accounted for elsewhere at the time. Johnson, p. 130–132, 342; A secondary source, Hila Gilbert, named Mitch Bouyer and Louis Richard as the guides of the Townsend Train in her book *"Big Bat" Pourier*. Understanding the events that transpired on the wagon train and Louis Richard's character and expertise as an interpreter help to make this possibility believable. He was however, only seventeen-years old at the time and no evidence has been discovered that either proves or discounts the possibility that Louis Richard was one of the guides. Gilbert, p. 19; Ricker, "Baptiste Pourier," tablet 15, p. 130–131; Census of Fort Fetterman, Albany County, Wyoming Territory, 1870.

10. This account of the Townsend fight was told by E. O. Railsback, a member of the Townsend wagon train, to Elmer Brock in 1939 and 1940. Additional details were provided by: Brock, J. Elmer, *Powder River Country*, (Margaret Brock Hanson, editor and publisher, Frontier Printing, Inc., Cheyenne, Wyoming, 1981), p. 24–25; Doyle, p. 7–8; Johnson, p. 132–134.

11. This rendition of the Coffinbury wagon train story is from the diary of David Weaver, as cited by Dorothy M. Johnson. Johnson, p. 135–137.

12. Ricker, "Baptiste Pourier," tablet 15, p. 100–101; The legendary Joseph Alfred "Jack" Slade had come west from Illinois following an unsolved murder there. He gained most of his notoriety as the superintendent of the Sweetwater division of Ben Holladay's Overland Stage Company. While in his employ Slade whipped the division into shape by killing anyone who did not perform to his wishes. Eventually Holladay fired him at the request of the Army. Slade then moved to the "diggin's" near Virginia City, Montana. He was hung by the Vigilance Committee in Virginia City on March 10, 1864, after repeatedly menacing the populace there. It is not known if Slade's wife, Virginia, was still at the ranch when the Richards and Pourier stayed there. Nevin, *The Expressmen*, p. 139.

13. Lowe, p. 107–114, 145–212; Doyle, p. 8–9.

14. Ricker, "Magloire Mosseau," tablet 28, p. 66–67.

15. Letter cited by Hila Gilbert. Gilbert p. 19.

16. McDermott, "John Baptiste Richard" in *Mountain Men*, 2:301–302; McDermott, "Joseph Bissonette" in *Mountain Men*, 4:58; Murray, Robert A., p. 22; Gilbert p. 18–19.

17. Among the chiefs who were camped on Sand Creek at the time of Chivington's raid were John Richard's old friends Slim Face and Left Hand. Cragin; Bryans, p. 135–136; Milner and Forrest, p. 131–135; Utley and Washburn, p. 234–235.

This 1842 sketch of Fort Laramie, drawn by an unknown artist, depicts the fort and the surrounding countryside. (*Wyoming State Archives, Department of State Parks and Cultural Resources*)

10

Beginning of
the Storm

O VER THE NEXT few years, Indian depredations along the North Platte
River and the Bozeman Trail reached an all time high. The year 1865
marked the beginning of a storm, primarily headed by the Sioux and
Northern Cheyenne, which would rage on for over a decade. In the preceding years the tribes of the northern plains and Rocky Mountains had
seen more and more infringement by the white man, primarily due to
mining activities, but also from emigrant traffic along the major westward
trails. Perhaps it was insight that prompted John Richard to leave the crossing of the Platte, but more likely his move was prompted by inside information received from some of his many friends among the Indians. The
survivors of the Sand Creek Massacre were speaking of vengeance.

The first significant retaliation for Sand Creek took place on May
20, 1865, when Bill Comstock, a white renegade, led two hundred
warriors in an attack on Deer Creek Station. During the battle that
ensued over the next few hours, three or four Indians were killed before
they withdrew. The defenders suffered no fatalities in the skirmish.
Colonel Preston B. Plumb then led his 11th Kansas Volunteer Cavalry
in pursuit of the attackers across the Platte. After killing one Indian and
wounding others during the chase, Plumb returned to the station. He
lost one man during the pursuit, the only military fatality.[1]

Joseph Bissonette lost another twenty horses during the attack on Deer
Creek Station. He then packed up his family and belongings and
returned to Fort Laramie. John Richard was evidently distraught by the
events and the politics of Indian affairs developing along the North
Platte. When released from Fort Laramie where he was still held over
the incident involving weapons, he returned to the bridge only long
enough to organize his affairs. He left his bridge, store, and saloon and
moved on, establishing a new trading post and road ranch on the

175

Overland Trail at the crossing of Rock Creek, about twenty miles northwest of the present city of Laramie. Big Bat Pourier and Buckskin Jack Russell also left Richard's Bridge for the season. Buckskin Jack went to work for Jules Ecoffey and Adolph Cuney at their Deer Creek Ranch. Pourier continued on with Richard to Rock Creek. Richard's Rock Creek road ranch quickly became a community, much the same as Richard's Bridge had.

Hiram and Lizzie Kelly moved from Fort Laramie also going further south, first to Fort Halleck, five miles west of present Elk Mountain, Wyoming, then to the Cache la Poudre near present Fort Collins, Colorado.[2]

⋈ ⋈

A detachment of men from Platte Bridge Station were camped on Reshaw Creek to guard the post's livestock there. After the fight at Deer Creek, the military found it impossible to maintain telegraph communication to the east, as well as to all points west of Sweetwater Station. On May 29, 1865, the military strengthened its presence at the Reshaw Creek guard camp and sent six men to Richard's Bridge. Sergeant Isaac "Jake" Pennock was with the guard camp. The men sent to the bridge had orders to keep watch from one of the empty houses, to observe any movements of Indians, and to stay out of sight during daylight hours. There was no unusual action at Richard's Bridge until July 3. That afternoon the guard camp received a dispatch from the post at Guinard's Bridge that the personnel there were under attack from the north bank of the river. Colonel Plumb and twenty men from the guard camp crossed Richard's Bridge to attack the Indians from the rear. When they arrived at the point of the attack, all they found were fresh tracks. Colonel Plumb led his men in pursuit of the Indians and engaged them before nightfall. Two soldiers and one Indian were killed in the resulting battle.[3]

Regiments of 11th Ohio and 11th Kansas Volunteers were scattered from Horseshoe Creek to Sweetwater Station, primarily trying to keep the telegraph lines in repair and emigrants safe. A fairly large number of troops were bivouacked along Reshaw Creek, including the Headquarters Company of the 11th Kansas and Colonel Plumb. This camp was some eight to ten miles from the Guinard's Bridge and three to four miles from Richard's Bridge. On June 12, two companies of troops were ordered in from this camp to garrison at Guinard's Bridge. Telegraph wires remained down east of Deer Creek and between Sweetwater Station and Platte Bridge Station. The regiment was also short on ammunition as the freight trains carrying their supplies had been delayed at Horseshoe Creek. Without adequate communication, they were uncertain when the supplies might arrive. The remainder of the Reshaw Creek encampment not destined to move to the bridge was ordered to start for Fort Laramie. These orders were rescinded the following morning before any of the regiment had started in motion.

The situation all along the North Platte River was tense. Twenty men had been sent to assist in a battle at Sweetwater Station, some fifty miles away. The station there had been under continuous sporadic attacks for several days. On June 26, 1865, Lieutenant William Y. Drew and his detachment were returning from Sweetwater Station when they ran headlong into a band of Indians just east of Red Buttes. A running battle ensued over the next six miles resulting in two men being wounded, but no fatalities. This little group expended sixty rounds of precious ammunition in their escape to the post. The following day, with scarcely any ammunition, Sargeant Pennock wrote, "I Company left here in a pretty ticklish position" for La Bonte Station. Unofficial word at the bridges was that the supply train with ammunition might arrive as early as the next evening.

On June 28, it began to rain and Headquarters Company departed for La Bonte under the veil of a torrential downpour. Two days later, the remainder of the 11th Kansas was still waiting for ammunition and supplies. This day Sergeant Pennock hazarded a visit to the saloon at Richard's Bridge. Pennock found that the two men at the saloon had no idea of what to expect from the Indians, and the conversation soon regressed to the weather. Pennock learned only that the rain of two days earlier had been harder than either of the men had ever seen in the territory. He returned to the camp on Reshaw Creek knowing little more than he had when he left. "Jake" Pennock's hope of gaining some insight from those who had extensive dealings with Indians was unfulfilled. That afternoon ammunition and supplies finally arrived.

At 9:00 a.m. on July 2, 1865, the camp on Reshaw Creek was roused from a peaceful morning by the sound of three signal shots being fired in rapid succession from the direction of their grazing horses some three quarters of a mile away. Except for a few men left to guard the camp, everyone scrambled for the horses. Within a short distance of their camp, as the soldiers crested the brow of a hill, they spotted a party of Indians about a half a mile away in the bottom of the valley. The soldiers fired a half dozen shots in the direction of the Indians, but the raiders were well out of rifle range, so the unit returned to camp. A small party of horsemen then rode out to ascertain the Indians' strength but quickly returned while under fire. The Indians were working their way up a number of ravines to within firing range of the camp. Small parties of soldiers engaged the approaching Indians at several points.

Sergeant Pennock was sent on one of these missions. They had proceeded about a half mile when advance men spotted a far superior force of Indians immediately over the next rise. While Pennock and his men descended the hill in an attempt to retreat, they were overtaken by the Indians who tried to cut the soldiers off from their camp. The soldiers fired on the war party with little effect and were driven farther from their camp. While the soldiers were trying to gain some position of defense, Sergeant Holding was wounded, and the shooter was immediately dispatched by a bullet to his chest. The shooter was believed to be a white renegade. Finally the soldiers gained a position to defend themselves and the Indians soon abandoned their attack, taking their dead and wounded with them. Pennock counted the spots of blood in the sand in an attempt to determine the injuries the Indians suffered. He and the squad made their way back to camp without further incident. Sergeant Holding's wound was minor. "This fight on Reshaw Creek, four miles from Lower Bridge," Pennock wrote in his diary.

The following day, July 3, Captain Greer sent a replacement telegraph operator to Sweetwater Station and a crew to repair the line to that point. They were accompanied by an escort group. Thirty-four men in all, they left the post at Guinard's Bridge at sunset. Sergeant Pennock was left in charge of the horse camp.

The evening of July 7, having heard no word from the telegraph crew for four days, Captain Greer, Lieutenant Clancy, and twenty-six men left the Guinard's Bridge to search for them. About two hours out, Captain Greer met the escort and repair crew returning. Miles of telegraph line was down and much of it had been carried off. The soldiers had not taken enough wire with them to make all the repairs. At this point the transcontinental telegraph was virtually useless. The Indians destroyed the line faster than crews could repair it. The horse herd was moved in to Platte Bridge Station for better protection. On July 11, 1865, a party of Indians attempted to stampede the horse herd, but was unsuccessful.[4]

On the following day an emigrant train consisting of some seventy-five wagons arrived at the bridge on their way to the Montana gold fields. Fearing an Indian attack along the Bozeman Trail, they opted for the longer route through Idaho.

In a state of drunkenness, Lieutenant Bretney and his men attempted a mutiny of Captain Greer. Failing to succeed, they then went to the wagon train camped a mile above the post and shot up their camp. Fortunately no one was killed, though the emigrants sent for assistance from the captain. While Captain Greer was attempting to restore order with the wagon train, Bretney chased the telegraph operator from his post at gunpoint. Fearing for his life, the operator ran to Sergeant Pennock for protection. When this fracas ended Bretney was held at gunpoint by some of the very men who had earlier joined him in his stupidities. At first light the wagon train pulled out at a rapid pace, fearing the crazed Lieutenant far more than any Indians. For some unknown and most likely inconceivable reason, Bretney and his cohorts were not arrested. On July 14, Sergeant Pennock received orders that he was soon to be mustered out of the Army. Before month's end he would be hoping to survive long enough to achieve this goal.[5]

⫷≫⦁⦗≪⫸

Shortly after their arrival at Rock Creek, Big Bat Pourier and Louis Richard hired out to Joseph McKnight as teamsters at thirty-five dollars per month. McKnight had an ambulance and six wagons and was continuing to haul freight to the gold fields of Montana up the Bozeman Trail. This time they took the cut-off Bridger had introduced that left the Platte River some forty miles below Richard's Bridge.

A quirk of fate was shining on their journey. Crossing Powder River country was potentially the most treacherous portion of this journey. To their good fortune, McKnight, Pourier, Richard, and the other teamsters of the company did not encounter any Indians along this portion of their trek. Unknown to them, most of the hostile Sioux and Northern Cheyenne of this region were concentrating their aggressions toward the soldiers along the Platte River, particularly those at Platte Bridge Station.[6]

⋖⋗ ⋖⋗

Jake Pennock wrote the story of the next few days at the fort in his diary in an eye-witness report that would be difficult to improve upon. Here are his words (without further editing) as published in *Annals of Wyoming* in 1951:

July 25, 1865—

"Fine breeze a.m. Considerable noise among the horses last night. Think Indians prowling. Too dark to see well. Immediately after dinner the cry of 'here comes the Indians' through camp. I ran out then sure enough they were coming up the other side of the river. The boys commenced shooting and made some very good shots, 75 rode along the bank yelling and hooting like mad men. We crossed the bridge ten mounted following them a couple of miles. We killed two if not 3 of them. They were gradually reinforced until we found we would be taken. We fell back to camp. They commenced crossing the river two miles below and ran into the cattle herd. Twelve or fourteen of the boys went after them and had a severe fight. Killing one a head chief, who was scalped. Also two or three mortally wounded. We finally drove them across the river. They killed one steer, but we stuck it and hauled it into camp. We fought them across the river until after dark, when we returned to camp. They did not disturb us during the night. About fifty or one hundred in sight.

July 26, 1865—

"Terrible day for our command and no knowing how it will end. At daybreak a few Indians was seen in the hills north of the river. Lieut. Britney and ten men arrived from Sweetwater before daybreak. Detachments of Co. "H" and "D" to be here by twelve or one o'clock. They camped three miles this side of Willow Creek. Capt. Greer received an order to send a detachment to meet Co. "H" and "D". I took charge of it by request of Capt. On reporting to Major Anderson found that Lieut. Collins of Co. "G" of the 11th Ohio was going along, twenty or twenty-five in all. We crossed the bridge and got about one mile from camp when from N.E.-S.W. and every point of the compass the savages came. It appeared as if they sprung from the ground. They completely surrounded us. There was no other alternative. Death was approaching on every side in its most horrible form. That of the scalping knife tomahawk of the Indian. We turned and charged in the thickest of them, drawing our pistols and doing the best we could. It was a terrible ordeal to go through. It really was running the gauntlet for dear life after a terrible break neck race of 3/4 miles we arrived at the bridge where our boys met us and to our support. In the charge we lost—five killed and twelve wounded. Lieut. Collins was killed.[7] Everything was in full view of the station. Over 1,500 Indians were around our little party. The Indians suffered dreadfully as our pistols were pushed right against their bodies and fired going great execution. We were forced to come back. Every horse was wounded in one or more places. Four were killed. They now cut the wire both east and west. Twenty men under Lieut. Walker went two miles east to repair it. Indians attacked and killed one and wounded two of our company. He had to retreat not getting the wire fixed at 1/2 past 11 o'clock. "H" and "D" Company came in sight west of us, the savages surrounded them, five boys crossed the river, three miles above, two were killed and three came in camp on foot. There horses being killed. One on horseback near the mountains, but several Indians were in close pursuit. All this we could see plainly from the station, but we could do nothing for them. "H" and "D" detachments corralled, or tried to corrall their wagons, but did not succeed very well. We could see the Indians in swarms charge down on our boys when they would roll volley after volley into them, it seemed as though the boys were in strong position, twenty in all being their number. About 4 o'clock the firing ceased and a smoke that of burning wagons commenced ascending. The enemy began going off north two and three until sundown not a living being was to be seen. We are sure all the boys were killed but from the length of time they held out and the number of Indians in solid masses upon them the Indians must have suffered terrible in killed and wounded. Two Snake scouts started at 1/2 past 9 p.m. with dispatches for Deer Creek. Would get there before day.[8]

July 27, 1865—

"Up at day break. Went on top post with glasses. Soon Indians commenced appearing on the ridge just opposite on north side of river. First one then two until by sunrise hundreds were in sight on all the hills. Some of them Halloed across in Cheyenne language. Telling the women to leave as they were going to burn us out and kill all the soldiers and men here. They are now going southwest for high ground towards Red Buttes, but few in sight at 8 a.m.[9] The Indians are very mad they told the Indians that they killed all men in "H" and "D" yesterday and was going to kill more white men today and our men killed and wounded heaps of Indians.[10] Copy of papers found on battle ground yesterday, viz. Blackfeet, Cheyenne, Arraphoes, Sioux and a few Comanches are here, now they want to fight four days more. It was taken prisoner down on Platte River. You killed Chief yesterday evening. They say they want no peace. There is over 1,000 they want stock and want to fight. They are moving to battle on this place.[11] A party of us crossed this afternoon to try to bring in our dead. We found Lieut. Collins and McDonald and one other man in a dreadfully mangles and cut up condition. Our scouts found discovered Indians in force about two miles off dancing encircled by their horses. Think this body 600 strong. Another body of men came in sight from the east. When we were recalled they proved to be a reinforcement of 50 men from Deer Creek. Our Indian scouts got there after day break. Lieut. Hubbard and Greer started immediately. Another party is just starting to bring dead bodies nearest river. The boys are all in safe. Brought in three dead bodies nearest river, 58 arrows were found in one body, 24 in body of Lieut. Collins and several in McDonalds. Two Indians showed themselves in the west on hills. The three boys that escaped from the train yesterday fought their way 7 miles, 60 Indians crossed the river and followed them, killing all of their horses and two out of the original that were cut off from the train at 1st charge of Indians, four of the Indians was killed and several wounded. The fighting were distinctly seen by all at the station. The three boys got into the bed of a brushy creek when the band of Indians pursuing them nearly all left, only fourteen continuing the pursuit of the three. The boys were Company "D" of our regiment, Henry Smith, Byron Swain and Corp. James Shrader. Co. "H"—13 killed, "L"—8, "I"—3, "K"—2 in Battle of Platte Bridge, Co. "J" 11 wounded "K" 2 wounded, address Henry Smith, Prescot, Kansas, Byron Swain, Corp. James Shrader, John Holding, Oaskasoosa, Kansas.

July 28, 1865—

"Sentinel on guard, fired shot at 2 o'clock a. m. Three Indians came near the post and ran as soon as fired upon. They were mounted. We all ran into the breastworks immediately, but at daybreak no one was in sight on the surrounding hills. No Indians appeared up to 2 o'clock p.m. A detachment started out to find our boys above. About five miles west from the station 20 dead bodies were found, the wagons burned. The Indians had a great many killed and wounded. They had to cut up a great many telegraph poles and split them to drag off their killed and wounded. The Indian scouts say there were 3,000 Indians at least went north from the Trail the telegraph lines destroyed as far west as the party went about six to eight miles."

So ends Sergeant Isaac "Jake" Pennock's version of the story of what became know as the Battle of Platte Bridge. On August 3, 1865, he wrote, "Homeward bound…passed Reshaw creek 7 miles from upper bridge…" Within a few days he and several of his Indian-fighting comrades were mustered out of the Army to be replaced by regulars returning from the Civil War.[12]

⋙⋘

In August Joseph McKnight, Louis Richard, and Baptiste Pourier arrived in Virginia City, Montana, with their freight wagons. They had encountered little trouble along the Bozeman Trail. The Indians that headed into the Powder River country following the Battle of Platte Bridge did not arrive in that area until after McKnight and his men had passed through the area. Upon their arrival in Virginia City, Pourier and Louis Richard both quit McKnight and went to work for the partnership of John Richard Jr., Mike McKenzie, and Al Long who with Mitch Bouyer were embarking on a trading expedition with the Crows. While engaged in trading along the Musselshell River, they were attacked by a Sioux war party. They fled on horseback and escaped serious injury, but left behind a valuable cache of furs.

After arriving back at Virginia City, John Richard Jr. and Big Bat Pourier joined McKenzie in another venture.[13] The company went to Salt Lake and purchased four wagonloads of flour from the Mormons there. They then returned to Montana with this flour which they sold to the miners at one hundred dollars per sack. They felt their luck had

In 1933, WIlliam Henry Jackson illustrated the fight at Platte Bridge. (*Wyoming State Archives, Department of State Parks and Cultural Resources*)

changed, so they gathered up Mitch Bouyer and Louis Richard, and returned to the Musselshell to recover their cache of furs. This done, they returned to Fort Laramie, and presumably sold their furs or shipped them via some eastbound freighter.[14]

⋘⋙

The winter of 1865–1866 dropped some of the heaviest snowfall ever in the area of the two bridges across the North Platte River. The new Fort Casper had recently begun expansion, and a logging and lumber camp called Camp Dodge had been established in the foothills of the nearby mountain to provide the materials and firewood for construction. Due to the excessive snows, however, the troops from Fort Casper were unable to reach Camp Dodge to replenish their supply of firewood. As the snow continued to deepen and firewood continued to diminish at Fort Casper, a detail was sent from the fort to blaze a trail through the snow seven miles down the valley to Richard's Bridge. Due to the close proximity of the military post, John Richard had not felt it necessary to leave a caretaker at the bridge through the winter. With no one present to argue against their decision, the command at Fort Casper ordered the bridge and several of the buildings of the settlement dismantled and brought to the fort to be burned for firewood.[15]

❧⚜☙

William G. Bullock had been an agent for Robert Campbell & Company, the post sutler at Fort Laramie. Seth Ward, the former partner of John Richard who was sutler there for many years, had evidently moved on to a higher position in the company. As early as 1862, Sioux chief Swift Bear, recognizing Bullock's lust for gold, had asked him why he did not go to the Hills (the Black Hills of Dakota, not the Laramie Mountain range) and get some. Bullock had ignored the Indian's suggestion, thinking it was superfluous. A few years later John Richard had paid a debt to Bullock in gold nuggets. When Bullock asked him where the gold had come from, Richard told him that his sons had taken it in trade from some Sioux who frequently hunted in the Black Hills. Bullock, who appears to have been a much better promoter and talker than a rugged frontiersman, let the fantasy of riches eat away at his thoughts until the spring of 1866. Then a wagon train of around 150 men arrived at Fort Laramie on their way to the gold fields of Montana. Bullock convinced the men that far more riches were to be had in the virgin mountains of the Black Hills—and without any competition from other gold seekers. Bullock had, of course, fabricated his monumental tale strictly on hearsay, but his story must have been convincing. The self-titled "Colonel" Bullock soon found himself the captain of an extensive expedition that planned to head into the Black Hills to search for gold.

The commander of Fort Laramie learned of the group's intent and most likely saved their lives when he put the kibosh to their plans. The miners were not easily convinced to revert to their earlier destination. The commander, however, explained that an escort of no less than a regiment of soldiers would be needed to save their scalps from hanging from a Sioux lance if they ventured into this sacred ground of the Sioux. To this Bullock and the miners demanded, as free white citizens, a sizable escort to accompany their expedition. When the commander told them that he could not send so much as a single man, much less even a patrol, to escort them into that region without a direct order from Washington, the roar subsided into a grumble. He cemented his statement by offering

This 1868 Alexander Gardner photograph shows, starting left, an unidentified man, Packs His Drum, John Finn, Amos Bettelyoun (standing), William Bullock (seated), Old Man Afraid of His Horses, Benjamin Mills, Red Bear, and James Bordeaux. (*Wyoming State Archives, Department of State Parks and Cultural Resources*)

to allow them to accompany the next troops that were sent up the Bozeman Trail to insure their safety across the Powder River country. The miners could not refuse, and Bullock was left seething at Fort Laramie as the wagon train pulled out for Montana.[16]

In March 1866, John Richard discovered the destruction of his bridge and most of the settlement that surrounded it. On March 21, 1866, Richard sent a voucher to the Quartermaster General demanding payment by the Army for his bridge. Judging by the flow of paperwork submitted by John Richard over the next several years, he never received any compensation for the loss of the bridge or its nearby dwellings. This paper trail of claims filed between 1866 and 1869 does support one substantial fact. Some historians have suggested that John Richard sold his bridge in 1864 or 1865. This must not have been the case. If so, he would not have been in a position to file the claims.[17]

In June of 1866, John Richard Sr. attempted to breathe life back into his operations on the North Platte River. Louis Richard may have been in charge at the old trading post when an advertisement appeared in an unidentified Denver newspaper. This further undermines the theory that Richard had sold the bridge:

To Freighters and Emigrants

RICHARD & CO. Fort Casper, Dakota Territory

Known as the Old North Platte Bridge, or California Crossing,

120 miles west of Fort Laramie.

Good accommodations for travelers.

This is the best and nearest road for Emigrants and Freighters

to Salt Lake, Virginia City Montana, and California.[18]

⋘⋙ ⋘⋙

In May 1866, John Richard Jr., Louis Richard, and Mitch Bouyer hired on with Henry E. Palmer[19] to trade for him in the Powder River country. On May 12, they departed from Fort Laramie on their expedition. When they arrived on Clear Creek, a tributary of Powder River near the present town of Buffalo, Wyoming, Palmer, Bouyer, and the Richard men erected a sod trading post. About a week later some twenty-five Cheyenne Indians arrived "to trade." While the men were sharing a pipe with the chief, they unwittingly fell into the captivity of the Cheyenne. With a portion of the band holding them prisoner, they watched as the rest of the warriors dismantled the trading post and replaced the sod from where it had been taken. This operation being completed, the chief turned to the men and lectured that no white man was allowed to break the earth in this favored Indian hunting ground. The chief ended his lengthy lecture by giving them the choice of returning to where they had come from or continuing on further north. The war party then left the men with all of their livestock and goods intact.

The dazed men loaded up their goods and, with hardly a word spoken between them, headed north. They continued on to Tongue River where they made camp, rested, recovered their wits, and assessed their next move. They decided that the next morning they would pack up and continue on north to trade with the Crows. Soon they fell in with a band of some seven hundred Arapahos and proceeded to the Big Horn River with them, trading as they traveled. When news reached the Arapahos of the trouble between Red Cloud and the whites, the Indians seized the traders as hostages. Once again they were held captive by a group of Indians that they did not know well, and once again they had no idea what their fate might be.

The Arapahos were far less congenial than the Cheyenne had been. After three weeks, the Arapahos grew tired of caring for their prisoners, and the men felt that they would soon suffer some horrific and torturous death. They were awakened one morning by the ruckus of the camp being prepared to move. As the last of Indians left the area, a warrior came to them and released them from their bonds. Much to their surprise, they were given their freedom, unharmed by their captors, but the Indians had taken all their trade goods, weapons, and livestock.

Now afoot and without food, they had to a decide which direction to travel, without delay. Fort Laramie was by far nearer than Bozeman, but if they chose to retrace that route they risked running into either the Cheyenne or Arapahos. Opting for the longer, but hopefully safer, route, the traders set off for Bozeman. They arrived at this destination without further delay or discomfort, except for empty bellies and sore feet.[20]

⬧⬥

It is not known what became of Palmer and his trading operation after this ordeal, and although the presence of Big Bat Pourier is not mentioned, it must be assumed that he had been along. After their arrival in Bozeman, Bat was involved in their next venture.

In July 1866, John Richard Jr., Louis Richard, Big Bat Pourier, Mitch Bouyer, and Lew Wahn constructed a ferry across the Big Horn River. These men felt that with their experience along the North Platte, they could build and operate a ferry at a profit. The site was near the mouth of Soap Creek a short distance from the most popular fording place along the river. They charged seven dollars per wagon to cross. Within a few weeks of operation, as a wagon train neared the crossing, a small war party raided in the night capturing the emigrants' horses. During the melee one of the men guarding the horses was wounded. He died the following morning. The emigrants sent men to Bozeman to purchase more horses, and while they were gone, the partnership made the decision to sell the ferry. The ferry was sold to A. C. Leighton, and the partners returned to Bozeman.[21]

⬧⬥

A few days later on August 18, 1866, Deer Creek Station sustained its last Indian attack. A marauding war party lay siege to the station and killed three men stationed there. The battle, decidedly in the Indians' favor, ended when they set fire to the station, and it burned to the ground. The station was not resurrected, and the site was abandoned to year round habitation for several years.

About that same time Captain N. C. Kinney was sent with troops from Fort Phil Kearny to establish Fort C. F. Smith on the Big Horn River. The site chosen was near the newly-constructed ferry, and the old ford was soon permanently abandoned. Almost immediately upon its completion, the new post was under near constant siege by the Sioux.[22]

When word reached Bozeman that Fort C. F. Smith was short on provisions, John Richard Jr., Louis Richard, Big Bat Pourier, and Mitch Bouyer contracted to haul several loads of potatoes to the fort.[23] On one of their return trips, the company camped with a band of Crow Indians. Their camp was raided by a party of Blackfoot Indians who stole their mules. John Richard Jr. and Mitch Bouyer gave chase and, as they were about to overtake the Indians, the renegades stabbed the mules and fled. Richard and Bouyer recovered the mules and managed to bring them back to their camp, but all of them died from their wounds. When the traders returned to Bozeman to replenish their supplies, the Crows moved their camp in search of more game. When the company returned, they found the Indians camped on the Yellowstone. The Crows had brought in a good supply of furs. The traders bartered for the furs and then continued to trade their way back toward the Platte.[24]

❈ ❈

In the spring of 1866, Hiram and Lizzie Kelly returned to the Fort Laramie area, and Hi contracted to supply beef to Everhardt, who represented Matt Ryan, a government stock buyer from Leavenworth, Kansas. Kelly secured an agreement to supply one hundred head of cattle which he intended to purchase in Colorado. Considering the state of turmoil, Kelly purchased a fleet horse for the trip from a lieutenant. He left Fort Laramie at dusk and reached the former Fort Walbach by dawn. There he camped in the nearby foothills waiting until the next nightfall before resuming his trip. He arrived at the ranch of E. W. Whitcomb and Joe Mason on the Cache la Poudre without incident and purchased his livestock. He hired Ab Loomis and John Colome and their riders to drive the cattle to Fort Laramie. While at Whitcomb and Mason's ranch, he received word that Everhardt needed another two hundred head of cattle. A few days passed while he acquired a herd and gathered a crew to take them down the trail. He needed to be back at Fort Laramie before the first herd arrived there, so he purchased "the fastest horse around," a mount raised on Crow Creek from a man named "Little Gary." With his two horses, he left the Cache la Poudre at dusk and by trading mounts throughout the night, he made the one hundred mile trip to Fort Laramie by morning, concluding his contract with Everhardt when the herds arrived.[25]

Taking the gains from his livestock dealings, Kelly then went to Nebraska City where he purchased five six-yoke bull teams with wagons and enough merchandise to fill them. He returned to the confluence of Horse Creek and the North Platte River, forty miles downstream from Fort Laramie, and purchased a store there from Todd Reynolds. He stocked the store with his fresh supply of goods, and he and Lizzie prepared to spend the winter.

When Joseph Bissonette had moved his family from Deer Creek back to Fort Laramie, they lived with the Bordeaux family. Bordeaux had built a log store and road ranch south of Fort Laramie near the confluence of Richeau and Chugwater Creeks. Kelly, Bissonette, and Bordeaux obtained a contract with Ed Creighton of Omaha to supply telegraph poles for the coming railroad. They hired two men to haul the poles from Bear Mountain to Kelly's store where they were stockpiled. On one of their trips, a band of Cheyenne killed and scalped the two teamsters and stole the mules. By the time the men were found, their bodies were frozen. Kelly took them to his store where they were buried.

Following this incident, Hi and Lizzie loaded up their merchandise and also moved to Bordeaux's road ranch for the winter. The next spring Kelly obtained the woodcutting contract for Fort Laramie. Bissonette reestablished his small farm and occasionally worked as an interpreter for the military. In the fall the Kellys moved near the headwaters of Horse Creek, twenty-five miles north of the new city of Cheyenne, and Bordeaux sold out to Cy Williams and his partner "Swolly," but the ranch has since been known as Bordeaux.[26]

⟨≋⟩⟨≋⟩

Bouyer, Pourier, and the Richard brothers had continued to trade with the Indians in Montana and as far south as Powder River, eventually working their way back to the Platte. The following spring they made their way back over the Bozeman Trail through Forts Phil Kearny and C. F. Smith.

James Bordeaux and his wife Marie, also known as Red Cormorant Woman, ran successful trading posts up and down the streams of Wyoming and Nebraska. (*Wyoming State Archives, Department of State Parks and Cultural Resources*)

In May 1867, John Richard Jr. and Mitch Bouyer rode into Bozeman with news that Fort C. F. Smith was in desperate trouble. They were seriously short on provisions, and all of their livestock had either died or been run off by hostile Indians. Ominous news spread that the Sioux were engaged in a huge sun dance on Powder River in preparation for an attack on Fort C. F. Smith. Richard and Bouyer led a party of volunteers back to the fort with supplies and ammunition. Accompanied by Pourier, they arrived at the fort on June 10, 1867. Then they waited, but nothing happened. The Sioux attacked Fort Phil Kearny instead of Fort C. F. Smith following the sun dance.

In August, the storm finally arrived at C. F. Smith. The Sioux attacked the hay cutting crew five miles south of the fort. During the Hayfield Fight, as it became known, A. C. Leighton, the contractor, suffered severe losses and was unable to complete his contract.[27] John Richard Jr. then contracted with the fort to furnish the balance of the hay. When the haying was finished, Richard then began cutting firewood for the fort. Big Bat Pourier obtained a contract to supply wild

Adolph Cuney (shown) was a partner of John Richard Jr. and Jules Ecoffey in the Six Mile Hog Ranch. (*Fort Laramie National Historical Site*)

game for meat to the fort. Following the fulfillment of these contracts, Pourier and the Richards returned to Fort Laramie. They set up camp on John Richard Sr.'s ranch on Richeau Creek. On November 12, John Richard Jr. and Pierre Chene translated Dr. Mathews's address to the Crow Council at Fort Laramie.[28]

⋘⋙

A mixed-blood boy named Baptiste Ladeau had meanwhile been working for Williams and Swolly at the Bordeaux road ranch. In March 1868, he got into a heated argument with Cy Williams. He quit and left the ranch headed for Fort Laramie. Cy Williams tracked him to Chug Springs. There near the spring, Williams killed Ladeau, his pony, and his dog. News of the senseless murder soon swept the area. The ruthless killing enraged the populace, particularly those with Indian blood. Feeling that the rope of a lynch mob soon would close around his neck, Williams fled to refuge in the village of his old friend Spotted Tail.

The Army grew tired of the continuing skirmishes with the Indians that had now continued for over three years. They contrived yet another treaty that would send the majority of the Indians to numerous reservations, but included the concession that the Bozeman Trail and all the forts along it would close. In April, the commanders of Fort Laramie hired John Richard Jr., Louis Richard, and their younger brother Charles E. Richard to travel to all of the Indian villages in the region and ask the chiefs to come to Fort Laramie for a peace conference. Among the villages visited by Charley Richard was that of Spotted Tail. While there he noticed Cy Williams but gave no indication of recognition. A few weeks later, with his mission for the Army completed, Charley Richard organized a band of mixed-blood men to avenge the death of Baptiste Ladeau. In early May, they arrived at Spotted Tail's village and called Williams out. Cy Williams was killed in the gunfight that ensued, but not before he managed to kill Charley Richard and wound two of the other avengers.

⟨≋⟩ ⟨≋⟩

On May 11, the Army was authorized to sell all the government stores and posts along the Bozeman Trail. W. S. McKenzie and Nelson Story wrote their partner, John Richard Jr. that they had purchased the remains of Fort C. F. Smith. They asked him to proceed to Montana with his freight outfit to help move these goods to Helena. With the recent death of his younger brother and the turmoil surrounding the Fort Laramie peace conference, Richard postponed this journey for nearly two months. Early in June, twenty-six Sioux lodges and 119 Arapaho lodges arrived at Fort Laramie to sign the treaty. On June 29, Peter Richard, brother of John Richard Sr., was hired to guide the Sioux and Arapahos to their reservations.[29]

⟨≋⟩ ⟨≋⟩

On July 6, 1868, the only civilian wagon train to cross the Bozeman Trail that year departed from Fort Laramie composed of freight wagons belonging to John Richard Jr. with Baptiste Pourier in command. Among the nineteen teamsters were Joseph Richard Jr., Louis Richard, Speed Stagner, Peter and Charles Janis, and Louis St. Cancellor. They arrived at Fort Phil Kearny on July 20 and left for Fort C. F. Smith on July 23. The train consisted of fifteen wagons, 167 cattle, seven horses, two mules, fifteen rifles, and five hundred rounds of ammunition. They met John Richard Jr., W. S. McKenzie, and Nelson Story on July 29, 1868 at Fort C. F. Smith as the fort was being evacuated, and they immediately began loading goods to take out.[30]

The following day a Sioux war party attacked the traders at the old fort. The warriors immediately threw the supplies into the Big Horn River. The traders would likely have been massacred had not Red Cloud and his brother Spider gone to the raiders' camp to call them off. Red Cloud told the warriors that these men were his relatives and consequently should not be killed. John Richard Jr. sent tobacco and trade goods to the warriors' camp, but most of the goods were destroyed anyway. The partners moved on to Helena where Richard turned his goods and outfit over to McKenzie. Then John Richard Jr. and his teamsters returned to Fort Laramie.

❖ ❖

While John Richard Jr. was engaged in Montana, Hiram Kelly contracted the removal of several families from Forts Reno and Phil Kearny to Fort Fred Steele, located near the crossing of the North Platte River on the Overland Trail. The partnership of Richard, McKenzie, and Story filed a claim of $50,000 in damages caused by the Indians at Fort C. F. Smith, but only received $1,250 for their losses.

It appears that John Richard Jr. severed his ties with McKenzie and Story after their calamity at Fort C. F. Smith. In the summer of 1868, Dr. H. M. Matthews contracted to supply the Crows with one hundred head of beef cattle. Matthews purchased the cattle from John Richard Jr. and contracted him to deliver them. On August 13, John Richard Jr. hired William G. Bullock as his personal accountant and financial manager. Bullock still also represented Robert Campbell & Co. of St. Louis as sutler of Fort Laramie. On November 19, 1868, Bullock received orders from Colonel William M. Dye denying any trade with Red Cloud or any other Indians off of the reservation. That December, Captain R. S. Lamotte of Fort Ellis, Montana Territory, claimed that John Richard Jr. had in fact delivered the contracted cattle to the Crows, but due to some misunderstanding between him and Dr. Matthews, Richard reclaimed the cattle and drove them to Fort Laramie. Captain Lamotte also charged John Richard Jr. with attempting to entice the Crows, Nez Perce, Blackfoot, Shoshones, and Sioux to unite and wage a massive war against the whites.[31]

In response to these charges, John Richard Jr. hired as his attorney General John B. Sanborn of the law firm of Sanborn & King in Washington D. C., who was a former Indian Peace Commissioner.

Sanborn wrote N. G. Taylor, the Commissioner of Indian Affairs, on Richard's behalf. In response to the cattle discrepancies Sanborn cited certified vouchers from both Richard and Matthews and statements from the appropriate Crow chiefs that proved the cattle had in fact been delivered and consumed by the Crows. On the charge of attempting to incite a war (nearly as serious as treason) Sanborn began by stating how ridiculous the idea of this possible union was. These tribes had been warring between themselves for generations and the likelihood that they would unite was, first and foremost, preposterous. He then cited Richard's track record—how he had supplied the forts along the Bozeman Trail and come to their aid in time of crisis. Sanborn described how Richard had convinced the Crows to travel all the way to Fort Laramie for a peace conference. Then he recounted that Richard had held council with Red Cloud and Man Afraid of his Horses, and though unable to convince these Sioux chiefs to attend the conference, he had brought their words to the commission.

By February the charges against John Richard Jr. had been dismissed, and he had been granted the sole license to trade with the Powder River Sioux north of the North Platte River. No one else had this privilege. Adolph Cuney, of Six-Mile Hog Ranch fame, and Allen T. Chamblin stood as guarantor's on the license. The employees named were Adolph Cuney, clerk, and Louis Richard and Baptiste Pourier, traders. John Richard Jr. felt that he was indebted to Red Cloud for saving his life at Fort C.F. Smith. No one had been permitted to trade with Indians except on their reservations since November 1868. The winning of this right by John Richard Jr. had given him a monopoly on trading with the bands of Red Cloud and Spotted Tail as well as several others who had yet to accept life on the reservation.[32]

Notes to Chapter Ten:

1. Bryans, p. 137; Sergeant Isaac "Jake" Pennock was a member of the 11th Kansas Volunteer Cavalry who kept a detailed diary. During the years of the Civil War the Army of the western plains was largely made up of these volunteer regiments. Many young men of this period, particularly those from the border states, joined volunteer regiments in order to avoid fighting against other members of their families on opposite sides in the Civil War. Pennock, p. 6.

2. The community of Rock Creek, near present day Rock River, Wyoming, became a booming business center boasting four saloons, a large hotel, and a blacksmith's shop. Gilbert, p. 20; Ricker, "Baptiste Pourier," tablet 15, p. 101; McDermott, "John Baptiste Richard" in *Mountain Men*, 2:302; Vaughn, p. 72; Murray, Robert A., p. 22–23; Bartlett, vol. III, p. 140.

3. McDermott, "Joseph Bissonette" in *Mountain Men*, 4:58; Pennock, p. 7–8.

4. Pennock, p. 9–15.

5. Pennock, p. 15–16.

6. It appears that McKnight, Pourier, and Louis Richard took the route from Rock Creek across the Laramie Mountain Range to the North Platte that later would become the Laramie–Fetterman road. They arrived in Virginia City, Montana thirty-five days after their departure from Rock Creek. Hila Gilbert stated in *"Big Bat" Pourier* that McKnight's train again crossed the Bridger Trail and that although the Bozeman Trail was becoming much more popular that Baptiste Pourier never took that route until 1867. It seems unlikely that this was the case. No wagon trains were recorded crossing the Bridger Trail in 1865 and no emigrant wagon trains crossed the Bozeman Trail that year. If this wagon train had crossed by the Bridger Trail they would have crossed the North Platte right in the middle of the Battle of Platte Bridge and the Battle of Red Buttes. Gilbert, p. 20–21; Lowe, p. 213; Ricker, "Baptiste Pourier," tablet 15, p. 101–102; Vaughn, p. 72.

7. Lieutenant Caspar W. Collins for whom the Post at Platte Bridge was later renamed Fort Casper. In 1936, the spelling was corrected to Fort Caspar.

8. Shoshone Indian scouts. The Shoshone tribe was often referred to as the Snakes, due to their living in the vicinity of the Snake River. The two scouts sent to Deer Creek were the mixed blood sons of Antoine Lajeunesse, Mitchell and Noel. They were paid one hundred and fifty dollars each to deliver the dispatch. Bryans, p. 137–138.

9. At this point it appears that Jake Pennock was updating his diary hourly. Presumably expecting to be massacred, he wished the details of the battle to be recorded for some future search party to discover.

10. The second group of Indians referred to were evidently Shoshone scouts who had talked to some of the hostile Indians.

11. Here Pennock's diary is confusing. They had either found a note with a message left for them among the bodies from the previous day's battle or captured a prisoner who gave them this story. Pennock's wording is difficult to decipher, but the earlier seems to be the case. Who wrote this note is more difficult to determine. Previous entries suggest that there were several white renegades among this group of Indians. It is possible that one of them left the note or perhaps an Indian who had learned to read and write penned it. Many "white

renegades" lived with tribes during this era. Some of these men have been identified, but many more never will be. The Civil War had ended just three months prior to this event. Many of the more radical Confederates refused to accept Lee's surrender. The stories of several bands of western outlaws begin from these roots. Some Confederates joined bands of hostile Indians, particularly the Comanche, in order to continue doing battle against American troops. Comanches were involved in the previous day's battle and that might suggest that the white renegades had come north with them. This theory is, of course, speculation, but worthy of consideration.

12. This version of the story of the Battle of Platte Bridge and the Battle of Red Buttes was chosen by the author because of its feel for the action of the battle as it progressed. Entire volumes have been written on the subject by scholars who have studied the incidents in great detail. The occurrence of these battles is significant to the story at hand. For the purpose of this book, it was not felt necessary to delve deeper into this subject. Pennock, p. 18–23.

13. Mike McKenzie and Nelson Story were partners of John Richard Jr. in several Montana ventures.

14. This incident involved a unique set of circumstances. The Musselshell River is far from what would be considered the normal realm of the Sioux so it is possible, if not likely, that this wandering war party was some of the group that had headed north following the Battle of Platte Bridge. Their attack on the Crows is not so unusual as these two tribes had been in conflict for generations. The fact that John Richard Jr. and Louis Richard were both a quarter Sioux and possibly acquainted with the very men who attacked them is once again a unique event. Obviously the Richard brothers were not willing to stick around and try to explain that they were friendly toward the Sioux while they had just been caught trading with enemies of their own tribe. Ricker, "Baptiste Pourier," tablet 15, p. 102–104.

15. Who was responsible for instigating the destruction of Richard's Bridge may never be known. The fact that Louis Guinard had developed a relationship with the command of Fort Casper tends to create the suspicion that he may have planted the seed of the idea that grew into the elimination of his competition for tolls on the Platte. Camp Dodge was located on the upper east side of what is now called Garden Creek. Cronin, Vaughn Stephen, *Casper Mountain: The Magic Yesterday and Today*, (Vaughn's Publishing, Casper, Wyoming, 1998) p. 33–35; Murray, Robert A., p. 23–24.

16. Spring, p. 24–25.

17. RG92 cited by Murray, Robert A., p. 24.

18. Cited by McDermott, *Frontier Crossroads*, p. 89.

19. Captain Henry E. Palmer had been the quartermaster and helped to organize General Connor's Powder River Expedition. After being mustered out of the

Army in 1865, he outfitted himself for a trading expedition into that area. Gilbert, p. 24.

20. Jones, Brian, p. 18–19; Gilbert, p. 24.

21. Gilbert, p. 21; Lowe, p.176–179; Doyle, p. 10; Ricker, "Baptiste Pourier," tablet 15, p. 107–108.

22. Bryans, p. 139; Doyle, p. 10; Jones, Brian, p. 19.

23. John Richard Jr. raised the potatoes on his farm at Bozeman that the partnership hauled to the fort. "John Jr. had already observed that you could grow small crops in this country and that there would be a high priced market for them at the mining town. Later, the soldiers at Fort C.F. Smith were glad that he had settled there." Gilbert, p. 19.

24. Ricker, "Baptiste Pourier," tablet 15, p. 104–106.

25. Bartlett, vol. III, p. 140.

26. Bartlett, vol. III, p. 140–141; McDermott, "Joseph Bissonette" in *Mountain Men*, 4:58; Jones, Brian, p. 20.

27. This is the same A.C. Leighton who purchased the ferry on the Big Horn River from the Richard brothers, Pourier, Bouyer, and Wahn. He was also the post sutler of the fort. Gilbert, p. 25–26.

28. Gilbert, p. 24; Ricker, "Baptiste Pourier," tablet 15, p. 109–114; Humphreys, A. Glen, "The Crow Indian Treaties of 1868: An Example of Power Struggle and Confusion in United States Indian Policy" *Annals of Wyoming*, (Spring 1971) vol. 43, no. 1, p. 75–76.

29. It is possible that this Peter Richard was the eighteen-year-old son of Joseph Richard. It is far more likely, however, that he was Joseph's forty-eight-year-old uncle. Jones, Brian, p. 20.

30. Johnson, p. 316–318; Peter and Charles Janis were sons of Antoine Janis III, brother of "Old Nick" Janis. Jones, Brian, p. 20–22; Ricker, "Baptiste Pourier," tablet 15, p. 113–118.

31. Bartlett, vol. III, p. 141; Jones, Brian, "John Richard Jr. and the Killing at Fetterman," *Annals of Wyoming*, (Fall 1971), vol. 43, no. 2, p. 239; Jones, Brian, *Those Wild Reshaw Boys*, p. 21–22.

32. Red Dog had chosen to accept the Treaty of 1868 and live on the reservation, but Red Cloud, Spotted Tail, and many others were still "at large." Ricker, "Baptiste Pourier," tablet 15, p. 122; Jones, Brian, "John Richard, Jr.," p. 239–240.

II

⤙THE OLDEST SON⤚

JOHN RICHARD Jr. had learned his lessons well from his father. Diversification had definitely been his father's key to success. From Indian trader to emigrant trader, from bridge builder to Denver merchant, from woodcutter to rancher, from whiskey smuggler to saloonkeeper, from farmer to hay contractor, all of his father's enterprises had proven to be at least sometimes successful. John Jr. had proven his finesse in dealing with both the military and Indians, although he'd occasionally had trouble with both. With only a year or two of formal education, he displayed the wit and wile needed to succeed on the western frontier and become a prominent businessman. From his years of working alongside his father he was well known and often well liked by his associates and customers. He suffered however, three weaknesses of character: women, whiskey, and a bizarre disregard for human life.

In April 1869, John Richard Jr. received a bank draft for $3000 from W. S. McKenzie, as his share of the profits from the sale of the goods salvaged from Fort C. F. Smith.

That same month William G. Bullock, Richard's accountant, who also worked as a representative of Robert Campbell & Co., straddled the fence. While drawing wages from Richard for his bookkeeping duties, he also wrote his other employer complaining that Richard had gained a monopoly on Indian trade north of the river. He stated that if Campbell was unable to attain a similar license for himself, he should do whatever was in his power to have Richard's trade license revoked. Bullock's request was granted, not by his employer obtaining a license, but by the cancellation of Richard's. John Richard Jr. again contacted attorney John B. Sanborn in Washington, D.C., to appeal this cancellation. He stated that he had not violated his trade agreement and that he had already purchased $10,000 in merchandise to trade with the Indians. "If I had don eanything out of the way I would not blame him for stoping me but I

General Crook's tent camp on the north side of the North Platte River in 1876. Fort Fetterman is on the bluff above the river. (*From sketches by the officers in the field, the Sioux Campaign.* Harper's Weekly, *July 22, 1876*)

have not give any cause and live up to the Law."[1]

While waiting for a response from the slow moving politicians in the east, John Richard Jr. went to Fort Fetterman to stir up some business. In May or June a large quantity of whiskey was flowing among the soldiers at Fort Fetterman. Colonel William McEntire Dye, commander of the fort, confronted John Richard Jr. about this. He asked Richard if he knew who had brought whiskey into the fort the previous day. Richard told Dye that he had seen four men on the road who had forty gallons of whiskey. He described the men to the colonel. Two of the men were arrested, and the whiskey was destroyed. Corporal Frances Conrad of Company E, 4th Infantry and several of his cronies were sufficiently aggravated with Richard's squealing on their source that they threatened to kill him as soon as Dye was relieved of his command. There were several witnesses to Conrad's threats including two employees of the post traders: clerk George Lake and bookkeeper Thomas Jefferson "T. Jeff" Carr. John Hunton and Frank Yates also heard the threats. Yates, who

was well acquainted with Conrad, warned Richard to take heed and consider the man very dangerous.[2]

During the summer, post traders Wilson and Cobb obtained the contract to supply hay and firewood for the fort and subcontracted it to John Richard Jr. and Hi Kelly. Hi Kelly was in charge of the wood-cutting portion of the contract, while John Jr. was in charge of the hay. Baptiste Pourier was hired to run the mule teams for the hay cutting crew at Deer Creek. John Jr. also had a freighting contract, hauling supplies to the posts along the Sweetwater, and Bat also worked as a teamster for Richard and Kelly that summer. John Richard Sr., too, was living in the camp near Fort Fetterman, presumably acting as camp guard and doing some trading with the roaming bands of Indians. Late that summer Baptiste Pourier took a leave of absence from his duties as a teamster to deliver the ballots from the Territorial Election at Fort Fetterman to Fort Laramie.[3]

That September, John Richard Jr. and Corporal Conrad had a second altercation at one of the establishments of dubious reputation located near Fort Fetterman, most likely Texas cowboy Harry Cain's One-Mile Hog Ranch. Richard was evidently sharing company with a "loose woman" when Corporal Conrad burst in and ordered him to leave. Unarmed and

Some historians believe this Alexander Gardner photograph, taken in 1868 in Fort Laramie, shows John Richard, Jr, on the far left. He sometimes worked as an interpreter and scout for the military. Others in the photograph are staff member of the peace commission. *(Minnesota Historical Society)*

caught in a rather compromising position, Richard begrudgingly complied. The corporal was smitten with the woman involved and was extremely jealous of her gentlemen visitors, plus he held a grudge against Richard. As Conrad forced him at gunpoint to exit the establishment, Richard vowed that he would get even for this embarrassment.[4]

In the early hours of September 9, a band of renegade Indians attacked the Richard camp and ran off much of the livestock. When this incident occurred, most of the men had already left to harvest firewood or hay for the day. John Richard Sr., his wife and daughters, and Hi Kelly's wife Lizzie were the only ones still in camp. John Richard Sr. eventually made his way to the fort, about three miles away, and requested assistance. No cavalry troops were then stationed at Fort Fetterman, so Captain Henry W. Patterson, who had taken over the command from Colonel Dye, sent 1st Lieutenant Breslin with thirty-five men to protect the camp and move it to a safer position closer to the fort. Corporal Conrad was likely among these troops that were sent to the Richard's camp. The soldiers terrified the women. During the moving of the camp, one of the wagons belonging to John Richard Jr. was overturned and much of the trade goods within were damaged or lost. As the soldiers made a half-hearted effort to reload the wagon, they stole whatever fit their fancy.[5]

When John Richard Jr. and the rest of the men returned to camp they found their belongings disheveled, destroyed, or stolen, and the women still dreadfully frightened. John Richard Jr. flew into a fiery rage. Hi Kelly, John Sr., and Baptiste Pourier managed to cool some of John Jr.'s temper, but not his vengeful anger. After a time John Richard Jr. went to Fort Fetterman. Before leaving for the fort he confronted Bat and told him not to interfere with him that day. Bat protested and John Jr. yelled, "You're not going to stop me this time!"[6]

Bat eventually lost the argument and gave his word that, come what may, he would stay out of the incident. While John headed to the fort, Bat followed with a load of hay to deliver. He wanted to get to the fort before John got himself into any kind of trouble. Bat suspected that Richard would confront the corporal and start a fight, landing himself in the guardhouse. To his surprise John met him near the blacksmith's shop at the fort proudly showing off a fine bay horse that he had just purchased from Speed Stagner for $150. To Pourier all seemed well, and he breathed a sigh of relief and went to unload his hay as Richard departed the post.[7]

Richard had noticed Conrad closely watching him from the porch of the sutler's store. Upon returning to his camp, Richard was warned by Thomas Reed that Conrad had been hanging around the sutler's store waiting for the opportunity to carry out his threat. Richard mounted his horse and returned to the post. T. Jeff Carr recalled, "Reshaw rode into Fort Fetterman singing the Indian death song. He rode up to the sutler's store and began firing his Winchester. Corporal Conrad was killed and several others narrowly escaped injury from the drunken Reshaw." Hearing the report from the rifle, Carr dashed from the store and wrenched it from Richard's hands. He also attempted to take his pistols, but Richard managed to escape. Baptiste Pourier was still unloading his hay when he heard the report of a rifle and turned to see John Richard Jr. casually leaving the post on his newly acquired mount. John Jr. had ridden up to the sutler's store where Conrad was lounging on the porch. Without speaking a word, he raised his Winchester and shot the man through. Corporal Conrad lingered until the following day before dying from his wounds. The result was as cold-blooded a murder as ever has been executed.[8]

Richard later claimed that he believed the corporal "was a desperado" intent on killing him at the first provocation or from ambush. Thus John Richard Jr. claimed that he had acted in self-defense and under mortal fear for his life. Amid the turmoil at the store, Pourier unloaded his hay as quickly as possible and returned to camp to report to the Richard family. Over an hour had passed since the shooting by the time Big Bat arrived back at the camp. To his surprise John Jr. was there calmly eating a meal. His horse was standing nearby carrying a few belongings. There had not yet been any attempt to arrest him. Pourier stood there in disbelief as Richard finished eating and came over to bid him farewell. He asked Pourier to help his mother keep an eye on his son and then rode off, headed for Red Cloud's village on Powder River. John Richard Jr. left behind all of his trade goods and some two thousand dollars in cash he had hidden in his trunk. These were soon to be confiscated by the military that arrived moments after his departure.[9]

Following Richard's flight to the north, Captain Patterson also confiscated Richard's freight wagons and livestock that were en route to the Sweetwater River country. Although it is recorded that these items were confiscated, there seems to be no record of their fate. It can only be assumed that some corrupt sutler, quartermaster, and or military officer disposed of his equipment and goods for personal gain. It also appears that little effort was made to pursue or capture Richard. A few days following the incident Captain Patterson did, however, issue a description and information regarding Richard in two separate reports: (1)"Richard is a very dangerous and smart man, if he has gone to join the Indians he will make a great deal of trouble." (2)"Richard is well known throughout all this country.... He is about twenty-five years of age, five feet eight or ten inches high, a dark moustache, slight figure, of good appearance and address, speaks English well."[10]

Hiram Kelly was obligated to fulfill the remainder of the hay contract at Fort Fetterman. After the dust settled, little time remained to meet this obligation, so Kelly traveled to Omaha to petition to be released from the hay cutting portion of the contract. The Army needed the hay and refused Kelly's request. In December, he was forced to purchase a hundred tons of hay from the Cache la Poudre valley in Colorado at $20 per ton. He spent the entire winter transporting it the two hundred miles to Fort Fetterman. He ended up losing over $5000 on the venture, a fact that did not endear him to the younger John Richard.

Following the events at Fort Fetterman, the Richard family returned to the ranch on Richeau Creek. In the fall of 1869, John Richard Sr. and his family, Hi Kelly, Baptiste Pourier, Joseph Hornback, Antoine Reynal and his family, and an old Mexican and his family all were residing on Richeau Creek. On October 10, Baptiste Pourier and Josephine Richard, and Louis Richard and Jennie Reynal all went to Fort Laramie. Frank Yates, who had become the trader and justice of the peace for the fort, married the two couples in a double wedding ceremony. There must have been something in the air that fall because about that same time Baptiste Garnier and Julia Mosseau were also married by a justice of the peace in Cheyenne.[11]

By December T. Jeff Carr had grown tired of life at Fort Fetterman and after quitting his job with Wilson & Cobb, he joined a company of freighters headed for Cheyenne. Among this company were Antoine Reynal and Magloire Mosseau. By this time John Richard Jr. had led a band of renegade Sioux in several attacks against the whites along the North Platte River. The freighters were unaware that their company had been selected as one of this band's targets. One night, while camped somewhere between La Bonte and Cottonwood Creeks, they were enjoying a meal of *buoyli,* a French soup that Reynal had made, when someone mentioned that they made easy targets of themselves by sitting so close to the fire. While this man spoke, Richard and his renegades had surrounded them and were quietly preparing to attack. In the light of the fire John Richard Jr. recognized Mosseau, Reynal, Carr, and several others. Richard called off the attack, telling the band that he knew many of these men, some were his friends, and most had been friendly toward him. The freighters continued their journey little aware how close to death they had come.[12]

Louis Richard and W. G. Bullock in the meantime were handling John Richard Jr.'s business affairs. The Fort Laramie Treaty of 1868 had put an end to the Bozeman Trail and the military posts along that route. It had also established the first of several Indian reservations or "agencies" as they then were called. However, several powerful chiefs had not signed or attended that conference, and the government was still intent on coming to an agreement with them, hoping to end the depredations in the territory. When Red Cloud and John Richard Jr. visited family on Richeau Creek that winter, W. G. Bullock was summoned to meet with them there. The particulars of this meeting are not known. In attendance were Red Cloud, John Richard Jr., John Richard Sr., Nick Janis, and W.G. Bullock. Here at this secret meeting on Richeau Creek a plan was hatched for one of the most important conferences to ever take place regarding United States Indian policy.

In exchange for a presidential pardon for the murder of Corporal Conrad, John Richard Jr. would amass the most influential chiefs who had not signed the Treaty of 1868, to form a delegation to visit President Grant in Washington. John B. Sanborn would be called upon again to start turning the wheels in Washington while Bullock would use his influence with Brevet Major General John E. Smith, the commander of Fort Laramie, to make the necessary arrangements.

On May 26, 1870, the delegation departed from Fort Laramie. Among the twenty-one people in this entourage were Red Cloud, Red Dog, Sword, Rocky Bear, Yellow Bear, Black Hawk, Red Shirt, Face, Standing Bear, General Smith, W. G. Bullock, and Jules Ecoffey. John Richard Jr. and James McClosky went as interpreters. Red Dog had wanted Leon Pallardie as interpreter instead of Richard, but Red Cloud overruled his choice.[13] Four Indian women also accompanied the delegation, possibly including Josephine (Richard) Pourier. According to Josephine, Red Dog was the first to speak to President Grant and said: "Your people are coming into my country and overrunning it, unsettling everything; doing as they please with everybody, taking a man here and a man there and doing just as they want with him; now here is a young man [John Richard Jr.], and I have brought him to you to do with just as you will; he got into some trouble with one of your men and killed him; now here he is and what will you do with him; will you cook him and eat him?"

To this President Grant told Red Dog to take Richard back with him and to "use [Richard's] abilities to attain to higher conditions." The pardoning of John Richard Jr. was a side issue to the delegation's conference.

President Grant wanted to set new policy regarding the Native Americans, and the main objective of this conference was to establish rapport with the chiefs. The pardon had been promised if Richard could convince them to come and was granted on the stipulation that he use his influence with the chiefs to help establish the agencies that would be necessary to maintain peace, as the government saw it, with the Indians.[14]

❖ ❖

That same spring, Big Bat Pourier hired on with the military as a scout and interpreter at $100 per month. This assignment was rather short lived, but Bat served similar capacities for the army over the next several years.[15]

Upon his return to Fort Laramie, the newly pardoned John Richard Jr. became a partner in the Six-Mile Hog Ranch belonging to Jules Ecoffey and Adolph Cuney, more commonly known as "Coffee & Cooney." This duo was of notorious reputation, but John Richard Jr. displayed no indication of following President Grant's request of "attaining higher conditions." At the same time it is easy to see the advantage Cuney and Ecoffey gained by bringing Richard into their business. Richard had a relationship of significant scale with nearly every band of the Sioux. Trade with the tribes had thus far been a miniscule portion of their business, and Richard had both the ability and contacts to vastly improve their profits.

By July 1870, the Union Pacific Railroad had reached Cheyenne. Hiram Kelly sold all of his draft cattle to a stock buyer named Prichard for $75 per head there. Prichard in turn sold them for $150 per head and shipped them to Paris to provide beef for the ongoing Franco-Prussian War. This was the first herd of cattle ever shipped by rail from Wyoming.[16]

❖ ❖

In August 1870, many members of the Richard family were again at Fort Fetterman. John Richard Jr. and his brother Louis had a trading camp near the post and were accompanied by their wives, Hubalola, Mary Louisa, and Jennie.[17] John Jr.'s personal property was valued at $6000 there. It had evidently been a very good season. He gave the actual fort and soldiers a wide berth. He did not wish to meet any of Corporal Conrad's friends who might desire to avenge his death.

Not far away was the trading camp of Louis Richard's father-in-law, Antoine Reynal. John's former wife, Louise (Merivale) and their two-year-old daughter, Milla, also lived at the fort with her parents, Joseph and

Mary Merivale. Joseph Merivale was employed by the military as a guide and interpreter. Speed Stagner worked there as a teamster. The sons of Joseph Richard, James and Joe Jr., worked for the hay contractor, as well as Joe Hornback from Richeau Creek, and Peter Janis. Joseph Richard Sr.'s widowed wife, Kane, and their two daughters were also living there.[18]

John Richard Sr. along with his son Peter and daughter Rosa remained in the Fort Laramie area as well as Baptiste Pourier and Josephine Richard Pourier. It is mysterious that John's wife, Mary, does not appear anywhere on the census of 1870 as it is known that she was still living at that time. Magloire Mosseau and his family were also in the Fort Laramie area, trading with the local Indians. James McClosky was employed by the military at Fort Laramie, and Gibson and Hopkins Clark were both clerks in the sutler's store.[19]

By the fall of 1870, Hiram and Lizzie Kelly had become well established on their ranch on Chugwater Creek, bringing in two hundred head of two-year-old heifers from Texas that year. John "Portugee" Phillips's holdings were also growing in the Chugwater valley, but Kelly did not feel he was as serious a competitor in the cattle business as William G. Bullock and his partner, Mills. Kelly, however, beat all competitors in obtaining the beef contracts for Fort Laramie in both 1871 and 1872.[20]

⟨⟩⟨⟩

John Richard Jr. soon returned to Fort Laramie. The Six-Mile Hog Ranch was a raucous establishment. John Richard Jr.'s presence there may have also brought additional business to the saloon and "dance-hall." His friends could stop by to speak to Richard and have an excuse to imbibe in the offerings. One night near the end of October, the Six-Mile Hog Ranch was the scene of a murder that later resulted in the first legal hanging in the Wyoming Territory. John Bouyer, the half-brother of John Richard Jr.'s former partner Mitch Bouyer, arrived at his home near Fort Laramie to find his widowed mother and sister bound and gagged. William Lowry and James McClosky, who had recently arrived from Fort Fetterman, had raped them.

The following night the twenty-six-year-old John Bouyer went to a dance at the hog ranch. For safety, the bartender checked the guns of all patrons as they entered. A short time later McClosky and Lowry joined the party. At about two o'clock the following morning, Bouyer retrieved his pistols from the bartender and left. After mounting up, he rode back to the door of the saloon and called McClosky and Lowry out, saying "he could whip them both." When the two men filled the door, Bouyer fatally shot them, Lowry in the chest and McClosky in the belly. He then fled to a nearby Sioux village. John Bouyer was eventually apprehended and taken to Fort D. A. Russell near Cheyenne for trial. He soon escaped imprisonment, but was again captured. On April 21, 1871, he paid for his crime, though possibly justifiable, when he swung from the gallows in Cheyenne.[21]

⋙ ⋘

In June, Red Cloud and several other chiefs were summoned to Fort Laramie to discuss the establishment of a new agency. Louis Richard and Joseph Bissonette were the interpreters for this meeting. Red Cloud insisted that the new agency be located north of the North Platte River. A spot was eventually agreed upon about a mile west of the Nebraska/Wyoming border. As part of the agreement, the Indians were given the right to choose whom they wished as traders for the new agency. In July 1871, Red Cloud Agency was formed and W. G. Bullock, John Richard Jr., and Jules Ecoffey were selected as their traders. Richard erected a trading post and a sod storehouse there, which he operated under the name of "Richard & Company." John Jr.'s brother Peter and their cousin Charles both worked as laborers for the agency. Also about this time, John Richard Jr. seems to have married Emily Janis, the daughter of Nick Janis, a long time friend and associate of the Richard family.[22]

⋙ ⋘

Early in 1872 the partnership of Cuney, Ecoffey, and, presumably Richard, built a new road ranch three-and-a-half miles southwest of Fort Laramie along the Laramie River. This new establishment, just off of the Fort Laramie military reservation, was soon known as the Three-Mile Ranch. The initial building was about fifty feet square and constructed of hewn-logs. The new road ranch began as a legitimate trading post, saloon, and hotel. After a poor start in its first season, however, the owners imported some young feminine help from Omaha and Kansas City to attract more business from the soldiers. It was not long before the fort declared the establishment off-limits, and the Three-Mile Hog Ranch was born.[23]

At the trading post at Red Cloud Agency, John Richard Jr. hired a young clerk named Hopkins Clark. Clark took care of the business end of running the trading post while Richard contracted to build a corral and derrick for slaughtering beef. In addition to the goods sold through the trading post, Richard also contracted to supply both hay and firewood. By March 1872, the Indians were getting bored with life at the agency and tensions were mounting daily. The threat of violence had escalated to the point that Richard and his men at Red Cloud Agency were beginning to fear that an uprising was imminent. Knowing that his few men would not be able to hold off an attack, Richard had Clark write to Jules Ecoffey to request military protection from General Smith at Fort Laramie. In the letter, Hopkins Clark told Ecoffey that among other ensuing problems the entire herd of livestock belonging to Joe Richard Jr. and Frank Salaway had been stolen.

The requested protection was slow to arrive, but a herd of beef cattle arrived in April to supply the Indians with food. Several herders came into Richard's store to relax when their work was done. One man left his loaded, cocked rifle on the counter. Richard remarked, "These boys will never learn to be careful with their guns," as he picked up the rifle, intending to unload it. Instead he accidentally fired it. The bullet passed through the coat of Louis Richard, who was standing nearby, and struck Hopkins Clark in the chest, killing him instantly. The report from the rifle drew immediate attention. When the Indians heard that Clark, who was well liked, was dead, they wanted revenge. Had it not been for Louis Richard keeping a cool head and showing the bullet-hole in his coat as he explained that it had been an accident, John Richard Jr., as well as others, might have been killed in the aftermath.[24]

A few weeks later an officer at Fort Laramie told John Richard Jr. to lay low for awhile. Troops from Fort Fetterman would soon be arriving and many friends of Corporal Conrad were among them. Taking his advice, on the afternoon of May 17, 1872, John Richard Jr., Billy Garnett, Louis Shangrau, and Peter Janis, a cousin of John Richard Jr.'s new wife, left Fort Laramie for the Red Cloud Agency, some twenty-five miles downriver from the fort. They planned to gather the eighty horses that were kept there and move them to new grazing. Seventeen-year-old Billy Garnett had previously been employed by Big Bat Pourier, who was then living three miles up the Laramie River with his wife. But most recently, Garnett had gone to work for John Jr.'s partners, Jules Ecoffey and Adolph Cuney, at the Three-Mile Hog Ranch. All of the men carried pistols, but Richard and Shangrau stopped at the Six-Mile Ranch and picked up their rifles also. They crossed the North Platte River on a skiff, and then told Billy Garnett to take the two horses and buggy that awaited them to Yellow Bear's camp, about four miles upstream from the Red Cloud Agency while the rest of the men floated down the river on the skiff.

When Garnett met the men downriver, John Richard Jr. was noticeably drunk and the case of whiskey that had been in the skiff upon their departure was now gone. John Jr., while staggering about, announced that he was going to Yellow Bear's lodge and collect Yellow Bear's daughter, the woman Richard once married as a teenager but had abandoned. Peter Janis goaded him on, saying that she would make good company for him while they herded the horses. Billy Garnett tried to reason with Richard saying that he had a fine wife in Emily (Janis), and that he should not dishonor her by being with another woman. Peter Janis interceded and ordered Garnett back to the buggy to care for the horses.[25]

Richard, Shangrau, and Janis proceeded to Yellow Bear's lodge, and Garnett laid back and followed with the buggy. As Billy neared the lodge, he saw the trio enter, Richard and Shangrau carrying their rifles. A number of Yellow Bear's band followed them into the lodge until it was too crowded for more to enter. A few minutes later Janis came out of the lodge and told Garnett that it looked like there was going to be trouble and for him to go inside. Garnett argued, saying the whole idea of Richard coming to get the girl had been Janis's and that he wanted nothing to do with it. Janis became belligerent and ordered young Billy into the lodge, while he stayed with the team.

When Billy entered the lodge it was packed with Indians. Richard sat cross-legged on the ground, holding his rifle and bragging of his exploits while living with Red Cloud's warriors on Powder River. Suddenly he turned to Yellow Bear and said he was there to collect his daughter. The chief replied that was not a problem except that she was at a dance at the agency. Several of the Indians confirmed this by stating that they had just returned from the dance and had seen her there. Richard did not believe them. He thought Yellow Bear was hiding her. The chief patiently repeated that the girl was not there, but Richard became angry and began toying with his rifle. Richard taunted Yellow Bear's mild and peaceful ways. He said that he had given the chief horses for the young woman and now he would kill them. Yellow Bear told Skinny White Man that if he wished to destroy the horses which he had once proudly owned, then he should do it.

Billy Garnett looked for a path of escape. Richard cocked his rifle, but the chief did not move toward the nearby gun. John Jr. then stood up as if to leave the lodge. As he neared the door, he turned and shot Yellow Bear. The Indians quickly reacted. Richard dropped his rifle and drew a pistol, but they clinched him as he fired and the shots went into the air. Several Indians stabbed him, and then one came up behind and shot Richard in the head.

Billy Garnett and Louis Shangrau were carried out of the lodge in the frenzy and fought for their lives. Peter Janis and the horses were nowhere to be seen. Shangrau knocked down an Indian trying to stab Garnett. Another Indian grabbed Shangrau's rifle and tried to wrench it from his grasp. Garnett told the Indian to let go; they did not want to hurt anyone, just to get away. The Indian let go, but as soon as he was safely out of the line of fire, the rest of the Indians opened up on them. The two men were showered by bullets as they ran for cover in the moonlight, but amazingly they were not hit. The Indians mounted up and searched for them, but under the cover of darkness, the traders were able to hide in the brush as groups of the horsemen passed. The white men worked their way toward the agency.

When Garnett and Shangrau arrived at the Red Cloud Agency the next morning, Peter Janis was already there. He had fled the encampment as soon as the first shot was fired. Billy Garnett was exhausted and fell into a deep sleep. In what he said seemed like only moments later, Baptiste Pourier roused him. Bat wept at the loss of his best friend and brother-in-law as Garnett recounted the events of the preceding day. When Emily Richard heard of the death of her husband she went to Yellow Bear's camp to retrieve his remains. There she found Richard's body lying in front of the lodge. The Indians had riddled his body with bullets before fleeing to the north, also leaving behind their unburied chief. She dragged Yellow Bear's body from the lodge and after shooting it, set it on fire.[26]

John Richard Jr., a member of the freemasons was buried in a masonic ceremony in the post cemetery at Fort Laramie. Following the death of John Richard Jr., Louis Richard moved from Red Cloud Agency back to Fort Laramie. Ecoffey and Cuney presumably took over their partner's operation at the agency.

⊰⊱·⊰⊱

During this time Henry Vandever Branham came to Fort Laramie to work for John Richard Sr., his uncle. Henry Branham was the youngest son of Charles B. Branham, John Richard's old partner at Fort Bernard, and Mary Elizabeth Richard, who had died when Henry was a young child. For the past several years he had lived with another aunt and uncle in Rulo, Nebraska, and now as a young man ventured further west to work in Richard's general store and trading post near the fort .[27]

The exact location of this latest trading post of John Richard's is unknown. It appears however that he had left Richeau Creek by this time. When surveyors arrived in July to plat the townships along Richeau Creek, they made no mention of any occupied dwellings in the area. It is known that a few years earlier the Richards lost numerous horses to raiding parties of Sioux and Cheyenne Indians, so it must be assumed that Richard had given up on ranching along Richeau Creek and reestablished himself as a trader in the Fort Laramie area.[28]

⊰⊱·⊰⊱

John Richard Jr. may have been dead, but the consequences had yet to come to a conclusion. The disrespect Peter Janis had shown toward John Jr. during the Yellow Bear incident would soon to be avenged by Richard's cousins. In the fall of 1872, Nick Janis had secured the firewood contract for Red Cloud Agency. His woodcutting camp was on Kiowa Creek, about twenty miles southeast of the agency. William and Peter Janis were staying with their cousin Emily Richard, the recent widow of John Richard Jr., at Red Cloud Agency. On December 20, they left with Swift Bear to visit their Uncle Nick's camp. Working at Nick's camp were Joseph Richard Jr., William Sullivan, William Dillon, James and Charles Richard, Paddy Miller, Nick's daughter Fillie Janis, and the Richard boys' widowed mother, Kane. These cousins of John Richard Jr. had said openly that John Jr. had been duped by Peter Janis into the situation that had cost him his life, and then Janis had fled the fight and left his companions to suffer the consequences. Emily Richard tried to stop her Janis cousins from going to the wood camp, warning them that there would be trouble.

On the afternoon of Christmas Day, Joseph Richard Jr. approached Peter Janis and William Sullivan, who had just finished loading a wagon with wood. Joseph invited them to his mother's lodge for a drink. When the two men entered the lodge, Kane Richard asked them to remove their guns, as whiskey and firearms did not mix. Looking around, Peter Janis saw that all of the other men were unarmed so obliged the lady by handing her his gunbelt containing its two pearl-handled six-shooters. After having his customary one drink, William Sullivan went outside. About four o'clock, Peter Janis emerged from the lodge saying that he was going to fight William Dillon. Janis was still unarmed, so Sullivan who was outside expected to see Dillon emerge and the two engage in a rough and tumble bout in the camp yard.

To Sullivan's surprise Joe Richard emerged just behind Janis carrying a pistol in each hand and immediately began shooting. Pete Janis, nearly twice Richard's size, wounded, and without a gun, clinched with Richard. William Janis then joined the fracas by trying to get the guns away from Richard. At this point James and Charles Richard both fired at William Janis hitting him in his back and in his head. Amidst Richard and Janis scuffling on the ground, Paddy Miller then opened fire on Peter Janis.

The two Janis boys lay on the ground either dead or dying. James Richard put another bullet into each of them. Fillie Janis tried to stop James Richard, but Charles Richard knocked her out cold with the butt of his pistol. The whole incident lasted only a few seconds and left Peter and William Janis both dead. It appears that the incident had been planned to kill Peter Janis in revenge for John Jr.'s death, including Kane Richard's ruse of disarming Peter Janis. Peter Janis was both young, tough, and considerably larger than any one of the Richards, but more importantly, he was deadly with the twin pistols that he so proudly carried.

Following their killing of the Janis brothers, the three Richards along with Paddy Miller disappeared into the Indian camps. Three days later a crippled mixed-blood Indian known only as Baptiste arrived at Emily Richard's with the bodies of her two Janis cousins. She asked him a dozen questions about the fight, but he refused to answer. At this point, she pulled her own gun and killed him.

The bodies of the Janis brothers were placed on scaffoldings at Red Cloud Agency and buried in "Indian fashion." Later Antoine Janis came and collected his sons' remains. They were then taken to Fort Laramie and buried in the post cemetery. No charges were filed as a result of the killings of the Janis brothers or Baptiste, the man who delivered the bodies. The *Cheyenne Daily Leader* condensed the general feeling of whites two weeks later: "No regret at the fatal result of these Indian amusements is felt in this community. On the contrary, our people are disposed to consider these brawls, blessings in disguise, as they free us from a set of hangers on to the Indian reservations, who are and have been the cause of our Indian difficulties. We do not object to their continuing this pastime, and are satisfied to leave the half-breeds among the full-breeds, as an element of discord, disseminating feuds among their brethren, the Indians. With the half-breeds among the Sioux and the epizootic among the Indian ponies, the white man is content to abide the result."[29]

The episode was only one of the brutal murders around Fort Laramie which Magloire Mosseau, a contemporary of Richard, summed up in an interview in 1906: *"The misery and mystery which would be revealed if only the ground around Fort Laramie could speak would be a shocking recital. The murders and other crimes were numerous and unexplained."* [30]

Notes to Chapter Eleven:

1. Jones, Brian, "John Richard, Jr.," p. 238–239, 241.

2. Affidavit of John Richard Jr., Washington, D. C., June 4, 1870, Case File No. C–274. Cited by Jones in "John Richard, Jr.," p. 251–252; Census of Fort Fetterman, Albany County, Wyoming Territory, August, 1870.

3. Ricker, "Baptiste Pourier," tablet 15, p. 118; Coutant, C.G., "Thomas Jefferson Carr, A Frontier Sheriff," *Annals of Wyoming*, (July 1948), vol. 20, p. 165; Jones, Brian, "John Richard, Jr.," p. 242; Gilbert, p. 32.

4. Brown, Larry K., *The Hog Ranches of Wyoming: Liquor, Lust, & Lies Under Sagebrush Skies*, (High Plains Press, Glendo, Wyoming, 1995), p. 28, 85–88; Frank F. Aplan reportedly stated that the "loose woman" in question was in fact John Richard Jr.'s estranged wife, Louise Merivale Richard. John Jr. was "married" several times and it is difficult to determine his marital status or to whom he may have been married at the time. Mr. Aplan's source for this information is unknown so it is consequently difficult to confirm. This information was in a letter dated January 13, 1963, from Frank Aplan to Brian Jones and cited by Jones. Jones, Brian, *Those Wild Reshaw Boys*, p. 23, 43–44; Descendants of Baptiste Pourier stated that when John Jr. arrived at the fort, he found Louise Merivale Richard living with "another man." Richard at that

point took his two-year-old son, Alfred (or Alexander), from Louise and left him to live with his grandparents. Gilbert, p. 36; Ricker, "Baptiste Pourier," tablet 15, p. 118–119.

5. Jones, Brian, "John Richard, Jr.," p. 242–243; Ricker, "Baptiste Pourier," tablet 15, p. 118–119.

6. Ricker, "Baptiste Pourier," tablet 15, p. 119–121; Gilbert, p. 30.

7. Ricker, "Baptiste Pourier," tablet 15, p. 119–121; Jones, Brian, *Those Wild Reshaw Boys*, p. 22 & 44; Gilbert, p. 30.

8. Coutant, "Thomas Jefferson Carr," p. 165; Ricker, "Baptiste Pourier," tablet 15, p. 119–121; Jones, Brian, "John Richard, Jr.," p. 245; Gilbert, p. 30.

9. There are five distinct sources for the information used in providing the details in the killing of Corporal Conrad. These are Baptiste Pourier, Thomas Jefferson Carr, John Richard Jr., the military reports, and family lore cited by Hila Gilbert. According to T. Jeff Carr, John Richard Jr. had ridden into the post with the intention of killing Joseph Merivale, who was then employed as a guide and scout by the post. Merivale had heard John Jr. was coming and had secured himself safely in his house, next door to the sutler's store. If Louise, John Richard Jr.'s estranged wife and mother of his two-year-old son, was the "loose woman" involved when Conrad backed Richard out of the hog ranch at gunpoint in his birthday suit, Merivale may have suspected that Richard intended to kill him for allowing Louise to consort with the corporal. Merivale may also have been involved in the "whiskey deal" that so enraged Corporal Conrad to begin with. Baptiste Pourier stated that "a loose woman" was involved. If he declined to name the woman as John's former wife in the interview, it may have been to protect her and her daughter from a disrespectful past. Louise Merivale Richard must have had two children with John Richard Jr.—a son born about 1867 and a daughter born about 1868 named Milla. T. Jeff Carr may not have known that Louise was Richard's former wife or consequently that Joseph Merivale was Richard's former father-in-law. Although John Richard Jr. failed to implicate a "loose woman" or Joseph Merivale, his story too bears a ring of truth. The claim that he truly felt he was acting in self-defense is highly unlikely, but his story does not vary greatly from those of the others. If Captain Patterson had just recently taken over command of the post from Colonel Dye, it is certainly possible that he was unaware of the earlier incident involving the whiskey. If Conrad was "romantically involved" with Louise Merivale Richard this undoubtedly added to the tensions between Richard and him. It is this author's belief that all five stories must be sifted and blended to reveal the truth of this tragedy. Yet many questions are left unanswered, perhaps to remain a mystery indefinitely, or perhaps awaiting a time when more information emerges. Jones, Brian, "John Richard, Jr.," p. 251–253; Ricker, "Baptiste Pourier," tablet 15, p. 119–121; Jones,

Brian, *Those Wild Reshaw Boys*, p. 22 & 44; Coutant, "Thomas Jefferson Carr," p. 165–167; Gilbert, p. 30 & 39.

10. Ricker, "Baptiste Pourier," tablet 15, p. 121; Record group 94, 98, and 393, National Archives, cited by Jones. Jones, Brian, *Those Wild Reshaw Boys*, p. 23, 43–44 and Jones, Brian, "John Richard, Jr.," p. 243.

11. Jones, Brian, "John Richard, Jr.," p. 245; Bartlett, vol. III, p. 141; Ricker, "Interview of Baptiste Pourier," p. 121–122, 125–126; Julia Mosseau was the daughter of Magloire Mosseau. Ricker, "Magloire Mosseau," tablet 28, p. 56–58; Frank Yates appeared on the 1870 census of Fort Laramie as Justice of the Peace. Census of Fort Laramie, 1870.

12. It appears that this company of freighters was hauling the hay from Colorado to Fort Fetterman for Hiram Kelly. T. Jeff Carr found out about their narrow escape a few years later. John Richard Jr. reportedly told the story from the Indians' side. It is not known if he related it directly to Carr. In this unique circumstance, the men's closeness to the campfire allowed Richard to see them well enough to identify them and consequently saved their lives. Coutant, C.G., "History of Wyoming Written By C. G. Coutant, Pioneer Historian and Heretofore Unpublished, Chapter 4 and 5," *Annals of Wyoming*, (April 1940), vol. 12, p. 149; Coutant, "Thomas Jefferson Carr," p. 167.

13. Jones, Brian, "John Richard, Jr.," p. 251; Leon Pallardie was Francois Leon Pallardie. He was born in St. Charles, Missouri, January 31, 1831. He was the son of Pierre Pallardie and Eulalie Loue Serre and either the brother or nephew of Antoine Pallardie, who was married to John Richard Sr.'s sister, Leanore. Monroe correspondence.

14. Man Afraid of his Horses had also intended to join the delegation going to Washington, but backed out at the last minute. Whether or not Josephine Pourier attended the delegation is not truly known. She may have repeated the words of Red Dog to Judge Ricker as she recalled hearing them spoken or it may have been as her brother, John Richard Jr., had told them to her. Ricker, "Baptiste Pourier," tablet 15, p. 122–125; Jones, Brian, *Those Wild Reshaw Boys*, p. 23; General Smith also submitted a testimonial on Richard's behalf. He had known Richard from his dealings with Fort C.F. Smith in Montana from 1867–1868. In his testimony General Smith stated that he felt Richard could be a useful ally, but would be a dangerous adversary if he were to remain an outlaw among the Sioux. Jones, Brian, "John Richard, Jr.," p. 249.

15. Baptiste Pourier worked as a scout, hunter, guide, or interpreter nearly continuously from 1870 to 1876. Ricker, "Baptiste Pourier," tablet 15, p. 129–140; Jones, Brian, *Those Wild Reshaw Boys*, p. 23–24; Brown, Larry K., p. 70–75.

16. Larson, p. 268; Briston and Dubois, p. 3.

17. Hubalola and Mary Louisa were presumably the two sisters of Yellow Bear whom John Richard Jr. had married the previous year while living with the

hostile Indians on the Powder River. Jones, Brian, *Those Wild Reshaw Boys,* p. 25–26.

18. Only Hubalola is listed in the census as a wife of John Richard Jr.. Mary Louisa is listed as a domestic servant, living in the same household. Considering available information, we must assume that the James Merivale, listed in the census as guide and interpreter, was in fact Joseph Merivale. He was listed in this census as fifty-five years of age and born in Mexico. Census of Fort Fetterman, 1870; James H. Bury, who was at Fort Fetterman that year stated that Joe Merivale was the guide and interpreter there. David, Robert, "Interview of James H. Bury, ca. 1920," (Unpublished notes, "The Bob David Collection," Goodstein Library, Special Collections, Casper College, Casper, Wyoming); "T. Jeff" Carr also stated that Joseph Merivale was living at the fort at the time of the killing of Corporal Conrad. Coutant, "Thomas Jefferson Carr," p. 165–167.

19. Census of Fort Laramie, 1870; Jones, Brian, "John Richard, Jr.," p. 238.

20. Mills later sold his share of the partnership in the Bullock ranch to pioneer rancher John Hunton. Hunton in turn eventually bought out Bullock. Larson, p. 268; Bartlett, vol. III, p. 141; Briston and Dubois, p. 3. The 1870 Fort Laramie census states the value of personal estates: the estates of Hiram Kelly, stockman, and "Portagee" [Portugee] Phillips, stock dealer, are listed as $5,000 each. W. G. Bullock, merchant, is listed at $8.000. Census of Fort Laramie, 1870.

21. Brown, Larry K., p. 61–64.

22. Jones, Brian, *Those Wild Reshaw Boys,* p. 24, 26; Cunningham, Don, 1868–1874, "Chapter One, Red Cloud Agency Days: Fort Robinson Illustrated," *Nebraskaland Magazine,* (Nebraska Game and Parks Commission, Lincoln, Nebraska, January–February, 1986), vol. 64, no.1, p. 14; McDermott, "John Baptiste Richard" in *Mountain Men,* 2:303

23. Brown, Larry K., p. 77–81.

24. John Richard Jr., with his ruthless nature, may have murdered Hopkins Clark for any of a number of senseless reasons. The several eyewitness accounts, however, all state that this was an accident and occurred as it is reported here. We must assume that John Richard Jr. was in fact innocent of any wrongdoing in this instance. Jones, Brian, *Those Wild Reshaw Boys,* p. 24–25.

25. It seems peculiar that Peter Janis would encourage John Richard Jr. to thwart his marriage to Peter's cousin Emily. Although Emily's father, "Old Nick" Janis, had been an associate and close friend of the Richards, it seems that Peter did not share this good will toward the Richard family. There may have been some old animosity between him and the younger John Richard. It appears in fact that Peter Janis felt that the womanizing John Jr. was not good enough to marry into the Janis family. He knew Richard quite well and possibly hoped that in this drunken state he could easily be convinced to reclaim

one of his former wives, thus ending the marriage to Peter's cousin. Jones, Brian, *Those Wild Reshaw Boys*, p. 25–27; Jones believes the girl in question was one of Yellow Bear's sisters; however, Richard family descendants have clarified that John Jr. had once been married to Yellow Bear's daughter and that Richard's abandonment of her had begun the lifelong feud between Yellow Bear and John Richard Jr.. Gilbert, p. 17–18.

26. Jones, Brian, *Those Wild Reshaw Boys*, p. 24–27; McDermott, "John Baptiste Richard" in *Mountain Men*, 2:303.

27. Bettelyoun, p. 41; Jones, Brian, *Those Wild Reshaw Boys*, p. 39; Henry V. Branham's relationship to John Richard is established by several correspondences of Stewart Monroe to the author. Henry Branham was born in 1852 in St. Charles, Missouri. In 1863 he left the residence of his father and stepmother in St. Charles, Missouri, to live with Alexis St. Louis and his wife Susanne (Richard) St. Louis, sister of John Richard Sr., in Rulo, Nebraska. When he came to Wyoming is not exactly known, but he returned to Nebraska in 1873, then moved to California in 1874 where he lived the rest of his life. During his stay in Wyoming "Redskins" killed a cousin (John Richard Jr.). Monroe; McComish, Charles Davis, and Lambert, Rebecca T., *History of Colusa and Glenn Counties California*, (Historic Record Company, Los Angeles, California, 1918), p. 1001–1002.

28. Henry G. Hay and John B. Thomas surveyed the Township lines of T21N R67W, T21N R68W, and T22N R67W in July of 1872. Edwin James and James B. Thomas surveyed the section lines of the same townships in August through October of that same year. USGS survey records, United States Bureau of Land Management, Department of the Interior, Cheyenne, Wyoming; Ricker, "Baptiste Pourier," tablet 15, p. 126–130.

29. Jones, Brian, *Those Wild Reshaw Boys*, p. 27–29; *Cheyenne Daily Leader*, January 13, 1873, as cited by Jones. Jones, Brian, *Those Wild Reshaw Boys*, p. 28–29.

30. Ricker, "Magloire Mosseau," tablet 28, p. 39.

12

⟪Black Hills Gold and the Indian Wars⟫

TROUBLE HAD BEEN building between the whites and Native Americans in the region for many years. The Fort Laramie treaty of 1868 had quenched some of the tempers among the Indians and fueled others. Just when the majority of the Sioux people were beginning to adjust to reservation life, gold was discovered in one of their most sacred grounds, the Black Hills of South Dakota. The ensuing encroachment into Native lands sparked the fire that raged on for half a decade and included many of the most famous battles between the two races in American settlement history.

Red Cloud Agency was moved some seventy-five miles northeast to an area along the White River in Nebraska near the present town of Crawford. The march began in August 1873. Louis Richard was one of the many men who assisted in this move. The new location along the White River, with its established timber, good grass, and fresh flowing springs, was far superior to the old one. The military hoped that this new, more abundant reservation would resolve many of the problems at the former site. The new agency was a considerable distance from the transcontinental traffic along the Platte River, and the military predicted that this separation would deter some of the depredations along the emigrant route.[1]

⟨⟩ ⟨⟩

In early July 1874, Colonel George Armstrong Custer led the 7th Cavalry and a contingent of botanists, geologists, and other scientists on the first military exploratory expedition into the Black Hills of South Dakota from Fort Abraham Lincoln in North Dakota. The Fort Laramie Treaty of 1868 forbade any such entrance into the Hills, but this was of little concern to the politicians in Washington. The "Panic of 1873" had crippled the United States economy, and many believed the persistent rumors of gold in the region needed to be confirmed. On July 27, while encamped in Golden Valley near present day Custer, South Dakota, gold was officially discovered by the expedition. That evening Custer wrote his preliminary report of the discovery. So did the newspapermen who accompanied the expedition. When finished with his report, Custer sent Charley Reynolds on a hair-raising ride through hostile Indian country to deliver the news to Fort Laramie and consequently by telegraph to the world. No military force in the world would be able to impede the rush that Custer and the newspapermen had started with their exaggerated reports.[2]

⋖⊰⋗ ⋖⊱⋗

From the moment Custer's report of gold arrived at Fort Laramie, a crowd of no-account loafers around the fort saw an opportunity to get rich quick. To compound the problem, the troops stationed along the Platte River were given the responsibility of keeping all of these would-be miners out of the Black Hills until a treaty with the Sioux could be ratified. Among the crowd was California Joe Milner who coerced an ambulance driver named Gray into a partnership with the goal of striking out for the hills in search of gold. One Saturday night, using Gray's money, they purchased gold pans, shovels, picks, scales, quicksilver, and a month's worth of supplies from the sutler and loaded their goods onto mules behind the store. On their way out an officer of the fort stopped them. Joe told him that they were going up the Platte to trap beaver until they were allowed to enter the Black Hills. Finding their story believable, the officer allowed them go on their way.

The next day, while camped along the river, Joe and Gray played cards and imbibed in generous portions of whiskey. As the day drew on, the two men, both quite drunk, got into an argument over who should bring in the stock for feed and water. As the controversy grew more heated, Joe shot Gray in the arm with his rifle. Thinking Gray was mortally wounded and planning to finish him off, Joe cranked another round into the chamber and fired again, but missed. Just as Joe moved in on Gray, a boy who was passing by on horseback and had heard the shots crested a nearby hill. Joe hollered to him to come in, but the boy stayed his distance. Joe took a shot at the boy and yelled, "I guess you'll come in now!" Heeding the warning, the boy rode to the camp. Joe instructed him to ride to the fort and tell them that California Joe just shot his partner and to send a wagon over for him.

Around dusk the boy arrived at the home of John S. Collins, the Fort Laramie post sutler, with the news. Collins was unequipped to handle the situation. Since it was not a military matter, he sent the boy to Adolph Cuney who was a deputy sheriff. Cuney hitched up his wagon and went to the camp. After loading Gray, who was not that seriously hurt, into the wagon, Cuney instructed Joe to mount a mule and come along. After a short distance, Joe spurred the mule and galloped away. Cuney was relatively helpless to stop him as it had grown dark, and he could not give chase in a wagon.[3]

⬦⋅⬦

In November of that year world-renowned paleontologist, Professor O.C. Marsh, hired Louis Richard as his guide and interpreter on his first of several fossil-hunting expeditions in Nebraska and Wyoming. Professor Marsh was very pleased with Louis's knowledge and abilities. He spoke highly of his faithfulness and reliability. The two perhaps became too well acquainted however, and Louis talked freely. From casual conversation, Marsh soon realized that the Indians at Red Cloud Agency were being victimized by corruption within the agency system. In June 1875, Professor Marsh arranged for Louis Richard to travel to Washington, D. C., and testify about fraud and misdealing at the agency. With these sworn statements in hand Marsh campaigned to the Commissioner of Indian Affairs. The result was the appointment of a commission to investigate the dealings at Red Cloud Agency.[4]

In August this team of investigators traveled to the agency and began collecting evidence. They interviewed Louis again. In Richard's attempt to collaborate some of the testimony others had given, he occasionally contradicted some of his earlier statements. Soon the investigators were badgering Louis and questioning his credibility. Richard became frightened and confused. He had only been trying to cooperate with his friend Professor Marsh, and now he felt as if he was being accused of something. The young frontiersman, who could have stood his ground against almost any danger of the wilderness, was as defenseless as a fawn in a pack of wolves. With the wile of a team of east-coast prosecuting attorneys, the investigators went in for the kill. In his confusion, Louis Richard totally discredited himself, and both his earlier and present testimonies were thrown out. Richard was thankful that no charges were pressed against him and vowed never to speak so freely to easterners again. During this time the Council of the Oglala Sioux was held at the agency. Leon Pallardie, Jules Ecoffey, William Rowland, and Antoine

Janis were appointed as interpreters for this council. Louis Richard had been requested by Red Cloud as an interpreter, but he was tied up with the investigations.[5]

⋯

In the meantime another commission had been appointed to secure the mining rights of the Black Hills from the Sioux. When this commission reached Red Cloud Agency in September, they hired Louis Richard as their interpreter. A huge council was formed to negotiate the agreement. A majority of the Sioux chiefs who attended the council supported selling the land, but strong and powerful minorities opposed the idea. Arguing among the Indians took up most of the time of the council. On the third day, September 23, 1875, Little Big Man stormed into the meeting and threatened to shoot the commissioners. The Indian police wrestled Little Big Man out of the conference meeting, but a similar threat was made by a group of young warriors who then began taunting the crowd by riding around the group making war cries. Louis Richard turned to the commissioners and said: "It looks like hell will break out here in a few minutes. The Indians are all mad, and, when they start shooting, we'll be the first to catch it."

Most fortunately the shooting never began. Young Man Afraid of his Horses and his Indian police calmed the Indians while the soldiers escorted the commissioners and Louis Richard from the council area. A few days later an attempt was made to continue the council, but no agreement was ever made and miners continued to flood into the Black Hills. Hundreds of Indians left the agencies and began a series of attacks on the trespassers. They killed the miners if the opportunity arose and vandalized or destroyed their property if it did not. In the fall of 1875, the military was in a difficult position. The miners' intrusion into the Black Hills was clearly in conflict with the treaty of 1868, but the politicians in the East offered no help in attempting to slow the influx.

In December, a proclamation was issued. Dozens of messengers were sent to the bands that were off the reservation with the order that all Indians were to return to their agencies by January 31, 1876, or be treated as hostile.[6]

⋯

The previous spring Speed Stagner had spent his life's savings on young beef cattle which he drove to Powder River to begin a ranch. With the vast majority of the Indians then living at the various agencies, the hostile yet fertile valleys of Powder River had become somewhat placid. With a herd of eighty-five head of yearlings and two-year-olds and the ever-increasing demands of the agencies for beef, this seemed a venture that could not fail. Hiram Kelly and Portugee Phillips had proven the profitability of the cattle business along Chugwater Creek in a very short time. Stagner hoped to do the same on Powder River. Little did he know the events of that fall that would bring most of the hostile bands of Sioux back from the agencies to the very ground that had been so disputed in the past. Upon the return of the Sioux, Stagner's herd was wiped out in days. What few of his cattle survived were scattered far into the Big Horn Mountains, and Speed Stagner felt lucky to return to Fort Fetterman with his life.[7]

⊗ ⊗

California Joe Milner's former partner, Gray, quickly recovered from his wounds and resumed his former occupation as an ambulance driver. Shortly after travel was allowed into the Black Hills, Gray accompanied the wagon train of Major John Furey there and met up with California Joe along the trail. With old scores far from settled, Gray and Milner were involved in another gun-battle. This time Milner was wounded. After the dust had settled and Furey had heard the reason behind the altercation, he immediately evicted California Joe from the camp.[8]

During this time, John Richard was trading among the Sioux between Fort Robinson and Fort Laramie. Shortly after the order for all Indians to return to reservations went out, he and his nephew Alfred Pallardie were camped near the headwaters of the Running Water along the road between these two points. On this undisclosed night in late 1875, California Joe Milner and Tom Newcomb stopped by their camp for a visit and a few drinks. What happened next is yet unknown. The next day Tom Newcomb arrived at Fort Robinson with the news that California Joe had murdered both John Richard and Alfred Pallardie at their camp. Frank Salaway, an experienced tracker, was among those who went to investigate the scene.

The first thing the searchers found along the trail was the body of John Richard. He had walked or crawled some distance after receiving his mortal wounds at the camp, leaving a pronounced trail of blood in the snow. At the camp they found the body of Alfred Pallardie plus a set

The Running Water (now known as the Niobrara River) along which John Richard was killed. (*Author's Collection, taken in 2013.*)

of wagon tracks leading toward the river. Richard and Pallardie's wagon was a short distance away, overturned in the Running Water River. Trade goods were strewn about the camp. Wagon tracks and numerous sets of both moccasin and boot tracks covered the ground.

John Richard reportedly had carried a large quantity of gold, which was not found. Both men still had guns and ammunition with them. How many different sets of tracks were found is not known. Richard most often wore moccasins, but it is unknown what he wore that night. Two sets of high-heeled boot tracks were believed to be those of Milner and Newcomb, though Milner often wore moccasins.

When the searchers returned to Fort Robinson, California Joe was apprehended. He soon was released for lack of evidence, but not before accusing Tom Newcomb of the murders. The blame for this double murder was eventually officially laid on a group of Cheyenne Indians, due to the presence of the moccasin tracks.

⟨⟩⟩⟩∘⟨⟨⟨⟩

So ended the life of John Baptiste Richard on a lonely trail, on an uncertain date, under unresolved circumstances, and without commemoration.

If Indians were in fact the culprits it seems unusual that they failed to take the weapons, and equally strange that they took Richard's gold but not the trade goods. California Joe immediately left the vicinity of Fort Robinson, but Tom Newcomb remained in the area and worked for the Red Cloud Agency as the butcher for some time. Later that summer Newcomb ventured to Deadwood where he reportedly had a run in with California Joe, who took his rifle away from him. California Joe hung around Deadwood off and on for several months. He reportedly always had money, but never staked a claim in the area. Mostly he bought lots of drinks and lost money gambling, thus many saloon customers put up with his bragging tales of his own heroics and considered him a good fellow.[9]

⋖∰⋗ ⋖∰⋗

During the month of March 1876, Brigadier General George Crook led the first expedition against the "hostile" Indians—those who had not returned to their agencies. He left Fort Fetterman on March 1 headed north with his column and twenty scouts and was to be joined by another ten scouts from Fort Laramie. Frank Grouard claimed to have been the "chief scout" and responsible for hiring all of the others, but there is no indication that this was the case. It appears that Baptiste Pourier may have been the chief scout as he received $150 per month for his services instead of the usual $125. At Powder River, Louis Richard, John Shangrau, Frank Grouard, Big Bat Pourier, Little Bat Garnier, and Charles Janis were sent ahead. In their absence, the main column was attacked by Indians.[10]

When the advance scouts arrived on Tongue River, they found a dead Crow Indian hanging from a tree. His body had been mutilated, and they believed it to be the work of the Sioux. The scouts gathered to determine their next move in hunting for the Sioux. Frank Grouard could not agree with the others and set off on his own, saying that he could find the Sioux in three days without anyone's help. Soon realizing that the rest of the scouts were not following, Grouard returned to await General Crook's arrival. When the main command caught up with the advance scouts, the combined group pushed on to the Yellowstone River. There they found large trails leading back toward Powder River using a different route from that which the troops had used. General Crook then returned to Powder River by the Indian's path. When they neared Powder River country, Crook sent Colonel Joseph J. Reynolds with the

General Crook's Camp on Goose Creek during the summer campaigns of 1876. (*"Indian Story Land," Frank Leslie's Popular Monthly*)

scouts and six companies of cavalry ahead. They traveled by night with the scouts taking turns picking out the dimly lit trail on foot.

When daybreak arrived, Louis Richard, Frank Grouard, and the Shangrau brothers were a considerable distance ahead of the column. The men agreed that they were very close to the Indian's village, so Louis Richard and Louis Shangrau went on ahead. Meanwhile John Shangrau and Frank Grouard were sent back to alert Colonel Reynolds. About ten miles above Little Powder River, Richard and Shangrau spotted the village. Colonel Reynolds and his cavalry attacked the village the following morning and drove the Indians from their camp. Reynolds captured the horse herd and put the torch to the camp. By the time General Crook arrived with the rest of the troops, bad weather had set in. The Indians had counter-attacked and regained some of their horses, and Reynolds had withdrawn from the site of the former village. The expedition, considered a success, decamped and returned to Fort Fetterman to wait out the storm before another round of challenging the hostiles.

E CREEK.

When General Crook arrived back at Fort Fetterman all the scouts were released except Louis Richard, Baptiste Pourier, and Frank Grouard. It appears that Louis and Baptiste remained at Fort Fetterman while Frank Grouard was sent to Fort Robinson. In April, General Crook continued organizing his Big Horn and Yellowstone Expedition. Louis Richard, Baptiste Pourier, and Frank Grouard would work as his guides and interpreters. This time Grouard may have truly been the chief scout as he was paid $150 per month while Richard and Pourier were paid the customary $125. Crook was expanding on his policy of hiring Indian scouts, and he contracted nearly two hundred Shoshones. By the time the expedition reached Goose Creek, the Shoshones had yet to join the expedition, and Crook was beginning to get aggravated by this. He was extremely anxious to recruit Crows to join him because he felt their long enmity with the Sioux would be of great advantage.[11]

General Crook then asked Frank Grouard and Baptiste Pourier if they could find the Crows and recruit some additional scouts. They took thirty of the best men mounted on the best horses to carry out this mission. The party was organized under the command of Lieutenant Sibley. It included a civilian packer who volunteered for the duty, and

John F. Finerty, a newspaperman from the *Chicago Tribune* who was bored with the monotony of camp and went along "for adventure and to enlarge his knowledge."

The account of this episode is taken from an interview of Baptiste Pourier conducted by Judge Eli Ricker which the judge subtitled "The Sibley Scouts." The following extract is a summary of Ricker's wording. The dialogue and quotations are from Ricker's account.

> They started off in late afternoon and near sundown stopped and made coffee on a little dry creek just north of Goose Creek. After a short break they continued on to Tongue River where they arrived shortly after dark. Grouard wanted to camp there for the night, but Pourier questioned this decision. Bat felt that Indians had been watching them since they left Crook's camp and wanted to continue on until dark in order to conceal their camping location. Lieutenant Sibley understood the logic of Pourier's suggestion, and they continued north for about two more miles before stopping for the night. They spent the night without fire or unsaddling their horses. The men simply laid themselves out on the ground and held their reins in their hands as they slept.
>
> The men were up and moving before daylight without food or coffee. As the sky began to lighten they were near a steep broken hill. Grouard, who led, motioned Pourier to the front. He told Bat and the lieutenant to continue up the ravine while he dismounted and climbed the hill to look around with his glass. Before Grouard departed he told Bat to watch for him and if he waved his hat to come running. Soon after Grouard reached the summit of the hill, Bat saw him swinging his sombrero. Bat told the lieutenant to continue the men up the ravine while he spurred his mount back down the trail. He bailed off his horse where Grouard had left his and scrambled up the rocky slope to Grouard's side.
>
> "Take this glass" Grouard said, "and look and see if those are Indians or rocks over on that hill?"
>
> Bat looked through the glass. "Those are Indians—a war party of Indians."
>
> "Of course they are" Grouard replied. "They are Crows, I believe."
>
> "I believe they are Sioux," Bat answered. "But hold on, I can tell whether they are Sioux or Crows when they start."

Crows usually traveled in military order. The chief or leader of the band was always out front with the warriors taking their places in the order of their hierarchy. The Sioux moved around at will when mounted. A warrior might race ahead of the chief or leader then fall back; they moved without regularity, more as a mob instead of a column.

As soon as the Indians mounted it was plain to see they were Sioux. The fifty warriors moved out without any orderly fashion, running their horses toward Tongue River expecting to roust the soldiers they had obviously seen the night before. They had no trouble locating the trail the soldiers had left from the river toward the ravine. From their vantage point, Grouard and Pourier could see the Indian's village some four or five miles distant at the head of Box Elder Creek. The soldiers were on a trail the Indians used when they went to the mountains to cut lodge poles. When Frank and Bat caught up with the column, Bat told the lieutenant to hurry or the Indians would soon cut them off. Grouard took his position with the lieutenant at the front, and Bat fell in at the rear to watch behind.

Bat's attempts to urge the soldiers out of their snail's pace seemed to no avail. He yelled to Grouard, "Hurry up, or the Indians will overtake us!"

"We can't go any faster," Grouard yelled back. "The Indians haven't seen us!" The column soon filed down a steep hill and was again on Tongue River. Here, in a small meadow, they stopped.

"What are you going to do?" Bat asked.

"We've got to make some coffee for these men," the lieutenant answered.

"Frank, you know better than that." Bat yelled, "We'll be jumped for sure! What are you going to do? Going to take the saddles off, too?"

"Yes," the lieutenant answered, "we are going to unsaddle."

Bat swore. "Well, my horse is going to be tied to this tree," he said. "And I'm not taking the saddle off from my horse!" he added.

The soldiers built a fire and began brewing coffee. Bat surmised that the Indians would by now be ahead of them, set for an ambush. He could not resist the opportunity to poke fun at the adventure-seeking reporter. "Well, now you have something to send to your paper."

"Yes," Finerty replied, "This is the last 'scout' I will accompany for the sake of news and I hope," he went on, "that nothing more serious will occur than has already happened."

To this Bat replied, "Look out for things of stirring interest to come."

While the party stopped for coffee, Frank Grouard laid down on his saddle. He was suffering miserably from a case of venereal disease. The strenuous events of the morning had already taken their toll on his weakened body. After the troops finished their coffee, Bat had to rouse Frank, who had dozed off, and help him to his feet. As Bat saddled Grouard's horse for him, he pondered how they would survive the ordeal he felt was inevitably yet to come.

Soon they were again mounted and moving. As they reached the top of the next hill they saw two coup sticks left on the trail. Bat was enraged. "Oh! No, they didn't see us!" he mimicked. "Here are these sticks; they are ahead of us now!" Their stop on Tongue River had allowed the Indians to get the jump on them, just as Bat had warned.

"Go on ahead," he said to Grouard, "I'll drop back." As the column moved on they were soon in a heavy copse of timber. When Bat peered over his shoulder he saw three warriors coming up from behind. He spurred his horse forward and yelled to Grouard and the lieutenant as he advanced, "They're right behind us!" By the time he reached the front of the column, a half dozen Indians were on the trail ahead. They broke from the timber into a small meadow or park. A jumble of rocks and a low hill were not far from the trail on the right; to the left was scattered timber. As they entered the park, the rocks came alive with Indians.

"Look out!" Bat yelled "They're going to fire!" The men drove their horses into the timber on the left as bullets flew around them.

"Dismount!" Grouard yelled, "and tie your horses!" Bat was already on the ground some fifty yards away when Grouard yelled. Lieutenant Sibley did not question nor rebuke Grouard for giving orders. He repeated the command at the top of his lungs and lay prone in the timber as quickly as any seasoned mountain man. When the firing started, the Chicago reporter's mare was hit. Finerty hit the ground, scrambling for the nearest bush, tree, or rock to get behind. The soldiers were pinned in the trees and had yet to fire a shot. The Indians behind the rocks never let up firing and, as more warriors arrived on the scene, the volume of their roaring rifles increased. It was mid-afternoon when the attack began, and the minutes turned to hours with no sign that the storm of bullets was soon to let up. The soldiers had lain deadly silent in the woods from the onset. Neither a single gunshot nor spoken word had been heard from their side of the glen.

Late in the afternoon the roar of the Indian's guns momentarily ceased. A voice from the far side of the park yelled out, "Oh Bat! Come over here; I want to tell you something. Come over!" Bat knew the voice. It was Painted Horse. He did not answer nor move; Painted Horse repeated his call, no answer. The shooting began again. Bat knew that there was nothing to gain by answering the Indian. He had obviously been identified by at least one of the renegades, but so too had he now identified one of them. By refusing to parlay they might think him wounded or dead, but it was not be likely that this would entice them to make a stupid move. Bat knew that the Indians' numbers were steadily increasing, and the relative safety of the timber would soon be lost if they were surrounded. He also knew that there would be no escape from the inferno if the Sioux decided to burn them out. Bat painstakingly passed away the hours visualizing step by step every possible scenario he could think of for escape. There was no chance on horseback; as soon as they cleared the timber they would be picked off like ducks in a pond. They would have to leave the horses behind and crawl away a safe distance before trying to cover any serious amount of ground on foot.

Bat lay prone at the far end of the column from Lieutenant Sibley, Frank Grouard, and John Finerty. His mind was made up; no alternative offered a better chance of survival. He began to crawl on his belly the length of the column between brush and rocks to the commander. A considerable amount of time had passed when he got there. He asked the lieutenant, "What are you going to do?"

"There is nothing to do," he replied, "We can't do anything."

"We can do something," Bat said. "Let's leave our horses tied and get out of here. I've got my horse tied; he is my own private property, and he will stay there. If you were wounded, Lieutenant, we would pull out and leave you; if I was wounded, you would pull out and leave me; let's leave our horses and get out of here before any of us are wounded."

Lieutenant Sibley lay silently for a long time. Finally he answered, "That is all we can do. Go tell Frank about it."

Bat crawled to Grouard. "Frank," Bat said, "Let's get out of here" and he explained his plan.

Grouard listened carefully to Bat's plan. "That's the only show we've got." While Bat and Frank were talking, a warrior had been racing his mustang up and down the glen in challenge to the soldiers, so they might betray their position by firing at him. Frank motioned toward the warrior, "If we're leaving anyhow, let's get ready and shoot that Indian when he comes again." The two men raised their rifles and waited for the warrior to be directly in front of them. They fired simultaneously and as the bold rider rolled from his horse to fall dead on the ground, Grouard and Pourier scrambled on their bellies to attain new cover as bullets rained down on their previous position. These were the only two shots fired from the military side during the entire encounter. When safely concealed, Bat again turned to Grouard, "Now hurry up Frank, let's get out of here. Let's go to the lieutenant, and let's get out of here."

Both men then crawled to Lieutenant Sibley who spoke when they reached him, "Frank, what will we do?"

"What Bat told you," Grouard answered. "It's all we can do."

The lieutenant gave the command to the nearest man, and it was passed from man to man down the line. Each man was to get all the ammunition from his horse that he could carry and make sure the horse was tied fast so as not to reveal their departure. This operation went off without a hitch. The horses provided the illusion that the men still held their positions, but they had in fact congregated near the lieutenant's position.

Bat wanted no stragglers. He spoke to Grouard, "You go ahead and I'll go behind and see that all keep up." The entire party crawled away as one body. The Indians' fire did not slacken as the men moved out shortly before sunset. Before long the men were in an area that had suffered from fire in previous years, which provided a maze of jumbled fallen trees intermingled with brush. The concealment was excellent but the travel horrific as the tired and hungry men climbed over the fallen logs and the brush seemingly tore them to shreds with every thorny finger. At least they were now able to walk erect.

They struggled on and soon reached Tongue River which they crossed on a log that spanned the stream. While crossing Lieutenant Sibley lost his footing and fell into the river. Night was falling and so was the temperature at this elevation. The lieutenant, now soaking wet through and through, offered no complaint, however, as he urged his men to ascend into the foothills of the Big Horn Mountains. When darkness totally enwrapped the command and the scouts could no longer pick out a trail, the men halted where an overhanging cliff loomed above them. Most of the tired and hungry men slept as soon as they dropped. All were totally exhausted and had consumed nothing all day but the coffee of that morning. With the cliff and timber providing concealment, Bat kindled a small fire and soon beckoned the lieutenant to warm and dry himself over the tiny blaze. A guard was posted and changed hourly so that all the men were allowed to rest.

At first light they continued toward General Crook's camp. Pourier now led as principal guide, and Grouard took the rear though his disabling illness drained him. About mid-day the column came out of the heavy timber into a sparsely wooded area. Bat scanned the area and spotted a party of about thirty Indians ahead and above them, traveling in their same direction, presumably headed to scout out Crook's camp. The two scouts agreed that it would be best to lay back and let the Indians continue away from them, so Lieutenant Sibley ordered the men to fall back into the timber to better conceal themselves. The men were greatly suffering from hunger and exhaustion. Here they decided to lighten their loads, and they cached 250 rounds of ammunition. It had now been over two days since any of them had eaten.

When night fell they resumed their journey. Grouard had now grown so emaciated that he often had to be helped along the trail, but he did not complain. His recurring utterance was "I'm sorry I'm sick; I'll do the best I can." Bat thought Grouard repeated the chant to give himself the strength to continue. About eight miles into this night's trek, they arrived on the middle fork of Goose Creek. Grouard struggled but made the crossing. One of the soldiers did not. This soldier had discarded his shoes after they had fallen apart, and his feet were cut, bruised, and swollen. When they reached the stream he announced that he would go no further and crawled into the brush to await whatever fate might find him.

The men stripped and carried their clothing with them as they crossed the river to prevent it from being soaked in the cold water. Two soldiers fell while fording the stream and lost their rifles in the icy water. A short distance beyond the crossing, Bat again kindled a small fire for the men to warm and dry themselves. Lieutenant Sibley questioned the safety of a fire visible to Indians. Bat told him he would prefer to die from a bullet than from freezing to death. So they dried, dressed, warmed, and took a moment's rest before they continued on through the night.

They stopped often to rest as fatigue and hunger rapidly debilitated them. Their bodies were weak but their purpose gave them the strength to continue on. When dawn broke, the glazed look in the eyes of every man told the tale of their perils without need of words. Wild game was plentiful, but none of these famished men succumbed to the temptation of firing a shot, which would have alerted the enemy of their position.

At mid-morning they were resting when "Uncle Dave" Mears, a civilian packer with Crook who was searching for a missing mule, spotted them. When the men realized how close they were to camp they again resumed their march. Uncle Dave rushed ahead to alert the camp and soon the beleaguered party was met with horses. A company of cavalry was sent to rescue the man who had remained at the crossing the previous night on Middle Goose Creek. He was found and returned to camp.

Through all the toils of this ominous event not a single man was lost, or even severely injured. According to Baptiste Pourier, "Lieutenant Sibley was a young man just out of West Point, about medium height, spare as young men usually are, of handsome features, fine figure, intelligent, gentlemanly, refined, brave, and at all times as cool as if on dress parade." The seasoned Pourier obviously thought very highly of the young officer. Sibley respected the knowledge of these frontiersmen which likely saved the lives of his men in this most perilous escape.[12]

⋘≫⋙

Baptiste Pourier and Frank Grouard were not long in recovering from this physical ordeal. On June 2, Louis Richard, Grouard, and Pourier were sent to the Crow Agency to recruit Crow scouts and bring them to join the column. Nearly two weeks later Richard and Grouard rode into Crook's camp on Goose Creek with the Crow chief. Pourier was not far behind with two hundred scouts. Tom Cosgrove and Nelson Yarnell soon joined them with Shoshone scouts.

Louis Richard may not have been receiving the highest pay for his services, but that night he proved his worth as he interpreted for General Crook and his officers at the grand council of the scouts. To assure he was understood by all, he translated in no less than four Indian dialects as well as French. Two days later Crook started down the Rosebud, and the following day ran head on into Crazy Horse with disastrous results. After his fight with Crazy Horse, General Crook returned to Goose Creek to lick his wounds and regroup. While there, General Crook received word of the ill-fated reception Colonel George Armstrong Custer had received at the Little Big Horn. Louis Richard was then dispatched to Fort Fetterman. For unknown reasons, possibly because he was eluding hostile bands of Indians, he took a circuitous route. On July 6, 1876, he arrived at John Hunton's ranch on La Prele Creek and broke the news of Custer's tragedy to the rancher. Somewhere along the line Richard had collected another scout, Ben Arnold, and these two arrived back at General Crook's camp on July 10.[13]

On August 10, General Crook met Brigadier General Alfred H. Terry with the ragtag remnants of the 7th Cavalry near Tongue River. Both men were hunting Indians, with little success. There were none to be found. After a half-hearted attempt to follow Crazy Horse with their joint force of nearly four thousand men, the two generals again separated. General Terry and his troops made for the Yellowstone River while General Crook headed for Bear Butte. On September 9, Colonel Anson Mills, who Crook had sent ahead of the main column, ran into the band of Sioux under chief American Horse at Slim Buttes with slightly better success in the engagement. In the battle, American Horse was killed and a few prisoners were taken. By now Crook's supplies had run out and his dilapidated army limped into Custer City in the Black Hills for food and rest.[14]

Crook's cavalry had lost some one thousand horses on the expedition. The vast majority of the column was afoot. Crook needed horses and the nearest ones available were at Fort Laramie. Frank Grouard was sent to Fort Laramie to hire drovers to bring a herd of horses to the Black Hills for this footsore cavalry. According to Grouard it was at this time that he first met California Joe Milner. He hired Milner for the job on recommendation of several of his cronies. Grouard later stated that at the time he knew nothing of the murder of John Richard or California Joe's alleged involvement. This seems hard to believe since Grouard had just spent the last several months on the trail in the company of Louis Richard and Baptiste Pourier, John Richard's son and son-in-law. Nevertheless, California Joe had evidently either been at Fort Laramie or met Grouard somewhere along the trail and hired on for a job that would return him to the Black Hills.[15]

⋘⋙ ⋘⋙

By October of that year, Peter Richard and William Denver McGaa[16] had contracted to supply beef to Crook's forces. They soon left Fort Laramie with three hundred head of cattle that they delivered to General Crook at Custer City. Crook was outfitting for his Powder River Expedition. Billy Garnett was sent with Baptiste Pourier and Frank Grouard to Spotted Tail Agency to recruit scouts. Several Sioux and Arapahos were hired. "Sergeant" Three Bears was put in command of the Sioux and "Sergeant" Sharp Nose of the Arapahos. This was the first time that Sioux scouts had been hired to go after Sioux warriors. Louis Richard, Baptiste Pourier, Louis Shangrau, and Frank Grouard were all hired as chief scouts at $150 per month. Billy Garnett and William Rowland were interpreters. All of the Indians were issued revolvers and Sharps rifles at Fort Robinson. They then went to Fort Fetterman where they met up with General Crook who had arrived from Fort Laramie.

In mid-November, General Crook and his command departed Fort Fetterman for Powder River. The cavalcade consisted of eleven troops of cavalry, eleven companies of infantry, and over two hundred Indian scouts. When they reached the site of old Fort Reno, Tom Cosgrove, Leoi Lu Clair, and their Shoshone scouts joined them. Four hundred Indians were now in the command representing several factions of the Sioux, Cheyenne, Shoshone, Arapaho, Bannock, and Pawnee tribes. Many of these tribes had long been enemies, and General Crook immediately held a council with the entire assembly. The exact message he presented has long been lost to history, but he told the Indians that they must forget old battles and join as one. United they would defeat the hostile Sioux and Cheyenne that were destroying all chances for true peace between the whites and Indians.

Ten scouts were sent out the next day to locate the village of the hostile Indians. It was soon found that Crazy Horse and Sitting Bull were camped on Powder River. Crook moved his army to the Crazy Woman Fork when he learned that a large Cheyenne village was camped near the headwaters of Powder River. Louis Richard and Louis Shangrau were sent with five scouts to Fort Robinson to recruit more scouts. Richard and Shangrau, accompanied by five hundred Sioux scouts from the Red Cloud and Spotted Tail Agencies, were en route to Belle Fourche to meet Crook when a messenger met them. Colonel Ranald S. MacKenzie and the 4th Cavalry had attacked and captured Dull Knife's village, and the scouts were to return to Fort Robinson. Richard and Shangrau cut across country and met General Crook whom they accompanied back to Fort Laramie. By year's end Louis Richard was discharged from the service of General Crook and returned to trading at Red Cloud Agency with recommendations.[17]

⟨⟩• •⟨⟩

So ends the exploits of John Baptiste Richard. This man and his family were involved in many of the events that helped to shape the history of the American West. It is ironic that a man who lived on the very fringes of civilization with perils at every turn should die in such an unassuming manner while camped in apparent safety. Had John Richard chosen to assemble his assets and retire in St. Charles, Missouri, or Rulo, Nebraska, as some of his contemporaries had, he may have lived for many more years. He may have become frail in his old age. As his fortunes dwindled some overbearing dime novelist might have offered cash to share his tale for young adventures to read and idolize. He may have become a legend, but that was not his way.

John Richard was a man of action and compassion. He could not ignore the plight of many Native Americans whose entire lives were rapidly disappearing right before their eyes. The nature of his character required he try to assist his many friends and family adjust to life on the reservations. Neither could he have forced himself into a life in a rocking chair on a porch watching bustling people passing on a dusty street before him. He had to be doing, moving, achieving something. His death was far less glamorous than that of a valiant hero falling under a hail of some enemy's bullets, but he died in the country he loved. The westward expansion of the United States had begun long before John Richard was born and continued on for many years after he was gone. Where John Richard lived the majority of his life was a thoroughfare for this massive westward migration, yet it was the most rugged and last to be settled.

Notes to Chapter Twelve:

1. Cunningham, p. 15–16; Jones, Brian, *Those Wild Reshaw Boys,* p. 39.

2. Since the end of the Civil War the stock market had been on a continual rise. Fledgling businesses were maturing and the American economy boomed for nearly a decade. By definition a boom does not last forever, though the American public acted as if it would. Suddenly in 1873 progress caught up with itself and so did mortgages. On September 18, 1873, the banking firm of Jay Cooke and Company, one of the largest in the United States, failed. Other financial institutions fell like dominoes over the next few days and the Stock Exchange literally closed its doors. This depression lasted until 1877; they called it the "Panic of 1873." Ambrose, p. 344–352.

3. Collins, John S., *My Experiences in the West*, (Chicago: The Lakeside Press, R. R. Donnelley & Sons Company, 1970), p. 131–134.

4. Othniel Charles Marsh (1831–1899) is considered by many to be the father of modern paleontology. On his numerous expeditions into the western United States he discovered vast numbers of prehistoric skeletons. Besides dinosaurs, he discovered an ancient bird called the Hesperornis, the flying reptilian Pterodactyl, and early ancestors of the horse. "Othniel Charles," *Encarta 98 Encyclopedia*, (Microsoft, 1993–1997); Jones, Brian, *Those Wild Reshaw Boys*, p. 29–30.

5. Jones, Brian, *Those Wild Reshaw Boys*, p. 30–33.

6. Jones, Brian, *Those Wild Reshaw Boys*, p. 33–35; Ambrose, p. 357–364; Utley and Washburn, p. 265–266.

7. This herd belonging to Speed Stagner is believed to have been the first cattle to graze along Powder River. The Frewen Brothers who claimed this distinction did not arrive in that part of the country until 1878. Coutant, "Coutant Collection," box 4, folder 53, book 37.

8. Collins, p. 134.

9. Alfred Pallardie was the son of John Richard's sister Leanore and Antoine Pallardie. He was born January 7, 1849, the third of their four children. Monroe. The Running Water is now known as the Niobrara River. Tom Newcomb had

been the butcher for Red Cloud Agency and Fort Robinson. He was well liked by most everyone in the vicinity. Judge Ricker stated that Salaway gave him every detail of the particulars of the case, and the circumstances pointed the guilty finger toward California Joe. Ricker, however, who normally is an outstanding source of historic information, failed to mention many of the details. Ricker, Judge Eli S., "Interview of Frank Salaway, 8 miles Northeast of Allen, South Dakota, November 4, 1906," (Unpublished Manuscript, Nebraska State Historical Society Library, Lincoln, Nebraska), tablet 28, p. 66–67; Ricker, "Magloire Mosseau," tablet 28, p. 63–65; Milner and Forrest, p. 222–235; Jones, Brian, *Those Wild Reshaw Boys*, p. 33, 45; McDermott, "John Baptiste Richard" in *Mountain Men*, 2:303; DeBarthe, Joe: Edgar I. Stewart, editor, *Life and Adventures of Frank Grouard*, (University of Oklahoma Press, 1958), p. 171–173.

10. Charles Richard, Louis Shangrau, Ben Clark, Speed Stagner, Tom Reed, Joe Eldridge, and Buckskin Jack Russell were also among Crook's thirty scouts. Jones, Brian, *Those Wild Reshaw Boys*, p. 35; Vaughn, p. 72, 80, 142.

11. Jones, Brian, *Those Wild Reshaw Boys*, p. 35–36.

12. Ricker, Judge Eli S., "Interview with Baptiste "Big Bat" Pourier begun Sunday, January 6, 1907, The Sibley Scouts," (Unpublished Manuscript, Nebraska State Historical Society Library, Lincoln, Nebraska) tablet 15, p. 22–73.

13. Jones, Brian, *Those Wild Reshaw Boys*, p. 36–38; Ambrose, p. 384–412.

14. Ambrose, p. 416–417.

15. The time line for this event is difficult to establish. It is known that California Joe left Deadwood on August 1, 1876, the day before the murder of Wild Bill Hickok and did not return for several weeks. If this is the period in which this horse drive was made, it must be assumed that Grouard was sent to Fort Laramie prior to the engagement at Slim Buttes. Rosa, Joseph G., *They Called Him Wild Bill*, (University of Oklahoma Press, Norman, Oklahoma, 1964), p. 226–232; DeBarthe, p. 171.

16. William Denver McGaa later married Baptiste and Josephine Pourier's daughter, Mary "Lovie" Pourier.

17. Jones, Brian, *Those Wild Reshaw Boys*, p. 38–39.

13
❦ THE AFTERMATH ❦

W HILE THE LIFE of John Richard and some of his descendants was over, the legacy of his many accomplishments would continue for decades. Not only had he influenced many of the people he met, but he also impacted the land and development. As John Richard had spent his entire life adapting to the ever-changing markets of trading and transportation, so would those who followed him. Certain key players and places near the end of John Richard's life should not be left without further exploration.

❦ ❦

CALIFORNIA JOE. The investigation into the murder of John Richard and his nephew was short and inconclusive, but questions over the crime did not end for years. Many believed that California Joe Milner had literally gotten away with murder and not for the first time.

Moses Embree "California Joe" Milner was born in Kentucky in 1829. He was married and had four sons, but left his wife on a farm in Oregon while he pursued a career as a scout and gambler across the central plains and Rocky Mountains. California Joe was considered by a select few to be a good friend, while others considered him untrustworthy, often even an enemy. His first known position as a scout was in the Mexican War from 1846–1848. During this time he became noted as an expert rifle shot. He also gained the reputation as a man who was not above murdering anyone he felt had threatened him, often before confirming the facts.[1]

Following the Mountain Meadows Massacre in 1857, Joe encountered a party of Mormons at Fort Bridger. There he murdered two of the party, claiming revenge for the massacre. He soon fled Fort Bridger, fearing retaliation by the Avenging Angels, a legendary vigilante group of renegade Mormons. He wound up in what is now Montana. Outside of Virginia City, he met up with a group he thought to be claim jumpers and supposedly acquired his nickname. Fearing for his life he told these men that his name was Joe and he was from California, and the name stuck. While in Montana he was closely associated with Jack Slade, the notorious ex-superintendent of the Overland Stage line. Shortly after the lynching of Slade, Joe fled Montana.[2]

By late 1864, Joe was in Colorado Territory. There he baited the Cheyennes and Arapahos to go to Fort Lyons for a peace conference. When this conference was aborted, he convinced the chiefs to camp near Sand Creek, about forty miles from the fort. Late that November, Colonel J. M. Chivington led his 1st Colorado Cavalry volunteers to Sand Creek where they easily annihilated the vast majority of those camped there, including men, women, and children. California Joe proclaimed his innocence as an instigator in this affair, but his actions were nevertheless suspicious.[3]

After the Civil War, Joe was in Hays, Kansas, where he became friends with the infamous James Butler "Wild Bill" Hickok, who also had been a former associate of Jack Slade. Their friendship is undisputed, though they did not spend much time together. Shortly before his death, Hickok claimed that his two pistols and California Joe were the best friends he ever had.

Research reveals a "Jo" Milner led a wagon train to Denver across the Platte River route. He brought with him four wagons loaded with flour, bacon, and other popular provisions to sell to the miners. He arrived in Denver on July 26, 1868. Colonel George Armstrong Custer appointed California Joe that same year as his chief of scouts. Custer however soon found Joe drunk and immediately demoted him.[4]

Over the next several years California Joe was usually found somewhere between Fort Hays, Kansas, and Cheyenne or Fort Laramie. He occasionally held a position as an Army scout but was most often found in one of the many saloons. He was reputed to always have money, though it is difficult to ascertain where he acquired it. He seldom received pay for military service and was not often a successful gambler. In 1874, he made a somewhat successful prospecting trip to California, then returned to Fort Laramie.

There he attempted a freighting business, but soon shot one of his partners, claiming they were trying to rob him. The man recovered from his wound, but a short time later Milner finished the job when he shot the former partner from ambush. Joe claimed this was in retaliation for a similar attempt made by the other man on his own life. This exploit was immediately followed by the partnership with Gray (discussed in the previous chapter) which also ended in an attempted murder by Milner.[5]

In 1875, California Joe found himself employed again by the Army in scouting for the Jenny Geological Expedition into the Black Hills of what is now South Dakota. When they returned to Fort Laramie that fall, Milner immediately began planning a return trip to the Black Hills to search for gold. It is possible that Joe murdered and robbed John Richard and Alfred Pallardie on the Running Water that winter to finance his prospecting. Richard's murder was officially attributed to renegade Indians, primarily based on moccasin tracks at the scene, even though Richard, Pallardie, and California Joe were all known to wear moccasins as often as not.[6] However, on this evidence and the testimony of California Joe, officials blamed Indians.

When we look at the rest of the evidence, California Joe's innocence is less certain. Joe was with Richard when he was last seen alive. Frank Salaway, an experienced tracker, helped search for John Richard and investigated the site, however, substantial details were not recorded. When confronted with the suspicions, Joe told the accusers that Tom Newcomb had killed Richard and Pallardie, then Joe immediately left for Deadwood. The murderer or murderers stole Richard's money and destroyed his wagonload of trade goods. If Indians had been the culprits, the trade goods would have been more valuable to them than the money.[7] California Joe next is reported in Deadwood with a large sum of money in his possession.

The mystery of California Joe continued when Wild Bill Hickok arrived in Deadwood. Hickok and Milner soon renewed their old friendship and were in constant company in the saloons about town. Rumors existed that there was a conspiracy to murder Hickok that he ignored. Milner mysteriously left for Montana the day before Hickok was murdered and did not return until after Hickok's alleged murderer, Jack McCall, had been acquitted in his first trial. When California Joe did return to Deadwood, he threatened to kill McCall in revenge, then again left town.[8]

In October of 1861, Tom Newcomb killed California Joe Milner at Fort Robinson. Three distinct versions of the killing emerged. Milner's grandson in his biography of California Joe places him at Fort Robinson in October, drinking in the Trader's Saloon when Tom Newcomb, the post butcher, entered. Upon seeing Joe, Newcomb drew his gun; Milner did likewise. But before any shooting could take place, others convinced them to put away their guns and share a drink. "Holdout" Johnson overheard part of the conversation between Milner and Newcomb and knew that it was about the murder of John Richard. Later that night, Tom Newcomb shot California Joe in the back at the quartermaster's corral with a Winchester. Joe died instantly and was buried in the post cemetery. Newcomb was jailed at the garrison, but was released on a technicality a few days later and never tried.[9]

Frank Salaway was a witness to the killing of California Joe and his story varies somewhat from that of Milner's grandson. Salaway said that following the murder of John Richard, California Joe quickly began spreading the word that Tom Newcomb had killed Richard. By the time Newcomb discovered the reason his friends were acting so peculiarly toward him, California Joe had left the area. A few months later, Joe was back at Fort Robinson and drinking in the Trader's Saloon, which conducted business from a dugout near the post. Several customers warned Joe that Newcomb intended to avenge Richard's death and the lies that had been told about him. California Joe told those who would listen that Tom Newcomb had not the sand to face a true man like himself and was probably hunting a hole to hide in. Someone repeated California Joe's insults to Tom. As Joe was coming out of the dugout, Newcomb appeared from around a nearby corner and said, "Here I am; hunt your hole!" Joe was armed but did not attempt to draw his revolver. Instead he tried to duck back into the dugout, and Newcomb shot him down.[10]

The third version of this story is from Frank Grouard who said the events following the murder were the exact opposite of what Frank Salaway reported. According to Grouard, Milner went to Fort Robinson the day after Richard's murder. There Tom Newcomb had Joe arrested for the murder. It was decided that no evidence pointed to Milner's guilt, and he was released and left town, but not before he threatened to get even with Newcomb. Accordingly, Newcomb lived in mortal fear of California Joe. "One morning as Joe was coming from breakfast, Newcomb hid behind the building where the former was messing, and just as the unsuspecting scout passed the corner of the building,

Newcomb leveled a double-barreled shotgun at him and pulled the trigger. The entire contents of the gun entered Joe's body, killing him instantly." Grouard goes on to admit that he was nowhere in the country at the time. The source of his information was hearsay, likely repeated by mutual friends of Milner and Grouard.[11]

A fourth version of the story is far less detailed. A resident of the Fort Laramie area at the time, John S. Collins, recalled: "The next heard of Joe was over at Red Cloud Agency, where he was killed in an affray with one Newcombe. The cause of this fracas was that Joe had been blamed for the killing of old man Reshaw (or Richard), and Newcombe, the only man supposed to know about the affair, might later expose him, so Joe undertook to kill Newcombe. Newcombe was the quicker of the two, and Joe fell dead on the spot." This version is the only one that ends in a two-way battle. It also implies Milner's guilt.[12]

California Joe Milner had gained notoriety as a scout in the west and was accorded merit in some circles. Unfortunately some considered him a hero. However, misplaced admiration is not uncommon; other western desperados have gained celebrity through cruel deeds that have mistakenly been depicted as heroic. Whether Milner was the murderer of John Richard and Alfred Pallardie will probably never be known. Perhaps at least one man felt so strongly that Joe was guilty that he resorted to vigilante justice. What is certain is that he was not a consistently honorable man. His death came with the same ruthless disregard that he had meted out to many of his own victims.

Magloire Mosseau was far from what would be considered a friend of John Richard and called him "an old rascal," but he did not dispute the general consensus that California Joe was a murderer and likely responsible for the death of Richard and Pallardie. He said "…a great many persons have been killed in the vicinity of [Fort] Laramie…and many have fallen at the hands of white men themselves." Several years later two well dressed, and seemingly well educated young men claiming to be the sons of California Joe arrived at Fort Robinson, where Mosseau then resided. They did not speak to any of the officers but asked numerous questions of the older civilians at the fort regarding the burial of Joe and the whereabouts of Tom Newcomb. After a time the two men left, but several weeks later they returned. They said that Newcomb had gone to the Pacific Coast but that they had "accomplished their mission."

Mosseau determined that these two likely were truly the sons of California Joe and that they had taken the life of Tom Newcomb.[13]

> *"If frontier posts and lonely places elsewhere could give up their secrets there would be a horrible record of crime revealed."*
> Magloire Alexis Mosseau, 1906.[14]

⊰⊱·⊰⊱

"HI" KELLY. Hiram B. "Hi" Kelly appears and reappears frequently in John Richard's life story. Kelly, however, acquired both fortune and political influence, at times living in luxury, while Richard continued the rough hewn lifestyle of a frontiersman and Indian trader. Kelly was born October 14, 1834, in Sheridan County, Missouri, one of ten children born to Hiram S. and Mahala Kelly. When he was fifteen, he and his father joined other forty-niners in the California Gold Rush. They celebrated Independence Day along with some three thousand other "rushers" at Independence Rock. Lacking other forms of fireworks, several of the miners loaded dynamite into cracks in the rock. The explosions destroyed hundreds of names left by their predecessors on the trails.

Hi and his father spent their first winter in Weavertown, California. They then traveled from one strike to another. After three years, they returned to Missouri, arriving back home in December 1852. While gone from home, Hi Kelly had grown to just over six feet tall, with a thin, wiry build and a fit and agile physique. In the spring of 1853, Kelly purchased a six-yoke bull team and freight wagon. He contracted with wagonmaster Poll Stone to drive them to Santa Fe. While with this company, he survived a narrow escape from Indians on the Arkansas River.[15]

In 1854, Kelly traded his oxen for a ten-mule team and contracted to run the Santa Fe Trail with wagon boss Van Eps. In 1855, Kelly tired of the monotony of freighting and began driving a mail coach from Missouri to Santa Fe. They made the monthly round trip in twenty-one days, giving mules and driver a few days to recuperate before repeating the excursion. In September 1856, while Kelly was hauling mail along the Little Arkansas River, some one hundred hostile Cheyenne Indians abducted Kelly and his assistants. They were placed inside a ring surrounded by fire. After a considerable parlay, Kelly bartered their freedom with their food and the threat that the military would retaliate for the obstruction of the mail. They traveled thirty miles before meeting a train of freighters from which they obtained food. Six years later Kelly

Hiram "Hi" B. Kelly was a noted figure in early Wyoming history and moved in and out of the life of John Richard. He was one of the first cattlemen in southeast Wyoming and controlled a vast amount of rangeland that he later sold to Swan Land and Cattle (*Wyoming State Archives, Department of State Parks and Cultural Resources*)

met up with one of these Cheyenne who told him that after they had been released, the Indians had changed their minds and attempted to overtake the mail coach. When the Indians caught up with them, however, Kelly and his men had already thrown in with the freighters so the Indians abandoned their recapture plans. In December 1857, Kelly's feet were badly frostbitten, and he gave up driving the coach and carrying the mails.[16]

Many of Hiram Kelly's exploits over the following twenty years have been chronicled in this book. He had a way of being in the thick of the action. In 1876, Kelly and his brother-in-law Tom Maxwell erected a large frame house about a mile south of the family's sod and log home. From this house Kelly and Maxwell operated the Chugwater Stage Station on the Cheyenne-Deadwood Stage Line. Tom Maxwell later operated a hotel from this home in addition to the stage station. In later years this home was the residence of the managers of the Swan Land and

Cattle Company. In 2013 it still stands, directly east of the present town of Chugwater, Wyoming.

In 1877, Kelly had a fourteen-room brick home constructed on the site of the old sod and log cabin that the family had occupied off and on since 1864. This home stood on the east side of the creek, a short distance from the present town of Chugwater, Wyoming. This new home was a mansion by all standards of any era. The house faced south and as visitors approached they would first see the large portico that supported an upper balcony above the entrance. Visitors entered through the massive double front doors into the main hall with entries into the two large parlors, each sporting massive fireplaces; an ornate staircase ascended from the main hall to the five family bedrooms on the second floor. On the main floor were also a formal dining room and an open porch, which faced east. To the rear were the kitchen, the butler's pantry, and an informal staircase, leading to two smaller bedrooms above the kitchen. While residing in this home, the Kellys always hired servants as well as tutors for their children. A short distance from the house stood a small, stout, adobe structure with wooden bars on the windows that once was used as a jail for road agents captured along the Cheyenne-Deadwood Trail. On a low hill just east of the house is a small family cemetery, in which several members of the Richard family are buried. This long vacant home was dismantled in 1974, and the bricks were used in an addition on a local church. Massive trees outline the yard that surrounded the old mansion.[17]

In 1879, Hiram Kelly bought the Donald McPhee Ranch. He had already acquired three nearby properties, the LC Ranch, the Hamilton Ranch, and the North Chug Ranch, plus he'd added the Y Ranch near LaGrange and the D Ranch, thirty-three miles north of Cheyenne, to his holdings. Later that year he obtained the contract to supply beef to Fort McKinney. To meet this need he brought four thousand head of cattle branded with the Cross H, which were located on the Crazy Woman Fork of Powder River. His range now included vast portions of eastern Wyoming and extended into parts of western Nebraska. With thousands of head of cattle and hundreds of employees he had, through hard work and tenacity, become a true cattle baron in most every sense of the word.[18]

April 28, 1884, Hiram and Lizzie Kelly left for Edinburgh, Scotland. There they sold their ranch consisting of 3,200 deeded acres plus associated grazing rights to the Swan Land and Cattle Company for $250,000.

Elizabeth Richard Kelly was the daughter John Richard's brother Peter and Lucy (aka Red Sack). She married Hiram B. Kelly. (*Wyoming State Archives, Department of State Parks and Cultural Resources*)

Before leaving Wyoming they purchased a quarter of a block on Ferguson Street (2410 Carey Avenue) in Cheyenne, directly across the street from the Capitol. They hired M. P. Keefe to erect a home there. Following their visit to Scotland, the Kellys toured Europe for most of the summer. They returned home to a sumptuous mansion that made their previous home on Chugwater Creek look like a country cottage. From elaborately carved walnut front doors to ornately styled arrowhead and tomahawk wrought iron gates and fences, no detail was overlooked. Matching cherry mantle pieces topped the fireplaces that warmed every room except the kitchen. The newel post and banister that adorned the stairway was a woodcarver's masterpiece. Crystal chandeliers hung from the ceilings of every room. The elegance of this three-story home demonstrated the stature to which the Kellys had risen. Hiram Kelly chose to retire at age fifty. He was a very wealthy man and for the next few years the Kellys spent a large share of their time entertaining friends and showing off their beautiful new home.[19]

Hiram Kelly had always been a man of action and this new lifestyle, which he had worked so hard to obtain, soon bored him. He became interested in mining and real estate investments, of which he knew very little, and soon his fortune began to dwindle. In 1902, the Kellys sold their Cheyenne mansion to Edgar Boice and moved to Seattle. Two years later they moved to Portland, Oregon, and, in 1906, to Denver. Four years later they moved to the suburb of Edgewater, Colorado. In Edgewater, Hiram Kelly remained active and agile. Though most of his money was gone, his mind was still sharp and his bright blue eyes still keen. Elizabeth "Lizzie" Richard Kelly passed away July 8, 1922. In later years, she spent many hours painting pictographs on leather. Several of her works were presented to the Colorado State Museum in Denver. Two years later, June 2, 1924, Hiram B. "Hi" Kelly passed away. The two are buried side by side in Fort Collins, Colorado.[20]

No better eulogy could be given than that by Daze Bristol, a Cheyenne newspaper woman whose brother was married to one of Kelly's daughters: "This was the career of a man who was born with little and died with little, but whose life was an example of the sturdy characters who built our great state and nation, a man whose contribution to Wyoming's story will always be remembered." The ranch Kelly built continued to grow under the ownership of the Swan Land and Cattle Company. At one point it was reputed to be the largest ranch in the United States, owning over half a million acres of deeded land and nearly two hundred thousand head of livestock.[21]

⋘≫⋙

THE SETTLING OF RICHEAU CREEK. John Richard began grazing livestock along Chugwater Creek in the mid-1840s. At times his herders ranged south to nearly Cheyenne Pass. As his seasonal operations expanded he eventually set up a semi-permanent headquarters on Richeau Creek resulting in the creek and surrounding hills bearing his name today. These frontier ranching operations of 1845-1870 would be the precursor for the massive herds of cattle that inhabited the vast ranges of the cattle barons of the 1890s.

John Richard was not the only one to recognize the richness of the Richeau Creek valley. In 1878, Robert Grant migrated with his family from Glasgow, Scotland, to the M-Bar ranch of John MacFarlane at Chimney Rock, Wyoming Territory, now known as Slater, Wyoming.

Mrs. MacFarlane was Mrs. Grant's aunt. While residing there, Robert Grant worked for John Hunton's LD ranch and soon realized the possibilities of Richeau Creek. He first homesteaded, however, on the east bank of Chugwater Creek, directly across from its confluence with Richeau Creek. Heavy rains the following spring flooded the family out of the dugout home that Grant had built, and they moved across to the west side of Chugwater Creek and filed on a new homestead. By this time it appears that none of John Richard's former associates remained on Richeau Creek. The families that were then homesteading in the vicinity were McPhee, Ramsey, Clay, Hunter, Rhemeyer, and Steele.[22]

⋘⋙⋘⋙

In 1880 Colin McDougall came to Wyoming and homesteaded on Richeau Creek. His claim included the dugout left some ten years earlier by John Richard. By 1884, Robert Grant had proven up on his claim on Richeau Creek and sold it to John Hunton. He took the income from the sale and purchased cattle. Then he filed a new claim on the north fork of the creek adjacent to McDougall. The Grants and McDougalls built spreader dams and dug ditches to irrigate the fertile valley. Many of these are still visible today. Educating their children was a primary concern of those living along Richeau and Chugwater Creeks. Initially the Grant and McDougall families helped to erect a schoolhouse on the M-Bar ranch. After Hi Kelly sold his ranch to the Swan Land and Cattle Company, many of their neighbors also sold to the large syndicate. The Grant and McDougall children then made up the majority of the students, so the school was moved to Richeau Creek. For a time classes were conducted from the McDougall and Grant homes, alternating every three months, until a schoolhouse was built between the two ranches.[23]

In 1890, Robert Grant built the stone house that in 2013 is still a residence used by the Grant family. He used local stone and manufactured his own mortar from limestone. He later built a large stone barn and several other outbuildings. In 1893, Colin McDougall erected a twelve-room frame house on his ranch. Colin McDougall sold this ranch a few years later, and it since has passed through several owners. The West family purchased this former John Richard ranch several years ago and at this writing live in the residence built by Colin McDougall.

Duncan Paul Grant, son of the elder Robert Grant, worked for many years for his father and the Swan Land and Cattle Company. For five years he and his brother, Bob, worked as wolf hunters for Swan. Wolf populations in that day had grown to such phenomenal populations that various packs would kill from twenty-five to thirty head of cattle at a time. In the springtime, when raising their pups, these packs killed cattle every day. For an operation the size of Swan Land and Cattle Company, which ranged from western Nebraska to Medicine Bow, Wyoming, daily losses mounted to the hundreds. Men like Duncan and Bob Grant contracted with the large cattle companies, receiving a bounty of four to twenty-five dollars for every wolf they killed. It was not a pleasant means of earning money, but a profitable one for those who had the tenacity to match wits with the wolves, and it was considered necessary. A good wolf hunter was considered valuable and the Grant brothers were good at their job. Duncan Grant captured a wolf pup, which he raised as a pet named "Howdy." Howdy lived for some time at the Grant Ranch, but was eventually stolen and sold to the Chicago Zoo.

When Robert Grant Sr. began to slow with age, the brothers quit working for the Swan Land and Cattle Company to help their father run the family ranch. When their father died he passed ownership of the ranch to Duncan. After an illustrious career as a cowboy and cattleman, Duncan Paul Grant passed away in his sleep while taking an afternoon nap on the family sofa. Duncan Grant was not of the personality to boast of his many achievements, but in his later years he could easily see that the lifestyle of his youth was no longer shared by the young men of the late 1900s. Prior to his death he painstakingly wrote down the details and recollections of events and methods used in ranching at the turn of the previous century, particularly along Richeau Creek.[24]

As the era of the big cattlemen and vast open rangelands gradually came to a close, ranchers began to adopt new methods of raising livestock. The changes have resulted in more efficient management and a higher quality of beef than could have been imagined in 1900.

John Richard probably would not recognize the land. As decades have passed, the valley along Richeau Creek has become much more lush than it was when John Richard first saw it. Ranchers have built diversion dams for irrigation and have cultivated portions of the wide meadows to improve hay and grazing conditions. In the Richeau Hills, the Bureau of Land Management, Wyoming Game and Fish, and local ranchers have worked together to greatly improve mule deer and other wildlife habitat.

⊰⊱·⊰⊱

A New Community at Richard's Bridge. After the abandonment of Fort Casper and Richard's Bridge, there is no record of habitation in the area for several years. When James H. Bury first passed the site of the old fort in the early 1870s, he wrote there was nothing there but the charred remains of the old adobe trading post. By the fall of 1882, Joseph M. Carey had located the regional headquarters for his CY Ranch at the former site of Fort Casper.

Joshua and Sarah A. Stroud, recognizing the vitality of one of John Richard's former grazing areas, established a road ranch near the crossing of Reshaw Creek, now known as Elkhorn Creek, on the Oregon Trail, approximately one mile southeast of the former site of Richard's Bridge. Since the Indian depredations of the 1860s and 1870s had considerably waned in the area, travel on the Oregon Trail had once again increased. It is often thought that after the completion of the transcontinental railroad, all travel along the Oregon and Overland Trails ceased. This is not true. Even though the railroad certainly diminished trail traffic, many emigrants could not afford the luxury of traveling by rail so still opted for the arduous journey west by wagon.[25]

When Joshua Stroud filed his Desert Claim for the homestead on October 17, 1883, he was already established there, and the site was known as Stroud's Station. Mrs. Stroud dispensed meals to the wayfaring travelers along the trail from the kitchen table of their modest cabin, and Stroud's Station was famous along the trail "for her fine culinary skill." When surveyors for the Wyoming Central Railroad arrived in the vicinity in 1885, Stroud's Station was chosen as the terminus for the railroad. With this in mind, Joshua and Sarah began platting the town of Strouds, Wyoming Territory, adjacent to the proposed railway, a few hundred yards north of Stroud's Station. Since this area was then part of Carbon County, they traveled to Rawlins, Wyoming, to file their plat. On July 20, 1888, their plat was approved for the new town of Strouds.

Joshua Stroud intended to sell the land of his new town to the railroad and the deal was all but concluded when the Carey family offered to give the railroad all the land they wanted for a town, four miles further west. When the railroad men approached Stroud with the Carey's offer,

Joshua flatly refused to consider giving away any portion of his ranch. He unfortunately did not share the foresight of the Careys who realized that as the new town grew they could sell additional portions of their land at greatly inflated prices.

Thus, the town of Casper, Wyoming, came to be. This late change occurred so suddenly that the new town had not been surveyed when newcomers began arriving to open businesses there. They camped in an area now referred to as Old Casper, about a mile east of the proposed town, for nearly a year until the new town could be platted. Joshua Stroud's town never materialized and with the proximity of the new town of Casper, even Stroud's Station was soon a thing of the past. Joshua and Sarah Stroud remained in the cattle business for many years. Around 1950 their ranch was purchased by Homer Lathrop and has since been known as Lathrop Ranch or the V Bar V. Joshua and Sarah Stroud's log cabin is still in very good repair and is likely the oldest standing structure in Natrona County, Wyoming.[26]

In 1889, Casper, Wyoming, was much the same as many other western towns anticipating the arrival of the railroad. Buildings of rough-sawn lumber sprang from the sagebrush as if by magic to house numerous new businesses. Cattlemen from near and far came to hear the latest news of the railroad's arrival while the cowboys employed by them flocked to the new saloons and dancehalls to test the latest wares. The town was instantly a thriving community and with community comes government. On April 21, 1890, Emanuel Erben was awarded the contract to construct a new town hall in Casper. He asked William Tranter Evans, a Welsh brick and stone mason from Grant, Nebraska, to make and lay the brick, while he would do the carpentry himself. Evans arrived in Casper a short time later. He soon found numerous businessmen waiting in line to contract his services. Before year's end he moved his family to Casper, for it seemed he would not be able to outlive the demand for his talents.

Over the next several years, W. T. Evans contracted to build schools, jails, churches, homes, and many of the commercial buildings of the downtown business district of Casper, Wyoming. In 1905, Evans filed for a homestead patent on a parcel of land three miles east of Casper and a quarter of a mile south of the former Richard's Bridge. There he established a ranch that included the site of Richard's Bridge, which he leased from the State. In 1921, at the age of sixty-nine, Evans retired as a mason and concentrated his efforts on ranching and enjoying the fruits of his many years of labor. The following year the Texas Oil Company took an interest in a portion of his ranch adjacent to property they had already purchased to construct an oil refinery. During speculation that the Texas Company would build there, Guaranteed Investment Company of Casper in a joint venture with W. T. Evans, subdivided and platted the Town of Evansville, Wyoming, on a portion of the Evans ranch. Construction of the refinery was soon underway and every lot in the new town was quickly sold. Two additions were also platted and soon sold. On May 15, 1923, the Town of Evansville was incorporated. The town boasted a church, electric lights, telephones, and a modern water system. The source of Evansville's once celebrated public water was Elkhorn Spring near Richard's old grazing camp. Over fifty years after John Richard left his bridge and the community that surrounded it, the town of Evansville took its place.[27]

⋘⋙

EPILOG. The fur trade and transportation could be said to be the West's first industries. With his fur trading, freighting, bridges, ferries, trading posts, and road ranches, John Richard played an important role in the development of both those industries. The livestock business quickly followed and was the mainstay of commerce in the West for many years. John Richard played his part in establishing and profiting from that business.

Petroleum and mining soon grew into powerful industries, and small veins of coal like that Richard used to fuel his blacksmith shops at Richard's Bridge were the first indication of the millions of tons of mineral beneath the surface.

John Richard was far from a saint, but he had many virtues. The colorful lifestyle and independent character of early trappers, traders, settlers, ranchers, merchants, and oilmen established a code for living that is still valued in the area. This unique frontier spirit, while romanticized, nevertheless plays an important role in the West's identity and spawned today's tourist industry.

John Richard influenced the development of nearly every phase of the economy in frontier West. The many aspects and adventures of John Richard's diverse life demonstrate how one little-known man can effect the course of history.

Notes to Chapter Thirteen:

1. Rosa, Joseph G., *The West of Wild Bill Hickok*, (University of Oklahoma Press, Norman, OK, 1982), p. 173, 196.

2. Milner and Forrest, p. 106–107, 125–129.

3. Milner and Forrest, p. 131–135.

4. Rosa, *The West of Wild Bill Hickok*, p. 196; It is not certain whether this Jo Milner was California Joe. If so, it does give reason for his move from Kansas back to the Rocky Mountain region at that time. Cragin, F. W., "Interview of Sylvester Monroe Buzzard on May 18, 1921," (Unpublished Notebooks, Cragin Papers, Colorado Springs Pioneers Museum, Colorado Springs, CO.), notebook XIV, p. 7; Ambrose, p. 288–297.

5. Milner and Forrest, p. 207–218; Collins, p. 131–134.

6. Milner and Forrest, p. 222–235; Jones, Brian, *Those Wild Reshaw Boys*, p. 45; McDermott, "John Baptiste Richard" in *Mountain Men*, 2:303.

7. Ibid.; Judge Ricker states that Salaway gave him every detail of the particulars of the case and the circumstances pointing the guilty finger toward California Joe. Ricker, however, who normally is considered an outstanding source of historic information, failed to mention many of these details. It is possible that Salaway did not want to share the fate doled out to Newcomb by California Joe's sons and requested that these details be omitted. A note in Ricker's own handwriting on page seventy-five of this same interview states "page 74 taken out purposely." Page seventy-three and seventy-five both contain incomplete sentences regarding the massacre at Wounded Knee Creek. It can only be surmised that Salaway requested the removal of some ticklish disclosure that had been recorded on page seventy-four. Ricker, Judge Eli S., "Frank Salaway," tablet 28, p. 66–67.

8. It is quite likely that it was during this absence from Deadwood that Joe went to work for Frank Grouard driving the herd of horses from Fort Laramie to Custer City for General Crook. DeBarthe, p. 171; Rosa, *They Called Him Wild Bill*, p. 226–232.

9. Milner and Forrest, p. 279–282; In 1947 all of those bodies buried in the military cemetery at Fort Robinson were exhumed and reinterred at Fort McPherson, near Maxwell, Nebraska.

10. About a year after the killing of California Joe, Tom Newcomb worked for Frank Salaway. Salaway said that he was a good fellow and a good worker. Following the murder of John Richard, Newcomb had in fact said that he would kill California Joe on sight for reporting that he had killed Richard. Ricker, *Frank Salaway*, tablet 28, p. 66–68.

11. DeBarthe, p. 171–173.

12. Collins, p. 134.

13. Ricker, "Magloire Mosseau," tablet 28, p. 63–65, 69. Thomas E. Newcomb was born in Kentucky, September 1847. He was shot in the back with a shotgun blast and left for dead in Montana around 1880. He survived his wounds, was married in 1886, and later became one of Yellowstone National Park's first rangers. United States Census, 1900, index and images, FamilySearch (https://familysearch.org/pal:/MM9.1.1/MM5z-CDN : accessed 19 May 2013, Thomas Newcomb, 1900.

14. Ricker, "Magloire Mosseau," tablet 28, p. 40.

15. Bartlett, vol. III, p. 139–142; Larson, p. 268.

16. Bartlett, vol. III, p. 141–142; Briston and Dubois, p. 1.

17. Larson, p. 268. A portion of the old Kelly Ranch, which includes the old homesite and cemetery was owned by Mrs. Jim Brown and operated by her daughter and son-in-law Amy and Steve LeSatz. They were gracious enough to allow the author access to the old home and cemetery sites, in 1998. The ranch is owned by Lance Garbowski in 2014.

18. Briston and Dubois, p. 3; Coutant, *Coutant Collection*, box 4, folder 53, book 37.

19. Larson, p. 268; Bartlett, vol. III, p. 141.

20. Bartlett, vol. III, p. 141–142; Larson, p. 268; Briston and Dubois, p. 3–4.

21. Larson, p. 268; Osgood, p. 97–98, 192, 222.

22. Grant. In 1872 federal surveyors made no mention of anyone residing in that vicinity. Henry G. Hay and John B. Thomas surveyed the Township lines of T21N R67W, T21N R68W, and T22N R67W in July of 1872. Edwin James and James B. Thomas surveyed the section lines of the same townships in August through October of that year. USGS survey records, United States Bureau of Land Management, Department of the Interior, Cheyenne, Wyoming.

23. Grant; Beach, Cora M., *Women of Wyoming*, Casper, Wyoming, (1927), p. 261; Beach, Cora M., *Women of Wyoming, Volume 2*, (Lusk, Wyoming, 1929), p. 321.

24. Grant.

25. David; Beach, *Women of Wyoming*, p. 253: Owen, W. O., Deputy Surveyor, Field Notes of the Subdivision Lines of T33N, R78W, USGS survey records, Bureau of Land Management, Cheyenne, Wyoming.

26. Beach, *Women of Wyoming*, p. 253–255: Casper Zonta Club, *Casper Chronicles,* (Written and Published by the Casper Zonta Club, Casper, Wyoming, 1964), p. 8–14; Tract Book from the Federal Land Office, Douglas, Wyoming, USGS

survey records, Bureau of Land Management, Cheyenne, Wyoming; Application and Approval for the Plat of the Town of Strouds, Transferred records from Carbon County, Wyoming, (Natrona County Courthouse, Casper, Wyoming).

27. Glass, Jefferson, "The Founder of Evansville: Casper Builder W. T. Evans," *Annals of Wyoming*, (Autumn, 1998), Vol. 70, No. 4, p. 20–28.

Appendix A
❧Richard Family Genealogy❧
Compiled by Stewart Monroe & Jefferson Glass

FIRST GENERATION
1. Jean Francois Xavier RICHARD.
Born in 1787, Jean died in 1846. Occupation: Trapper/Trader.

About 1810 when Jean was 23, he married Rosalie COTE, daughter of Alexis COTE Sr. (1724–1808) and Elizabeth DODIER. Born about 1790, Rosalie died in July 1833.

They had the following children:

2	i.	Jean Baptiste (1810–1875)
3	ii.	Leanore "Ellinore" (1812–)
4	iii.	Rosalie (1818–)
5	iv.	Pierre "Peter" (1820–)
	v.	Agnes Eulalie "Julia"—Born about 1822.
6	vi.	Mary Elizabeth (1823–1855)
7	vii.	Joseph B. (1823–1864)
	viii.	Susanne—Born on June 13, 1829.[1]
	ix.	Louisa—Born on May 15, 1831.
	x.	Victorie—Born in July 1833.

SECOND GENERATION
Family of Jean Francois Xavier RICHARD (1) & Rosalie COTE

2. Jean Baptiste RICHARD aka "John Baptiste RICHARD Sr."
Born on December 14, 1810. John died late in 1875. Occupation: Trapper/Trader.

About 1843 when John was 32, he married Mary GARDINER, daughter of William GARDINER and White Thunder Woman. Mary was born on April 5, 1823.

They had the following children:

8	i.	John Baptiste (1844–1872)

    ii.   Louis—Born about 1847, Louis died on July 10, 1898.[2]

    iii.   Peter S.—Born in 1850.

    iv.   Charles E. (Twin) Born on November 9, 1852, Charles died in May 1868.

9   v.   Josephine (Twin) (1852–)

    vi.   Rose—Born in June 1859.

3. Leanore "Ellinore" RICHARD

Born on September 22, 1812.

On April 27, 1840 when Ellinore was 27, she married Antoine P. PALLARDIE, son of Pierre P. PALLARDIE Sr. (1771– ?) and Marie Josephine LABUSSIERE. Antoine was born in 1806.

They had the following children:

    i.   Jean Francois—Born in October 1840.

10   ii.   Mary Philomene (1844–)

11   iii.   Rosalie (1846–1920)

    iv.   Alfred—Born on January 7, 1849, Alfred died late in 1875.

    v.   Charles Benedict—Born in August 1852.

4. Rosalie RICHARD

Born on July 15, 1818.

On February 11, 1839 when Rosalie was 20, she first married Charles B. BORDEAUX. Born about 1815, Charles died before 1850.

They had one child:

    i.   Charles Felix—Born on February 19, 1843.

In 1853 when Rosalie was 34, she second-married Constant PRINAT.

5. Pierre "Peter" RICHARD

Born on September 4, 1820. Occupation: Trapper/Trader.

On May 6, 1857 when Peter was 36, he first married Sarah Jane ST. CIN, daughter of Francis Xavier "Daniel" SINCENNES (1804–1873) and Marie "Mary" CRELY (1818–1920). Sarah was born in 1837.

Peter second married Red Sack also known as Lucy.

They had the following children:

    i.   John Al—He died in 1891.

12   ii.   Elizabeth "Lizzie" (1849–1922)

6. Mary Elizabeth RICHARD

Born in 1823, Mary died about 1855.

On August 2, 1843 when Mary was 20, she married Charles B. BRANHAM. Born on November 22, 1811, Charles died on August 2, 1893; he was 81.

They had the following children:

      i.   John (1845-1863). Possibly also called John Brenon.

      ii.   Amanda—Born in 1849.

13   iii. Henry Vandever (1852–).

7. Joseph B. RICHARD Sr.

Born in 1823, Joseph died on July 5, 1864. Occupation: Trader/Merchant.

About 1846 when Joseph was 23, he married Cane Woman (Kane), daughter of Whirlwind. Cane Woman was born about 1830.

They had the following children:

      i.   Joseph—Born about 1847. Occupation: Teamster.

      ii.   Charles—Born about 1850.

     iii. James—Born about 1854. Occupation: Laborer.

     iv. Louisa—Born about 1858. (Louisa married Bill "Old Bill" ALLMAN.)

      v.   Suzanne—Born about 1863. (Suzanne married Ben JANIS, son of Nicholas "Old Nick" JANIS (1827–1902) and Martha.)

THIRD GENERATION
Family of John Baptiste RICHARD Sr. (2) & Mary GARDINER

8. John Baptiste RICHARD Jr.

Born about 1844, John Jr. died in 1872. Occupation: Trader.

About 1862 when John was 18, he first-married a daughter of Yellow Bear.

In 1864 when John was 20, he second married Louisa MERIVALE (also spelled Merrivile), daughter of Joseph (sometimes José or James) MERIVALE (1815–) and Mary (1832–). Louisa was born in 1849.

They had two children:

      i.   Alfred or Alexander— Born about 1867.

      ii.   Milla F.—Born in 1868.

In 1869 when John Baptiste was 25, he third married Hubalola, born about 1852. They had no children.

In 1869 when John Baptiste was 25, he fourth married Mary Louisa, born about 1848. They had no children.

In 1871 when John Baptiste was 27, he fifth married Emily JANIS, daughter of Nicholas "Old Nick" JANIS (1827–1902) and Martha. They had no children.

9. Josephine RICHARD

Born on November 9, 1852.

On October 10, 1869, when Josephine was 16, she married Baptiste Gene "Big Bat" POURIER, son of Joseph POURIER Sr. (1790–1843) and Mary (Marie) AUBUCHON (–1876). Bat was born on July 16, 1843. He died on September 17, 1928, when he was 85.

They had the following children:

  i.   Alice—Born on July 8, 1870.[3]
  ii.   Elizabeth—Born in 1874. (Elizabeth married Charles JONES.)
  iii. Joseph—Born in 1878. (Joseph married Etta McGAA.)
  iv.   Louis—Born in 1880. (Louis first married Ella MONTEAUX. He second married Mamie DURAY.)
  v.   Mary "Lovie"—Born in 1884.[4]
  vi.   Peter—Born in 1888. (Peter married Hattie STANDING BEAR.)
  vii. Rose—Born in 1890. (Rose married William TIBBETTS.)
  viii. Charles—Born in 1892. (Charles first married Bessie PROVOST. He second married Louise.)
  ix.   Ellen—Born on November 22, 1895, she died on August 13, 1990.[5]
  x.   Florence T.—Born on September 5, 1897. She died after 1986.[6]
14 xi. John Baptiste
  xii. Emile[7]

Family of Leanore "Ellinore" RICHARD (3) & Antoine P. PALLARDIE

10. Mary Philomene PALLARDIE

Born on June 30, 1844.

On April 11, 1863 when Mary was 18, she married William H. SELBY Sr..

They had the following children:

  i.   Charles
  ii.   Fredrick
  iii. James E.
  iv.   William H.—Born in 1876, William died in 1936.

11. Rosalie PALLARDIE

Born on September 17, 1846, Rosalie died on January 20, 1920.

About 1867 when Rosalie was 20, she married Eli PLANT Sr.. Eli was born on September 19, 1826. He died on November 8, 1899.

They had the following children:

i.	Mary Nora—Died on June 29, 1871.
ii.	Eli—Born in 1868. Eli died on May 29, 1890.
iii.	Louis—Born in 1872. (Louis married Cecelia.)
iv.	Charles—Born on February 18, 1875. (Charles married Henrietta COMPTON.)
v.	Susan Amelia (Suzanna) (1878–1937) **(15)**
vi.	Rose—Born on March 27, 1881.

15 before v.

Family of Pierre "Peter" RICHARD (5) & Red Sack aka Lucy

12. Elizabeth "Lizzie" RICHARD

Born about 1849, Lizzie died on July 8, 1922.

In 1864 when Lizzie was 15, she married Hiram B. "Hi" KELLY, son of Hiram KELLY and Mahala. Hiram was born on October 14, 1834. He died on June 2, 1924.

They had the following children:

i.	Kate
ii.	Cora
iii.	Clara
iv.	Chug
v.	Will
vi.	Charles
vii.	Ben
viii.	Jack

Family of Mary Elizabeth RICHARD (6) & Charles B. BRANHAM

13. Henry Vandever BRANHAM

Born on September 1, 1852.

Henry married Margaret Agnes ST. LOUIS, daughter of Joseph Colbert ST. LOUIS (1804–1863) and Mary Margaret LUCIEN (1833–1916).

They had the following children:

i.	Charles J.—Born about 1877, he died on September 22, 1936.

16 ii. Rosalie "Rose" (1878–1941)
17 iii. Lillian (1880–)
    iv. Chester H.—Born on June 15, 1880, he died on January 31, 1961. (Chester married Miss COOPER.)
    v. Hazel Belle (1885–) (Hazel married James Frank GARNETT.)

FOURTH GENERATION
Family of Josephine RICHARD (9)
& Baptiste Gene "Big Bat" POURIER

14. John Baptiste POURIER
John Baptiste married Josephine ECOFFEY, daughter of Jules ECOFFEY. They had one child:
    i. Emil Albert (1902–1990)

Family of Rosalie PALLARDIE (11) & Eli PLANT Sr.

15. Susan Amelia (Suzanna) PLANT
Born on May 31, 1878, Susan died in 1937.

On June 4, 1901 when Susan was 23, she married Stephen Washington CUNNINGHAM, son of Benjamin F. CUNNINGHAM (1832–) and Mary GEMMILL. Stephen was born on February 1, 1874.

They had the following children:
    i. Mary Rosalie
    ii. Mildred
    iii. Alyce Irene

Family of Henry Vandever BRANHAM (13)
& Margaret Agnes ST. LOUIS

16. Rosalie "Rose" BRANHAM
Born on December 8, 1878, Rose died on March 9, 1941. Occupation: Corsetiere.

Rose married Charles F. BELIEU.

They had the following children:
    i. Zelma (1908–1965)
    ii. Charlotte Lillian (1910–1995)

17. Lillian BRANHAM

Born about 1880. Occupation: Corsetiere.

Lillian married John P. BEGUHL.

They had the following children:

    i.   Charles Armine (1907–1993)

    ii.   Hazel

Notes to Appendix A:

1. On August 2, 1843 when Susanne was 14, she married Alexis ST. LOUIS, son of Jean Baptiste ST. LOUIS and Marie Angelique HEINEMAN. Alexis was born in 1828.

2. Occupation: Scout, Interpreter, Clerk and Camp Guard. On October 10, 1869 when Louis was 22, he married Jane "Jennie" REYNAL, daughter of Antoine REYNAL (1809–). Jennie was born about 1850.

3. Alice married Joseph BROWN Jr., son of Joseph BROWN Sr. and Jeanie ADAMS. Joseph was born on July 13, 1869.

4. In 1902 when Lovie was 18, she married William Denver McGAA Sr., son of William McGAA and Jeanie ADAMS. William Denver was born on March 8, 1859. He died after 1912.

5. Ellen first married William SWALLOW. In 1915 when Ellen was 19, she second married David L. STEELE. He was born about 1885.

6. In 1915 when Florence was 17, she married Thomas TIBBETS, son of Benjamin TIBBETS & Suzie BULLOCK. Thomas was born on December 19, 1897. He died in August 1980.

7. Emile married a daughter of Joseph BISSONETTE (1818–1894) and Julie HUBERT.

BIBLIOGRAPHY

Books:

Ambrose, Stephen E. *Crazy Horse and Custer: The Parallel Lives of Two American Warriors*. Garden City, New York: Doubleday & Co., 1975.

Arnold (Connor), Ben. *Rekindling Camp Fires: The Exploits of Ben Arnold (Connor)*. Bismarck, North Dakota: Capital Book Co., 1926.

Baker, Hozial H., ed. *Overland Journey to Carson Valley & California*. The Book Club of California, 1973.

Barry, Louise. *The Beginning of the West*. Topeka, Kansas: Kansas State Historical Society, 1972.

Bartlett, I.S., ed. *History of Wyoming*. S.J. Clarke Publishing Company, Vol. III, 1918.

Beach, Cora M. *Women of Wyoming*. Casper, Wyoming: 1927.

———. *Women of Wyoming: Volume 2*. Lusk, Wyoming: 1929.

Bettelyoun, Susan Bordeaux. *With My Own Eyes*. Edited by Emily Levine. Lincoln, Nebraska: University of Nebraska Press, 1998.

Brock, J. Elmer. *Powder River Country*. Edited by Margaret Brock Hanson. Cheyenne, Wyoming: Frontier Printing, Inc., 1981.

Brown, John. *The Autobiography of Pioneer John Brown*. Edited by John Zimmerman Brown. Salt Lake City, Utah: Stevens & Wallace, Inc., 1941.

Brown, Larry K. *The Hog Ranches of Wyoming: Liquor, Lust, & Lies Under Sagebrush Skies*. Glendo, Wyoming: High Plains Press, 1995.

Brown, William Richard. *William Richard Brown: Diary*. Edited by Barbara Wills. Mokelumne Hill, California: Barbara Wills, granddaughter, 1985.

Bryans, Bill. *Deer Creek: Frontier Crossroads in Pre-territorial Wyoming*. Glenrock, Wyoming: Glenrock Historical Commission, 1990.

Bryant, Edwin. *What I Saw in California: Being the Journal of a Tour*. Minneapolis: Ross & Haynes, Inc. 1967.

Burton, Sir Richard F. *The City of the Saints and Across the Rocky Mountains to California.* Edited by Fawn M. Brodie. New York: Alfred A. Knopf, 1963.

Casper Zonta Club. *Casper Chronicles.* Casper, Wyoming: Casper Zonta Club, 1964.

Chalfant, William Y. *Cheyennes and Horse Soldiers.* Norman and London: University of Oklahoma Press, 1989.

Cipriani, Count Leonetto. *California and Overland Diaries.* N.p.: Champoeg Press, 1962.

Collins, John S. *My Experiences in the West.* Chicago: R. R. Donnelley & Sons Company, Lakeside Press, 1970.

Coutant, C. G. *The History of Wyoming from the Earliest Known Discoveries.* Laramie, Wyoming: C. G. Coutant; printed by Chaplin, Spafford & Mathison, 1899.

Cronin, Vaughn Stephen. *Casper Mountain: The Magic Yesterday and Today.* Casper, Wyoming: Vaughn's Publishing, 1998.

DeBarthe, Joe. *Life and Adventures of Frank Grouard.* Edited by Edgar I. Stewart. Norman, Oklahoma: University of Oklahoma Press, 1958.

DeVoto, Bernard. *Across the Wide Missouri.* Boston: Houghton Mifflin Company, 1947.

———. *The Year of Decision, 1846.* Boston: Little, Brown and Company, 1943.

Edwards, Lewis C. *Who's Who in Nebraska, 1940.* Richardson County, Nebraska: NEGenWeb Project, [1940].

Franzwa, Gregory M. *Maps of the Oregon Trail.* Gerald, Missouri: The Patrice Press, 1982.

Gilbert, Hila. *"Big Bat" Pourier: Guide and Interpreter, Fort Laramie 1870-1880.* Sheridan, Wyoming: The Mills Company, July, 1968.

Hafen, LeRoy. *Decline of the Fur Trade.* N.p.: The Arthur H. Clark Company, Vol. 1, n.d.

———. *Reports From Colorado.* N.p.: The Arthur H. Clark Company, Vol. 13, n.d.

———, ed. *Mountain Men and the Fur Trade of the Far West.* N.p: The Arthur H. Clark Company, n.d.

Hammond, George P., ed. *The Adventures of Alexander Barclay, Mountain Man.* Denver, Colorado: Fred A. Rosenstock, Old West Publishing Company, 1976.

Hanson, Charles E. Jr., ed. *The David Adams Journal.* Chadron, Nebraska: The Museum Association of the American Frontier, 1994.

Hendry, Mary Helen. *Tales of Old Lost Cabin, and Parts Thereabout*. Lysite, Wyoming: Mary Helen Hendry, 1989.

Hyde, George E. *Spotted Tail's Folk: A History of the Brule Sioux*. Norman, Oklahoma: University of Oklahoma Press, 1961.

Jackson, W. Turrentine. *Wagon Roads West*. London and New Haven: Yale University Press, 1952.

Johnson, Dorothy M. *The Bloody Bozeman*. New York and Toronto: McGraw-Hill Book Co., 1971.

Jones, Brian, *Those Wild Reshaw Boys*. London: English Westerners Society Special Publication No. 2 (From *Sidelights of the Sioux Wars,* Francis B. Tauton, ed), 1967.

Jones, Daniel W. *Forty Years Among the Indians*. Los Angeles, California: Westernlore Press, 1960.

Kelly, Charles, ed. *Journals of John D. Lee*. Salt Lake City, Utah: Western Printing Company, 1938.

Larson, Robert R., *Kelly, Hiram B*. N.p., n.d.

Lecompte, Janet. *Archibald Charles Metcalf*. N.p.: The Arthur H. Clark Company, Vol. 4, n.d.

———. *Pueblo-Hardscrabble-Greenhorn, The Upper Arkansas, 1832–1856*. Norman, Oklahoma: University of Oklahoma Press, 1978.

Lewis, Jon E. *The Mammoth Book of the West: The Making of the American West*. New York: Carroll & Graf Publishers, 1996.

Loomis, Noel M., and Abraham P. Nasatir. *Pedro Vial and the Roads to Santa Fe*. Norman, Oklahoma: University of Oklahoma Press, 1967.

Lowe, James A. *The Bridger Trail, An Alternative Route to the Gold Fields of Montana Territory in 1864*. Spokane, Washington: The Arthur H. Clark Company, 1999.

Luttig, John C.. *Journal of a Fur Trading Expedition on the Upper Missouri 1812–1813*. Edited by Stella M. Drumm. New York: Argosy-Antiquarian Ltd., 1964.

McComish, Charles Davis, and Rebecca T. Lambert. *History of Colusa and Glenn Counties California*. Los Angeles, California: Historic Record Company, 1918.

McDermott, John D. *James Bordeaux*. N.p.: The Arthur H. Clark Company, Vol. 5, n.d.

———. *John Baptiste Richard*. N.p.: The Arthur H. Clark Company, Vol. 2, n.d.

——. *Joseph Bissonette.* N.p.: The Arthur H. Clark Company, Vol. 4, n.d.

——. *Frontier Crossroads, The History of Fort Caspar and the Upper Platte Crossing.* Casper, Wyoming: City of Casper, 1997.

Microsoft Corporation. *Encarta 98 Encyclopedia.* N.p.: Microsoft, 1993–1997.

——. *Marsh, Othniel Charles.* N.p.: Microsoft, 1993–1997.

Milner, Clyde A. II, Carol A. O'Connor, Martha A. Sandweiss, editors. *The Oxford History of the American West.* New York–Oxford: Oxford University Press, 1994.

Milner, Joe E., and Earle R. Forrest. *California Joe: Noted Scout and Indian Fighter.* Caldwell, Idaho: The Caxton Printers, Ltd., 1935.

Mokler, Alfred James. *History of Natrona County Wyoming: 1888–1922.* Chicago: R. R. Donnelley & Sons Company, The Lakeside Press, 1923. Reprint, Mountain States Lithograph, under the direction of Kathleen Hemry, 1989.

Morgan, Dale, ed. *Overland in 1846: Diaries and Letters of the California–Oregon Trail.* Georgetown, California: The Talisman Press, vol. II, 1963.

——. *The West of William H. Ashley.* , Denver, Colorado: Fred A. Rosenstock, The Old West Publishing Company, 1964.

Moulton, Candy, and Ben Kern. *Wagon Wheels.* Glendo, Wyoming: High Plains Press, 1996.

Murray, Robert A. *Trading Posts, Forts and Bridges of the Casper Area.* Casper, Wyoming: Wyoming Historical Press, 1986.

Myers, John Myers: *The Saga of Hugh Glass: Pirate, Pawnee, and Mountain Man.* Lincoln and London: University of Nebraska Press, 1963. Reprint, Bison Books, 1976.

Nevin, David. *The Expressmen.* New York: Time-Life Books, 1975.

——. *The Old West.* New York: Time-Life Books, 1975.

——. *The Texans.* New York: Time-Life Books, 1975.

Osgood, Ernest Staples. *The Day of the Cattleman.* University of Minnesota, 1929. Reprint, Chicago and London: University of Chicago Press, 1970.

Parkman, Francis Jr. *The Oregon Trail.* New York & Boston: Books, Inc., n.d.

Platte County Extension Homemakers, ed. *Wyoming: Platte County Heritage.* Wheatland, Wyoming: Platte County Extension Homemakers Council, 1981.

Raat, William Dirk. *The Mexican War.* N.p.: Microsoft, 1993–1997.

——. *Marsh, Othniel Charles.* N.p.: Microsoft, 1993–1997.

Raynolds, Captain William F. *Report on the Exploration of the Yellowstone River.* N.p.: United States Army Corps of Engineers, 1868.

Rosa, Joseph G. *They Called Him Wild Bill.* Norman, Oklahoma: University of Oklahoma Press, 1964.

———. *The West of Wild Bill Hickok.* Norman, Oklahoma: University of Oklahoma Press, 1982.

Ruxton, George Frederick. *La Bonte: Hunter, Free Trapper, Trail Blazer and Mountain Man of the Old West, 1825–1848.* Edited by L. C. Bishop. N.p.: Earl T. Bower & L. C. Bishop, 1950.

Service, Alex. *The Life and Letters of Caspar W. Collins.* Casper, Wyoming: City of Casper, 2000.

Spring, Agnes Wright. *The Cheyenne and Black Hills Stage and Express Routes.* Glendale, California: The Arthur H. Clarke Company, 1949.

Taunton, Frances B., ed. *Sidelights of the Sioux Wars.* London: English Westerners Society Special Publication No. 2, 1967.

Thwaites, Reuben Gold, ed. *Andre Micheaux's Travels.* Glendale, California: Arthur H. Clark, Vol. 3, 1966.

———. *Early Western Travels.* Glendale, California: Arthur H. Clark, 1966.

———. *Nuttall's Journal.* Glendale, California: Arthur H. Clark, Vol. 13, 1966.

Urbanek, Mae. *Wyoming Place Names.* Boulder, Colorado: Johnson Publishing Company, 1967.

Utley, Robert M., and Wilcomb E. Washburn. *The American Heritage History of The Indian Wars.* New York: American Heritage Publishing Co., Inc./Bonanza Books, 1982.

Vaughn, J. W. *The Reynolds Campaign on Powder River.* Norman, Oklahoma: University of Oklahoma Press, 1961.

Wade, Mason. *Francis Parkman: Heroic Historian.* New York: Viking Press, 1942.

Webster, Noah. *Webster's New School & Office Dictionary.* Cleveland & New York: The World Publishing Company, 1943.

West, Elliott. *The Contested Plains: Indians, Goldseekers, & the Rush to Colorado.* Kansas: University Press of Kansas, 1998.

———. *Bison Hunters to Black Gold.* Casper, Wyoming: Wyoming Historical Press, 1986.

Periodicals:

Briston, Dave and William R. Dubois III, "Highlights in the life of 'Hi' Kelly." *Bits and Pieces: Your Own Western History Magazine*, Vol. 5, no. 9 (1969).

Collister, Oscar. "Life of Oscar Collister, Wyoming Pioneer." Edited by Mrs. Charles Ellis. *Annals of Wyoming* 7, no. 1 (July 1930).

Coutant, C.G. "History of Wyoming Written By C. G. Coutant, Pioneer Historian and Heretofore Unpublished, Chapter 4 and 5." *Annals of Wyoming* 12 (April 1940).

Coutant, C.G. "Thomas Jefferson Carr, A Frontier Sheriff." *Annals of Wyoming* 20 (July 1948).

Cunningham, Don. "1868-1874, Chapter One, Red Cloud Agency Days." *Fort Robinson Illustrated. Nebraskaland Magazine* 64, no. 1 (January-February 1986).

Dean, Julie. "1880-1890, Chapter Three, Transition Years." *Fort Robinson Illustrated. Nebraskaland Magazine* 64, no. 1 (January-February 1986).

Doyle, Susan Badger, Ph.D. "The Bozeman Trail, 1863-1868." *Annals of Wyoming* 70, no. 2 (spring, 1998).

Frontier Times and New Oregon Trail Reader (Evansville, Wyoming) 1, no. 1 (Summer, 1966).

Glass, Jefferson. "The Founder of Evansville: Casper Builder W. T. Evans." *Annals of Wyoming* 70, no. 4 (autumn, 1998).

Henderson, Paul, ed. "Rev. J. McAllister diary." *Annals of Wyoming* 32, no. 2 (October 1960).

Humphreys, A. Glen. "The Crow Indian Treaties of 1868—An Example of Power Struggle and Confusion in United States Indian Policy." *Annals of Wyoming* 43, no. 1 (spring, 1971).

Jones, Brian. "John Richard, Jr. and the Killing at Fetterman." *Annals of Wyoming* 43, no. 2 (fall, 1971).

Morgan, Dale L. "The Mormon Ferry on the North Platte." *Annals of Wyoming* 21 (n.d.).

Myer, Nathaniel. "Journey Into Southern Oregon: Diary of a Pennsylvania Dutchman." Edited by Edward B. Ham. *Oregon Historical Society Magazine* (n.d.).

Nicholas, Thomas A. "Platte Bridge and the Oregon Trail in the Civil War Period—1855–1870." *Casper Star Tribune,* (February 19, 1961).

——. "A New Look at Richard's Upper Platte Bridge and Trading Post at Evansville Wyoming." *Casper Star Tribune* (1963).

——. "Timbers From Old Reshaw Bridge Found." *Casper (Wyoming) Star Tribune.* (October 9, 1966).

Pennock, Sgt. Isaac "Jake". "Diary of Jake Pennock." *Annals of Wyoming* 23, no. 2 (July 1951).

Sloan, William K. "Autobiography of William K. Sloan." *Annals of Wyoming* 4, no. 1 (July 1926).

Workman, William. "A Letter From Taos, 1826." Edited by David J. Weber. *New Mexico Historical Review* XLI (1966).

Unpublished and Informally Published Materials:

Anderson, Kevin, and Jefferson Glass. "Oral History of William Trevor Evans." Cassette and typescript. Special Collections, Goodstein Foundation Library, Casper College, Casper, Wyoming, 1998.

Bradway, J. R. "Diary." Library of the State Historical Society of Wisconsin.

Brown, J. Robert. "J. Robert Brown's Journal." Western Americana Collection, Beinecke Rare Book and Manuscript Library, Yale University Library, New Haven, Connecticut.

Chouteau, Pierre Jr. "Chouteau Papers." Missouri Historical Society, St. Louis, Missouri.

Church of Jesus Christ of Latter Day Saints. "Family Search, International Genealogical Index." Salt Lake City, Utah.

Collins, Colonel William O. "Order book of Colonel William O. Collins, October 27, 1862 to April 8, 1863." Morgan Library, Colorado State University, Fort Collins, Colorado. Copy in Special Collections, Goodstein Foundation Library, Casper College, Casper, Wyoming.

Coutant, C. G. "Coutant Collection." Notebooks. Box 4, Folder 53, Book 36 and Book 37. Box 5, Folder 48, Book 16. Wyoming State Archives, Cheyenne, Wyoming.

Cragin, F. W. "Cragin Papers." Notebooks. Colorado Springs Pioneers Museum, Colorado Springs, Colorado.

——. "Interview of Tom Autobees on July 28, 1908 at Avondale, Colorado." Notebook I. Colorado Springs Pioneers Museum, Colorado Springs, Colorado.

——. "Interview of Sylvester Monroe Buzzard on May 18, 1921." Notebook XIV. Colorado Springs Pioneers Museum, Colorado Springs, Colorado.

———. "Interview of William T. Eubank on August 18, 1908 at Denver, Colorado." Notebook I. Colorado Springs Pioneers Museum, Colorado Springs, Colorado.

———. "Interview of Luz Trujillo Metcalf Ledoux on February 13, 1908 at Las Vegas, New Mexico" Notebook VII. Colorado Springs Pioneers Museum, Colorado Springs, Colorado.

———. "Interview of Jesse Nelson." Notebook VIII. Colorado Springs Pioneers Museum, Colorado Springs, Colorado.

———. "Interview of Josiah F. Smith on July 18, 1903 at Pueblo, Colorado." Notebook XVII. Colorado Springs Pioneers Museum, Colorado Springs, Colorado.

———. "Interview of Vincente Trujillo on November 9, 1907 at Avondale, Colorado." Notebook X. Colorado Springs Pioneers Museum, Colorado Springs, Colorado.

David, Robert. "Interview of James H. Bury—ca. 1920." Notes. The Bob David Collection, Goodstein Library, Special Collections, Casper College, Casper, Wyoming.

Drips, Major Andrew. "Fort Pierre Letter Book." "Drips Papers." Missouri Historical Society, St. Louis, Missouri.

Empey, Tom. Interviews by author. Notes, 1996-1998.

Grant, Duncan Paul. "Memoirs 1881-1975." Robert Grant Family Collection, Grant Ranch, Richeau Creek Rd., Wheatland, Wyoming.

Judson, H. M. "Diary 1862." Nebraska State Historical Society, Lincoln, Nebraska.

Kern, Ben, Interviews by author. 1997-2002.

Lander, F. W. "Preliminary report of F. W. Lander, Report of the Secretary of the Interior, 35th Congress, Feb. 23, 1859." National Archives.

Leaneagh, Joan, Correspondences with the author. 1999.

MacKinnon, William. Correspondences with the author. 2001.

Monroe, Stewart. Correspondences with the author. 1999-2001.

Murray, John. "Journal." T-177, Box 1, Folder 12. Special Collections, Washington State Historical Society.

Phelps, Captain John Wolcott. "Diaries of John W. Phelps." Rare Books and Manuscripts, New York Public Library, New York.

Reber, Thomas. "The Journal of Thomas Reber" MA Thesis. Edited by Albert M. Tewsbury. Claremont College.

Richards, James L. and Warren K. Gordon, Correspondences with the author. 1999.

Ricker, Judge Eli S. "Ricker Collection." Notebooks. Nebraska State Historical Society Library, Lincoln, Nebraska.

———. "Interview of Magloire Alexis Mosseau, Buzzard Basin, Pine Ridge Reservation, South Dakota, on October 30, 1906." Tablet 28. Nebraska State Historical Society Library, Lincoln, Nebraska.

———. "Interview with Baptiste 'Big Bat' Pourier began Sunday, January 6, 1907—The Sibley Scouts." Tablet 15. Nebraska State Historical Society Library, Lincoln, Nebraska.

———. "Interview of Baptiste Pourier, Wounded Knee Creek, January 7, 1906." Tablet 15. Nebraska State Historical Society Library, Lincoln, Nebraska.

———. "Interview of Frank Salaway, 8 miles Northeast of Allen, South Dakota, November 4, 1906." Tablet 28. Nebraska State Historical Society Library, Lincoln, Nebraska.

Scott, George C. "These God Forsaken Dobie Hills: Land Law and the Settlement of Bates Hole, Wyoming 1880-1940." MA. Thesis. University of Wyoming, 1978. Copy in Special Collections, Goodstein Foundation Library, Casper College, Casper, Wyoming.

Smith, Dr. John. "Diary 1853." Portions of this diary were hand-copied for the author by Susan Badger Doyle, Ph.D., Huntington Library.

Government Documents

Application and Approval for the Plat of the Town of Strouds. Carbon County, Wyoming, Natrona County Courthouse, Casper, Wyoming.

Census of Fort Fetterman. Albany County, Wyoming Territory, 1870.

Census of Fort Laramie. Laramie County, Wyoming Territory, 1860.

Census of Fort Laramie. Laramie County, Wyoming Territory, 1870.

Census of Rulo, Richardson County, Nebraska Territory, 1860.

Census of St. Charles, St. Charles County, Missouri, 1850.

USGS survey records. United States Bureau of Land Management, Department of the Interior, Cheyenne, Wyoming.

❧ INDEX ❧

ᴀ<small>ʙᴏᴜᴛ ᴛʜᴇ</small> Aᴜᴛʜᴏʀ

J<small>EFFERSON</small> G<small>LASS</small> <small>BELIEVES</small> in the hands-on study of history. He has traveled thousands of miles and hiked hundreds of miles on the routes used by western frontiersmen.

He's been fascinated with oral histories of the Oregon Trail from his earliest childhood. In his native Oregon, he knew families who proudly displayed heirlooms that their ancestors had carried in wagons across the country on that famous thoroughfare. It was only natural for him to become engulfed in the history of the region when he relocated to central Wyoming over thirty years ago. For most of that time he has been a resident of Evansville, Wyoming, and lives a few hundred yards from the site of Reshaw's Bridge.

His interest in history prompted him to found the Evansville Historical Commission and to serve as its chairman for several years. It was then that he began his research on local history including John Richard and his bridge. He wrote "Founder of Evansville: Casper Builder W.T. Evans," published by the *Annals of Wyoming* in 1998. In 2000, he assisted the Bishop family in research that would result in Bishop Family Home in Casper being on the National Register of Historic Places. He then wrote a second article for *Annals of Wyoming*, "Marvin Lord Bishop Sr., Pioneer Sheep Rancher," published the same year. Jefferson later served on the board of directors for the Cadoma Foundation which preserves and protects Wyoming's historic buildings (www.cadomafoundation.org).

In 2002 he wrote, "Crossing the North Platte River: A Brief History of Reshaw's Bridge-1852-1866" for *Annals of Wyoming*. By this time he had been compiling material for the story of John Richard for several years and had written drafts of this book. In 2012 he was commissioned by WyoHistory.org to write a entry on Reshaw's Bridge for their website (www.wyohistory.org).

✥ NOTES ON THE PRODUCTION OF THE BOOK ✥

The text is set in type from the Adobe Garamond family.
Display type is Old Book, Regular and Old Style,
from the International Typeface Corporation.
Additional ornaments are from
Adobe Woodtype and LHF Noel's Ands.

The text is printed on sixty-pound Tessaroni Grande,
a white, acid-free, recycled paper.
The book is covered with ten-point stock,
printed in four colors, and coated with matte film lamination,
by Versa Press, Inc.